A Dictionary of
ANCIENT NEAR EASTERN ARCHITECTURE

A Dictionary of
ANCIENT NEAR EASTERN ARCHITECTURE

GWENDOLYN LEICK

with illustrations by Francis J. Kirk

R

ROUTLEDGE

LONDON AND NEW YORK

First published in 1988 by
Routledge
11 New Fetter Lane, London EC4P 4EE

Published in the USA by
Routledge
a division of Routledge, Chapman and Hall, Inc.
29 West 35th Street, New York, NY 10001

Set in 9½ pt Ehrhardt
by Columns of Reading
and printed in Great Britain
by T.J. Press (Padstow) Ltd
Padstow, Cornwall

Library of Congress Cataloging in Publication Data
Leick, Gwendolyn, 1951–
    A dictionary of ancient Near Eastern architecture.
    Bibliography: p.
Architecture, Ancient—Middle East—Dictionaries.
    2. Architecture—Middle East—Dictionaries.   3. Middle
    East—Antiquities—Dictionaries.   I. Title.
    NA212.L45   1988   722'.5'03   87–23375

British Library CIP Data also available
ISBN 0-415-00240-0

This book is dedicated to the memory of Walter Segal (1907-85)

CONTENTS

ILLUSTRATIONS

PLATES

FIGURES

MAPS

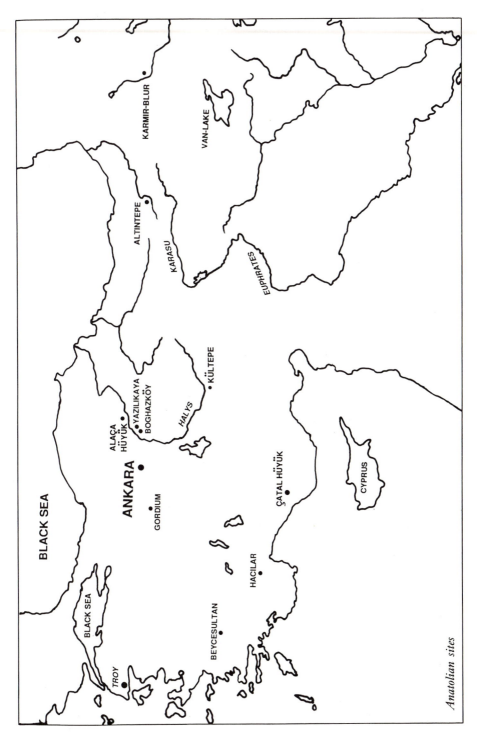

BLACK SEA

KARMIR-BLUR

VAN-LAKE

ALTINTEPE

KARASU

EUPHRATES

KÜLTEPE

YAZILIKAYA
BOGHAZKÖY

ALAÇA
HÜYÜK

HALYS

ANKARA

GORDIUM

ÇATAL HÜYÜK

CYPRUS

HACILAR

BLACK SEA

BEYCESULTAN

TROY

Anatolian sites

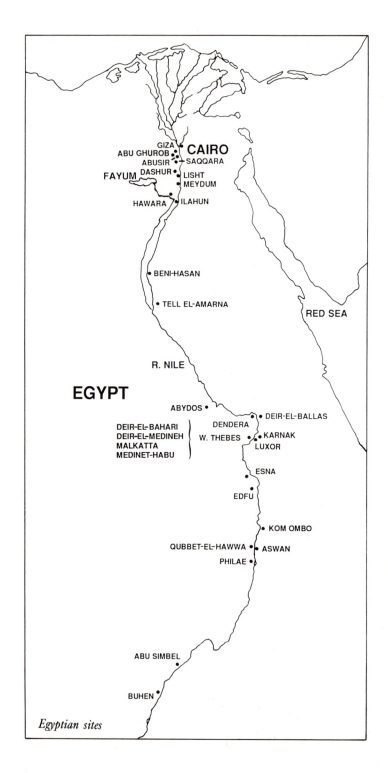

GIZA
ABU GHUROB • CAIRO
ABUSIR •
DASHUR • SAQQARA
FAYUM • LISHT
MEYDUM

HAWARA • ILAHUN

• BENI-HASAN

• TELL EL-AMARNA

RED SEA

R. NILE

EGYPT

ABYDOS •

DEIR-EL-BAHARI   • DEIR-EL-BALLAS
DEIR-EL-MEDINEH   DENDERA
MALKATTA   W. THEBES • KARNAK
MEDINET-HABU   LUXOR

ESNA

EDFU

KOM OMBO

QUBBET-EL-HAWWA • ASWAN
PHILAE •

ABU SIMBEL

BUHEN •

Egyptian sites

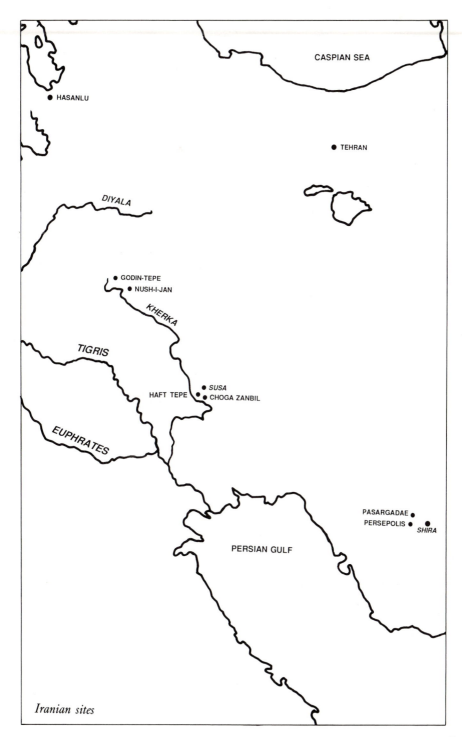

CASPIAN SEA

● HASANLU

● TEHRAN

DIYALA

● GODIN-TEPE
● NUSH-I-JAN

KHERKA

TIGRIS

HAFT TEPE ● *SUSA*
● CHOGA ZANBIL

EUPHRATES

PASARGADAE ●
PERSEPOLIS ● ●
SHIRA

PERSIAN GULF

Iranian sites

xvii

BASTAM

LAKE URMIYA

HASANLU

TIGRIS

TELL BRAK

TELL ARPACHIYA
KHORSABAD
TEPE GAWRA
NINEVEH
JARMO
NIMRUD
KAR
TELL AL-RIMAH
TUKULTI-NINURTA
ASSUR
NUZI

EUPHRATES

R. DIYALA

TELL ABADA

MARI

R.KURKHA

TELL HARMAL
TELL ASMAR
'AQAR QUF
TELL AGRAB
KHAFAJE
ISCHALI

SIPPAR
TELL UQAIR

KISH
BABYLON

NIPPUR

URUK
LARSA

UR
AL UBAID
ERIDU

PERSIAN GULF

Mesopotamian sites

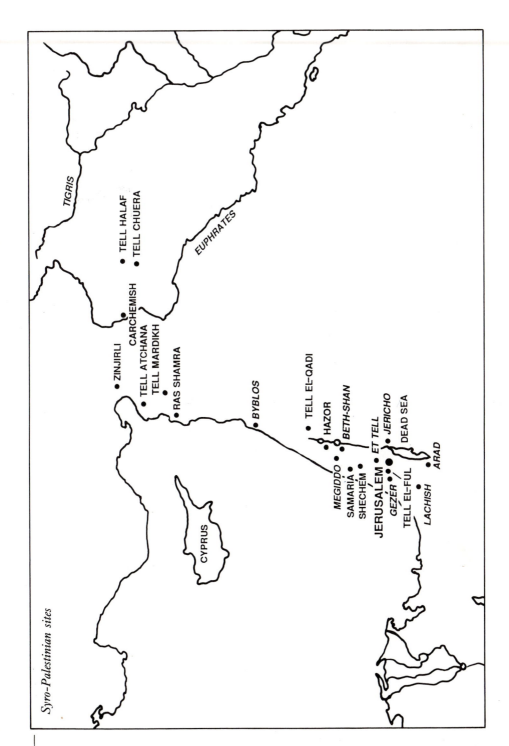

Syro-Palestinian sites

TIGRIS

TELL HALAF
TELL CHUERA

EUPHRATES

CARCHEMISH

ZINJIRLI
TELL ATCHANA
TELL MARDIKH
RAS SHAMRA

BYBLOS

TELL EL-QADI
HAZOR
BETH-SHAN

CYPRUS

MEGIDDO
SAMARIA
SHECHEM

ET TELL
JERICHO
DEAD SEA

JERUSALEM
GEZER
TELL EL-FUL
LACHISH
ARAD

abacus

In a TRABEATED building the flat square stone tablet between the vertical support and the horizontal element. It is documented only in Egyptian stone-architecture. In Achaemenian columns, the abacus was replaced by zoomorph IMPOSTS. There was no structural distinction between shaft and abacus as they were sometimes both carved from a single block. The width is generally the same as the largest diameter of the shaft, the height a third or half its length. The abacus could be decorated with hieroglyphic inscriptions, but remained generally unobtrusive.

Abu Ghurob

Egypt, see map p. xvi. On this site in the vicinity of ancient Memphis, German archaeologists discovered in 1898/99 the remains of the largest and best-known SUN TEMPLE. Dating from the V Dynasty (c. 2565-2420 BC), it was built by Niuserre (c. 2456-2425 BC). The whole complex consisted of a valley-building beside the canal, a 100m-long, covered CAUSEWAY leading up to the actual sanctuary and, outside the girdle-wall, a brick sun-boat.

The sanctuary was reached through a gate-building abutting against the narrow side of the rectangular enclosure which contained treasure-chambers, magazines and slaughter-houses. The central feature of the site was a huge OBELISK of limestone raised on a platform 20m high which could be reached by an internal passage. The squat shape of the obelisk has been reconstructed on the basis of hieroglyphic signs occurring in a list of names of V Dynasty sun temples. In front of it was a large court with an alabaster altar, presumably intended for blood sacrifices as it was equipped with drainage spouts on four sides. Next to the obelisk was a small chapel decorated with relief representations of sacred rituals.

Bissing, F. von, *Das Re-Heiligtum des Königs Ne-woser-re* I (Berlin 1905)

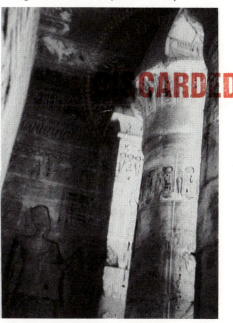

Abacus and papyri-form column from mortuary temple at Medinet-Habu (XIX Dynasty)

Abu Shahrein (ancient Eridu)

Mesopotamia, see map p. xviii. This site lies on a high sand dune in the midst of the southern Mesopotamian marsh area. The chief deity worshipped there in historical times was Ea, god of wisdom and the 'sweet-water ocean'. The place, however, had been occupied since pre-historic times and altogether eighteen levels were enumerated by the excavators, who have drawn particular attention to the almost unbroken sequence of temple buildings.

The simplest and earliest structure (level XVIII), thought to have been a 'shrine', was a small rectangular chamber (12.10m × 3.10m) with a recess (1.10m × 1m) containing an altar or pedestal facing the entrance. At level XI the main room had become larger (4.50m × 12.60m) with several subsidiary rooms and corridors surrounding it. Each face of the outer wall was articulated by rhythmical alterations of RECESSES and BUTTRESSES, one of the earliest examples of this feature which was to become characteristic for Mesopotamian temple architecture. The last temple(?), built during the Obeid period (levels VIII-VII), rose on a platform containing the levelled remains of earlier structures and is distinguished by its clear, symmetrical layout. Access to the cult-room is either by vestibules on the N and S side respectively or through double doors facing altar and pedestal. The subsidiary rooms surrounding the main chamber protrude at the corners of the building. All the exterior walls were again heavily corrugated by buttresses.

The ZIGGURAT of Eridu was built towards the end of the 3rd millennium BC, on the site of the Early Dynastic temples. During the Ur III period (c. 2113-2004 BC) it was rebuilt, presumably to resemble the ziggurat of Urnammu at UR.

Safar, F., Mustafa, M.A., Lloyd, S., *Eridu* (Baghdad 1981)

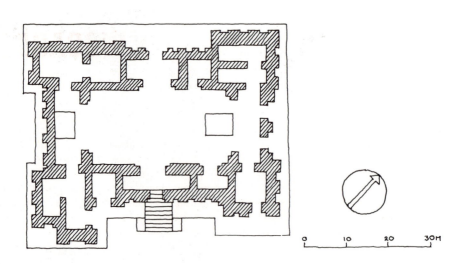

Abu Shahrein: temple VII (after Lloyd)

Abu Simbel

Egypt, see map p. xvi. The original site of the two temples built by Ramesses II (XIX Dynasty) is now submerged by the waters of the Aswan dam. An international rescue operation transferred the rock-cut temples to a purpose-built artificial hill between 1966 and 1972.

The Great Temple is dedicated to the deified pharaoh Ramesses II (c. 1304-1237 BC) and to the gods of state. The most striking aspect of this building is its facade, in the shape of a single-tower PYLON, which serves as the backdrop to four colossal seated figures of the king set on an inscribed pedestal, a pair on either side of the central doorway. The grandeur of this sculptural facade – the colossi are over 21m high – was intended to impress the Nubian subjects of Egypt towards whose homeland the temple was oriented. The interior of the temple was entirely cut out of the rock and displays the standard sequence of gradually diminishing vestibules and hypostyle halls. The inner sanctum is oriented to the east so that the rising sun illuminates the dark interior.

A short distance away is the smaller temple of Hathor, dedicated to Ramesses' consort Nefertari. Her statue wearing the costume of the goddess appears between the two standing colossi of her husband. The interior arrangements of this temple are simpler, consisting of one hypostyle hall plus vestibule and two smaller chambers. The inner sanctum contains the image of the goddess in the form of a cow emerging between two Hathor columns.

Macquitty, W., *Abu Simbel* (London 1965)

Abusir

Egypt, see map p. xvi. Ancient necropolis of the V Dynasty (c. 2565-2420 BC).

Only four of the eleven PYRAMIDS originally erected there can be made out today and even these are badly preserved. They were constructed of a core of small stones encased in local sandstone. The relatively best preserved is the pyramid of Sahure, originally complete with MORTUARY TEMPLE, valley temple, CAUSEWAY and a small subsidiary pyramid characteristic for this period. The valley temple had a portico (on the E face of the building) supported by eight monolithic columns with date palm capitals. The T-shaped hall and the walls of the causeway were decorated with reliefs showing the pharaoh triumphant over his enemies. Reliefs also covered the walls of the mortuary temple. A passage connected the central porticoed courtyard with its palmiform columns to the pyramid enclosure. Magazines to store precious objects used for the funerary cult were reached from two recesses with a monolithic column in the shape of a papyrus cluster. They were two storeys high, each with its own stairway. The central part of the building contained a small chamber with statue-niches. The actual sanctuary was an oblong room with a FALSE DOOR set in the west wall at the base of the pyramid. This type of plan was used for mortuary temples throughout the last dynasties of the Old Kingdom.

There are also numerous private tombs of the MASTABA type; e.g. the Mastaba of Ptahshepses, a large complex containing a square pillared courtyard, offering-chapels with niches, burial chambers and sunken oval pits which supposedly contained sun-barges. The second portico preserves two columns featuring the earliest examples of lotus capitals.

Nearby is the site of the SUN TEMPLE of Userkaf, and maybe more as yet unexcavated sun temples of other V Dynasty kings.

Morgan, H. de, *Revue archéologique* 3, ser. 24 (1894), 18-33

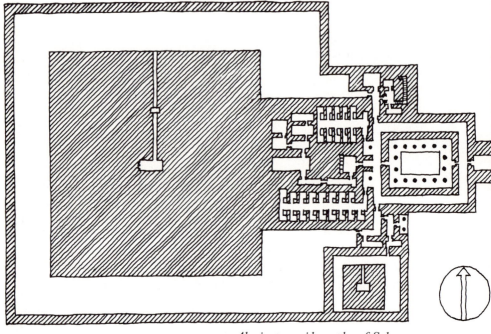

*Abusir: pyramid complex of Sahure
(V Dynasty) (after Edwards)*

*Palmiform capital from the sanctuary of
Sahure (Abusir)*

Abydos

Egypt, see map p. xvi. An important early dynastic necropolis and cult-centre of Osiris which remained a prestigious burial-place throughout Egypt's history. If the actual tomb was located elsewhere, a CENOTAPH or dummy tomb could be purchased at Abydos. This practice was instigated by the kings of the early dynasties and has caused much controversy about the location of the real burials of these kings, which has not been settled.

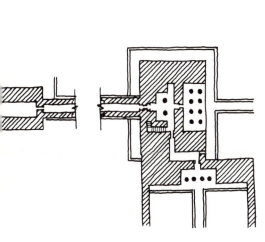

'Osireion': cenotaph of Seti I (XIX Dynasty)

There are two archaic royal burial-grounds, Umm el-Qa'ab (I Dynasty, *c.* 3100-2890 BC), and to the north, Shunet el-Zabib (II Dynasty, *c.* 2890–2780 BC). The typical Abydos tomb consisted of a sunken burial-pit heaped over with a mound of sand. A panelled brick wall surrounded the whole precinct like a fence and a stone stela proclaimed the name and title of the royal owner of the tomb. Underneath the architecturally undefined mound, the burial chambers were of increasing complexity. The walls of the pit had originally been lined with timber panelling to retain the pressure of the soil. Later, brick and then stone were used. As the pits grew larger in order to store more offerings and funerary equipment, the space was divided into several chambers with load-bearing brick or timber walls which supported the roofing beams. As the builders acquired more skills in work-ing with brick or stone, the interior arrangement became more complex and there was considerable variation in the ground-plans.

Helck, H., 'Zu den Talbezirken in Abydos', *Mitteilungen des Deutschen Archäologischen Instituts Abteilung Kairo MDAIK* 28 (1972) 95-99

Kaiser, W., 'Zu den königlichen Talbe-zirken der 1. und 2. Dynastie in Abydos und zur Baugeschichte des Djoser Grabmals', *MDAIK* 25 (1969) 1-2

Kaiser, W., Dreyer, G., 'Umm el-Qaab', *MDAIK* 37 (1981) 241ff; 38 (1982) 17-24

Kemp, B.J., 'Abydos and the Royal Tombs of the First Dynasty', *Journal of Egyptian Archaeology* 52 (1966) 13-22

Peet, T.E., *The Cemeteries of Abydos III* (London 1914)

Petrie, W.M.F., *The Royal Tombs of the First Dynasty* (London 1900)

Petrie, W.M.F., *The Royal Tombs of the Earliest Dynasties* (London 1901)

While of the ancient tombs very little remains today, the XIX Dynasty Temple of Seti I (*c.* 1318-1304 BC), built in fine white limestone and decorated with some of the best painted reliefs of the New Kingdom, is still one of the most impressive monuments of Pharaonic temple architecture. It was completed by Seti's successor Ramesses II and dedicated to the deified king and six divinities (Ptah, Re Harakhte, Amon, Osiris, Isis and Horus). To accommodate them all, the temple has an unusual sevenfold arrangement with seven shrines or chapels side by side, reached through two successive broad HYPOSTYLE HALLS divided by six pairs of columns, two and three rows deep. The shrines are comparatively large, decorated with painted reliefs and roofed by false (carved) barrel-vaults. There is an additional private sanctuary of Osiris behind his shrine. A passage leads from the second hypostyle hall to a tract containing magazines and storerooms which forms an L-shaped annex. A broad stone stairway with a false vault leads to the temple roof.

Calvery, A.M., *The Temple of Sethos I at Abydos* I-IV (London, Chicago 1933-58)
Capart, J., *Abydos, Le temple de Seti Ier* (Brussels 1912)

Behind the temple lies the cemetery and the so-called Osireon, thought to have been a cenotaph for Seti I. Its main feature is a large rectangular pillared hall of red granite masonry surrounded by two transverse halls and small niches.

Frankfort, H., *The Cenotaph of Seti I at Abydos* I-II (London 1933)

Near the temple of Seti I is a temple built by Ramesses II (*c.* 1304-1237 BC), which repeats the pattern of a Theban MORTUARY TEMPLE with an open courtyard surrounded by OSIRIDE PILLARS. Like the temple of Seti, this building contains many well-preserved painted reliefs of excellent quality.

Achaemenian architecture

Originating in the mountainous plains of Persia, the Achaemenian dynasty (550-331 BC) achieved the political, and to a certain degree cultural, unification of the whole Ancient Near Eastern world. It produced the last of the great ancient Oriental civilisations and it was the first to confront and challenge Greece. When Alexander the Great conquered this Persian empire, he was inspired by the cosmopolitan ideals of Cyrus and continued the fruitful policies of cultural and religious tolerance instigated by the Achaemenian kings.

The arts of the Persians are characterised by a consciously applied eclecticism in which the stylistic or structural traditions of different nations and countries merge to constitute an 'imperial style'. This is most beautifully documented in the monumental architecture of the great Achaemenian cities of PERSEPOLIS, SUSA and PASARGADAE. Little is known about the vernacular tradition of this period, and the religion of Zoroaster did not require complex temple buildings. Elevated platforms and tower-like structures containing the sacred fire were sufficient.

The rock-cut royal tombs of Persepolis and Naqsh-i-Rustam combine pictorial images and architectural scenario in their flat porticoed facades surmounted by large raised reliefs.

The most important architectural projects realised by the Achaemenian kings were the PALACES which were carefully planned and executed, with meticulous attention to detail. Surrounded

Columns and gate, Persepolis

by quadrangular enclosures oriented to the points of the compass, these palaces consist of several independent architectural units which were grouped at right angles to each other. The evolution of palace architecture was completed in only thirty years. There was a continual development from the palace of Pasargadae, built by Cyrus the Great around 550/549 BC, to Susa and Dasht-i-Gohar (c. 520 BC) which culminated in the vast complex of Persepolis, planned and begun by Darius I in 518 BC. While the palaces of Susa were reminiscent of those in Babylon, with their abundance of polychrome glazed tile decoration and agglutinative ground plans, the palace complex of Persepolis was studiously eclectic. For example, doorways in stone were surmounted by Egyptian cornices, orthostat reliefs adorned the walls as in Assyrian palaces, the glazed tiles were made by Babylonian craftsmen, the tall columns were worked by Ionian specialists etc. This palace was probably used only for ceremonial occasions, especially the Persian New Year festival, which confirmed the royal authority before an audience composed of dignitaries and kings of all subject countries and provinces. The palace was built not only to accommodate and entertain these visitors and the royal entourage, but to provide the setting for the complicated rituals and processions. The whole complex with its elaborate architectural symbolism and its synthetic style can be interpreted as a three-dimensional model of imperial harmony in which diverse parts constituted a carefully balanced whole. In contrast to the hybrid style typical of the mercantile cities of the Levant, the imperial architecture of the Persians is highly original. The palace complexes lack the typical Ancient Near Eastern maze-like accumulation of relatively small rooms clustered around wide courtyards hidden behind impenetrable and thick mudbrick walls. Instead we have very large and generous interiors, made visually accessible by deep porticoes and large symmetrically placed doorways. The ramp-like stairways and monumental gates of Persepolis have a theatrical rather than defensive character. Indeed the whole building ostentatiously lacks ramifications of security.

Columned halls (see APADANA) and deep porticoes were the most important features of Achaemenian architecture; this TRABEATED style points to Greece as a source of inspiration and is in sharp contrast to the Near Eastern tradition of 'earth architecture'. Roofed with cedar beams, which could span 8m, supported by slender columns of great height (19m at Persepolis), interiors were vast and in spite of the extreme opulent interior decoration, seemed airy and generous compared with the small-roomed Greek adyton, or the dark and densely columned Egyptian hypostyle halls. The columns themselves with their strange, composite capitals are another example of the ingenious fusion of many stylistic elements, since they combine Ionian scrolls, Egyptian lotuses and Mesopotamian heraldic animals with a native type of split IMPOST.

The methods of construction were equally diverse. The foundations, external stairways, balustrades, door and window frames were made of stone in a manner reminiscent of the CYCLOPEAN MASONRY of East Anatolia. The curious technique of carving structural elements out of monolithic blocks (for instance several steps in each block in the great stairway at Persepolis) seems to indicate a certain unfamiliarity with this material. Timber was used for the flat roofs of columned halls, brick vaults, in the Elamite or Mesopotamian tradition, for narrower spaces. The walls were predominantly of mudbrick, occasionally decorated with moulded glazed bricks in the Babylonian manner. Painted stucco and tapestries, variegated stone and gildings, and architectural sculpture in the form of relief ORTHOSTATS and carved jambs (as in Assyria) were used to adorn the interiors in luxurious splendour.

Culican, W., *Imperial Cities of Persia: Persepolis, Susa and Pasargadae* (London 1970)

Ghirshman, R., *Iran from the Earliest Times to the Islamic Conquest* (Harmondsworth 1962)

Herzfeld, E., *Iran and the Ancient Near East* (Oxford 1941)

Kleiss, W., 'Zur Entwicklung der Achämenidischen Palastarchitektur', *Iranica Antiqua* 15 (1980) 199-211

adobe

Spanish word meaning mudbrick. It is occasionally used for Ancient Near Eastern building techniques, although it is generally applied to Latin American architecture.

adyton

A term derived from classical architecture (Greek: 'Holy of Holies') to describe the inner sanctuary reserved for the priesthood (see CELLA).

agglutinative

Describes structures built mainly in MUDBRICK which evolved by gradual lateral and/or vertical extension around a basic unit, eg one or more rooms and a courtyard. Further single elements (rooms) or units could be added on at will. The possibilities for building by agglutination became apparent as soon as rectangular house plans replaced the circular

ones (see HOUSE). It was particularly popular in Mesopotamian domestic and palace architecture.

Schmidt, J., *Die agglutinierende Bauweise im Zweistromland und in Syrien* (Dissertation der Fakultät für Architektur der Technischen Universität Berlin 1963)

'Ai *see* ET TELL

Alaça Hüyük

Anatolia, see map p. xv. The site was occupied from the Chalcolithic period (end of 4th, beginning of 5th millennium BC) onwards. The royal tombs of the following Copper Age (level III) yielded rich funerary equipment in silver and bronze (among them the famous stags with the sun-disks between their antlers).

Alaça Hüyük: sphinx gate

9

The architectural remains of interest date from the Hittite period (*c.* 19th-12th C BC). The fair-sized town (*c.* 4km²) was surrounded by a circular stone wall pierced by two substantial gates. The main gate, which is still preserved in the lower part, had monolithic jambs with carved sphinxes and relief-decorated orthostats. Streets and public buildings were carefully aligned and distributed around open spaces. There is evidence of a well-built system of canalisation. The main public building (the so-called Temple-palace) stood in its own *temenos* and incorporated a colonnade of stone pillars on either side of a corridor-shaped court. Although the plan is not quite clear it appears that a series of small chambers and parallel oblong rooms surrounded a square main room or courtyard.

Arik, R.O., *Les fouilles d'Alaça Hüyük* (Ankara 1937)
Kosay, H.Z., Akok, M., *Ausgrabungen von Alaça Hüyük:1940-48* (Ankara 1966)

Alalakh *see* TELL ATCHANA

altar

Summary designation for bench- or table-like structures associated with religious practices such as offerings and sacrifices. These could consist of many substances, like raw or cooked food, drinks, flowers, incense, textiles and fire, as well as live animals. There are open-air altars (eg BAMAH) but the majority were installed in religious precincts or temples. In archaeology, the presence or absence of an altar-like structure has traditionally been an important criterion for the religious designation of an otherwise unspecified type of building.

Altars in Egypt were often shaped like the hieroglyphic sign for offering, representing a mat with a piece of bread on it. The altar was rectangular or square with a central round slab made of limestone or alabaster (eg in ABUSIR, DASHUR: mortuary temple, KARNAK: Tuthmosis III). Another type was made of simple brick or stone masonry blocks with torus and cornice and a small ramp or a low parapet.

In Mesopotamia, solid or hollow bench-like brick platforms often imitated architectural features of the temple, such as recessed panelling. Portable altars, with or without wheels, were common in archaic temples (eg KHAFAJE, ASSUR: Ishtar temple). They too repeat elevational details such as windows, niches and doorways of the temple itself and are therefore of great archaeological interest.

In Palestine, 'horned' altars with raised corners on a block were common in Biblical times. 'Tabernacle' altars of the same shape were equipped with rings and staves and hollowed out for easy transport.

Monumental open-air fire altars with a flight of steps leading to a platform were built for the specific requirements of the Achaemenian religion.

Altintepe

Anatolia, see map p. xv. URARTIAN site (9th C BC) with an important temple of the SUSI type. The shrine was set towards the back of a square courtyard (27m × 27m) which was open to the sky but surrounded on all sides by a flat-roofed colonnade with twenty wooden columns on stone bases. This gracefully proportioned structure contrasted with the tall thick-walled (4.35m) temple building (13.80m × 13.80m). The single small CELLA (5m × 5m) contained the image of the state god Haldi. The cella and the walls of the colonnade were originally decorated with paintings, as in other

Egyptian altar, Karnak

Temple at Altintepe

Urartian sanctuaries (Arinberd, KARMIR-BLUR) which were inspired by the palatial wall-decorations of Assyria.

On the summit of the hill, south of the temple-palace, stood an interesting building (44m × 25.30m on the inside), with thick mudbrick walls on stone foundations. Eighteen columns in three rows of six stood on stone bases 1.50m in diameter. The columns were made either of wood or of mudbrick, as those at KARMIR-BLUR. The walls on the facade were reinforced with stone projections and the interior was decorated with wall-paintings. The excavator interpreted this structure as the reception hall of the palace and regarded it and similar ones from other Urartian sites as ancestral to the columned halls of the Medes and the Achaemenians (see APADANA).

The royal tombs were built to represent models of houses with actual doors connecting the underground burial apartments. The subterranean chambers had parallel stone walls filled with rubble, and were roofed either with flat slabs or a pseudo-vault. Above ground, a mudbrick superstructure resting on stone and PISÉ foundations enclosed a single large chamber. The habit of interring the king in a stone sarcophagus inside underground vaults may derive from Assyria. Next to the tombs was an open-air temple with four stelae and an altar surrounded by a stone wall on four sides. Such installations are associated with the Urartian funerary cult practices.

Özgüç, T., 'Altintepe, Architectural Monuments and Wall-paintings', I *Türk Tarih Kurumu Yayinlarindan* 24 (Ankara 1966); II (Ankara 1969)

Al-Ubaid

Mesopotamia, see map p. xviii. This site was investigated by Sir Leonard Woolley when he was digging at nearby UR. He discovered interesting Early Dynastic remains of a ZIGGURAT, a small settlement and the sanctuary dedicated to Ninhursag built by A-anni-padda (*c.* 27th C BC) of Ur. The temple stood on a platform of limestone foundations situated on a natural hillock and was approached by a flight of steps with a timber-panelled parapet. Nothing of the actual temple architecture remains, but a large copper relief of a demonic bird between two stags (now in the British Museum) was thought to have adorned the facade.

Hall, H.R., Woolley, C.L., *Ur Excavations: Vol. I, Al 'Ubaid* (Oxford 1927)

ambulatory

Some late Egyptian temples have open corridors or walkways which separate the temple building from the surrounding *temenos* walls (eg EDFU). Smaller shrines,

Ambulatory, mamissi *at Philae (Graeco-Roman period)*

such as peripteral chapels or MAMISSIS, had a covered ambulatory, often supported by pillars or columns round the main shrine.

Anatolian architecture

The geographical position of Anatolia determined to some extent its cultural affinities. The west shared in the Aegean tradition, the south was open to the Levant and Syria, as well as Mesopotamia further east. The central highlands were more cut off and developed a vernacular style of architecture which was ideally suited to the prevailing conditions. It has changed little over the millennia to the present day. In antiquity, much of the country was covered by forests of deciduous and evergreen trees which supplied high quality timber. Buildings in wood must have been much more common than the archaeological evidence suggests. The MEGARON, with its pitched roof, is generally thought to derive from a timber structure. The harsh winter climate of central Anatolia makes outdoor living less desirable, and therefore houses do not as a rule have courtyards as the central unit. Stone, mainly limestone, was also plentiful and so was clay. Since earthquakes were not infrequent, a method of constructing walls with a timber grid filled in with mudbrick, resting on stone foundations, is still in use in many rural areas of modern Turkey. The standard of domestic architecture was already high in the earliest period of Anatolian civilisation, the Neolithicum (7th millennium BC). The houses at HACILAR had two storeys and a large central room complete with wallcupboards, windows and fireplaces.

The history of Anatolia was turbulent; invasions and popular unrest, as well as natural catastrophes, were frequent occurrences. Rich in minerals, stones and timber, it was subject to colonial raids but in peaceful times pursued a lucrative trade

House in Ankara built in the traditional Anatolian manner

with all other Near Eastern countries. The earliest foreign trading community specialising in silver was composed of Assyrian merchants who settled at KÜLTEPE in the beginning of the 2nd millennium BC.

The Hittites dominated events during most of the 2nd millennium BC and they built numerous fortified towns preferably on exposed hill-sites. Masters in the art of FORTIFICATIONS, they flung crenellated ramparts with towers and bastions around the modest Anatolian settlements, turning them into formidable CITADELS. This tradition was continued during the Iron Age by the North Syrian neo-Hittite principalities and the warlike Urartians in the east. The Hittites were skilled workers of stone (as were the Urartians), and built strong walls with huge boulders of dressed rock or double casemate walls. The lower

13

courses of the exterior walls below the mudbrick superstructure were protected by upright stone slabs, which were decorated with reliefs in important buildings, particularly in neo-Hittite palaces like CARCHEMISH, Karatepe and ZINJIRLI (see also ORTHOSTAT). Monumental temples are rare in Anatolia. If the interpretation of the painted chambers at ÇATAL HÜYÜK as shrines is correct, then these were the earliest examples (6th millennium BC). Numerous open-air sanctuaries are known from all periods; the Hittites used to carve large scale reliefs of gods on rock-faces, particularly near springs and on mountain passes. The cult of the most popular of Anatolian deities, weather-gods and mother-goddesses, apparently did not require regular temples. The Hittite capital did of course have its established priesthood, and there were several large and small temples at Hattušaš (see BOGHAZKÖY). The cellae, however, in the middle of a vast complex of tall store houses and only indirectly accessible through a courtyard and vestibules, had large windows set low in the wall to let in light and air.

The Phrygians and Lydians, who established kingdoms in the first half of the 1st millennium, had little impact on the architecture of Anatolia. The Phrygians did develop curious rock-cut monuments with a gabled facade imitating a house and decorated with geometrical patterns. The internal arrangement of rooms also recalls the layout of houses. It is not certain whether they were intended as tombs or shrines.

Lloyd, S., *Early Anatolia* (Harmondsworth 1956)
Naumann, K., *Die Architektur Kleinasiens* (2nd ed., Tübingen 1971)

annulet

The slightly projecting ring around the shaft of a column.

antae

A term derived from classical architecture for the projecting lateral walls of a single-room building which provide an open porch. Columns between these walls are said to be '*in antis*' (see MEGARON).

apadana

In Achaemenian palaces, the columned hall of square plan flanked by one or more lower porticoes, which was used as an audience-hall. Square columned halls (although without porticoes) were used in Iran before the Achaemenians came to power, as can be seen in the citadel of HASANLU (beginning of the 1st millennium BC). The Medes seem to have carried on this tradition (see GODIN-TEPE, NUSH-I-JAN). An ultimate Urartian origin has also been proposed (eg the columned mudbrick structure of the palace at ALTINTEPE).

apse

Vaulted semi-circular or polygonal extension of a room or building, found mainly in private houses in the Syro-Palestinian area.

Thompson, H.O., 'Apsidal Construction in the Ancient Near East', *Palestine Exploration Quarterly* (1969) 69-86

'Aqar Quf

Mesopotamia, see map p. xviii. A still impressive ruin of a ziggurat dominates this site in the vicinity of Baghdad. A foundation of Kurigalzu I (late 15th C BC), it became the royal residence during the reign of the Kassite kings (*c.* 1519-1162 BC) in Babylonia. Only a

Ziggurat with restored baked-brick revetment,
'Aqar Quf

'Aqar Quf: vaults in the store rooms of the
palace (Kassite period) (after Baqir)

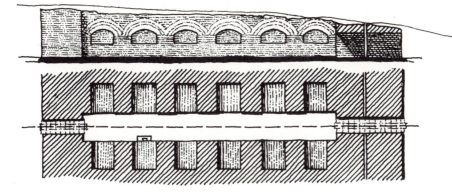

fraction of this town and its numerous fine buildings has been excavated. The ziggurat, however, is relatively well preserved and follows the standard Mesopotamian pattern. The present remains are 57m high; the plan is roughly square (69m × 67.60m). The mudbrick core is built up of layers interlaid with sand-imbedded reed matting and secured by plaited reed ropes running through the whole structure from side to side.

There were four major temples, also probably built by Kurigalzu, with huge gateways, paved brick pavements and very thick solid brick walls (average 3.50m).

Of great interest is the extensive palace. A large court ($64m^2$) is surrounded on three sides by units comprising one long room (or corridor) and a small room on each side. There were vaulted store rooms and passages and arched doorways. Traces of wall-paintings have been found, featuring a procession of officials. The 'White Building' in level II had massive mudbrick walls and a barrel-vaulted ceiling.

Baqir, T., *Iraq Supplement* 6–7 (1944-45); 8 (1946)

aqueduct

Artificial channel to transport water over certain distances to ensure supply in arid places. An aqueduct consists of a brick or stone bed or canal, bridges and tunnels, which overcome the different levels of the terrain. Best known is the one of NINEVEH, built by Sennacherib (704-681 BC). It was over 80km long and constructed entirely of limestone with pointed arches and bridges ornamented with recesses and buttresses. The excellently graded concrete surface could also serve as a road when the water was not flowing. The Urartians also built various artificial waterways. One in the vicinity of Van

transported drinking water over a distance of 75km (see URARTIAN ARCHITECTURE).

Jacobsen, T.H., Lloyd, S., *Sennacherib's Aqueduct at Jerwan* (Chicago 1935)

Arad

Palestine, see map p. xix. This site in the Negev was first inhabited during the Chalcolithic period but the major occupational levels date first from the 3rd millennium BC (Early Bronze I and II) and then from the end of the second and the first half of the 1st millennium BC (Iron Age).

Arad was flourishing during the period of the First Egyptian dynasty (*c.* 3100-2890 BC) when it was an important way-station for Egyptian caravans journeying to the Dead Sea. The town was surrounded by a curved wall strengthened by semicircular towers which followed the contours of the hill. The houses were well built and mostly of one type, with a broad central room furnished with a stone table, and adjacent kitchens and utility rooms in the courtyard. A DOUBLE SANCTUARY was found, of a BREITRAUM-cella type as in MEGIDDO. Towards the end of Early Bronze II, the settlement was destroyed and only the highest part was subsequently inhabited again.

From the 12th C BC onwards, Arad became a fortified outpost in the south of the Judean kingdom. It had a square citadel (*c.* 50m on each side) with strong casemate walls built in fine ashlar masonry typical for Israelite fortifications. A sanctuary within the citadel is claimed to have been a Jewish temple. It consisted of a courtyard and a broad chamber at the entrance of which were two pillars, maybe similar to 'Joachin and Boaz' of Solomo's Temple. A small room, more like a niche, protruded outwards from the wall opposite the entrance and contained two small stone altars and a '*masseba*' (cult-stone).

Aharoni, Y., Amiran, R., 'Arad, a Biblical City', *Archaeology* 17 (1964) 43-53

arch

Although the arch played a minor role in the Ancient Near East compared to its prominent position in Islamic architecture, it was probably more conspicuous than the archaeological records suggest. Arches are generally preserved only in subterranean tombs; but we know from contemporary architectural representations and from a few excavated examples, that they were used throughout the Near East, especially over large doorways and monumental gates where the span was too great for wooden lintels to support the incumbent mass of masonry.

The technique of building true arches was known since the 3rd millennium BC (eg the Royal Tombs at UR; the 'Vaulted Hall' at level VIII of TEPE GAWRA; Old Kingdom tombs as at GIZA, SAQQARA from the III Dynasty onwards) but cor-

Megalithic arch, Boghazköy (Anatolia)

belled arches, like corbelled vaults, were much more common. Arches were built predominantly in mudbrick, sometimes with specially shaped bricks for the voussoirs. Otherwise, regular rectangular bricks were used and the gaps between them were filled out with chippings. Stone arches are much rarer (one at Tell Taya: Agade-period – see *Iraq* 30, p. 247); in Egypt they were introduced in the Middle Kingdom and tended to be cut from already laid blocks in a corbelled roof.

The Hittites introduced the megalithic, parabolic arch, composed of two huge upright stone boulders inclined against each other until they met at the top (eg ALAÇA HÜYÜK, BOGHAZKÖY). The Elamites used arches and vaults a great deal, as did the Kassites in Mesopotamia.

Besenval, R., *Technologie de la voûte dans l'orient ancien* (Paris 1984)

architect

Like artists and   ıns, architects in the Ancient Near East remained anonymous. The credit for planning, financing and executing prestigious monumental projects went invariably to the ruler or king. There are large numbers of BUILDING INSCRIPTIONS from all areas of the ancient Orient in which royal building activities are proudly recorded. Gudea of Lagash (20th C BC) for instance, a Sumerian governor, claimed that divine inspiration by a dream provided the design for a new temple. One of the best-known accounts of royal building activities occurs in the Old Testament and concerns the Temple of Jerusalem built by Solomo (I Kings 6, 1-35 and II Chronicles 3, 1-14).

In Egypt, however, architects in charge of royal commissions could reach powerful positions and occasionally ended up deified. Although the title of such persons was 'Overseer of the King's Works', it is

not certain whether they were actually engaged in the creative part of the enterprise, as the western usage of the word 'architect' implies. Their own accounts on statues and in funerary inscriptions are silent on this interesting point. Most famous among them is IMHOTEP (III Dynasty), a high priest and official, who was in charge of the first monumental funerary complex entirely built in stone (see SAQQARA, monument of Djoser). He was later deified. Amenhotep, son of Hapu (XVIII Dynasty), was also granted divine honours.

Several architects responsible for major works during the New Kingdom are known by name; eg SENMUT (DEIR-EL-BAHARI, Hatshepsut), or Hatey (columns of hypostyle hall in KARNAK).

Bissing, Fr. W. von, 'Baumeister und Bauten aus dem Beginn des Neuen Reiches', *Studi in Memoria di Ippolito Rosellini* (Pisa 1949)

architectural representation

Pictures of buildings on documents, painted walls or various small objects contribute valuable data for the reconstruction of ancient buildings, particularly in regard to elevational details. It is, however, often difficult to interpret certain features due to the limitations of an art eschewing the use of perspective.

Sumerian architectural representations on seals, stone vessels or votive plaques depict rural structures made of vegetal materials, such as domed sheds and stables fashioned from bundled reeds, some of which had religious associations. The interpretation of more complex edifices such as temples or ziggurats, is more problematic as the artists only put in what they considered important. But it appears that temples, for instance, could have several storeys, or that their main hall was higher than the surrounding rooms.

Pylon, relief on the temple walls at Edfu

Assyrian palace-reliefs feature town-scapes, fortresses and temples from various parts of the empire, such as the shield-hung, spear-crowned temple of Musasir and the crenellated forts of Urartu or Elam.

Egyptian architectural representations on papyri, tomb-paintings and temple-reliefs represent mainly examples of domestic architecture: brightly painted columns and garlanded interiors. Foreign structures were also illustrated on reliefs recording military or commercial campaigns (eg fortifications in North Syria and Palestine on the temple walls of KARNAK and ABU SIMBEL; or thatched mud-huts in Punt on Hatshepsut's mortuary temple at DEIR-EL-BAHARI).

Davies, N. de G., 'The Town House in Ancient Egypt', *Metropolitan Museum Studies* I, Part 2 (1929)

Delougaz, P.P., 'Architectural Representations on Steatite Vases', *Iraq* 22 (1960) 90-95

Gunter, A., 'Representations of Urartian and western Iranian Fortress Architecture in the Assyrian Reliefs', *Iran* 20 (1982) 103-113

Heinrich, E., *Bauwerke in der altsumerischen Bildkunst* (Wiesbaden 1957)

architrave

Term borrowed from classical architecture where it denotes the lowest part of the

19

*Architraves in the temple of Luxor
(XVIII Dynasty)*

entablature. In Egyptian TRABEATED ARCHITECTURE, they were rectangular blocks held up by columns or pilasters, which carried the roofing-slabs of stone which replaced the wooden beams. Their width and height always corresponds to the upper part of the support. The disposition is longitudinal in the centre of a large space (eg in a hypostyle hall) and transversal to the row of supports in the subsidiary spaces (aisles or porticoes). Architraves are bound by means of clamps and peg-dowels in wood or stone. Two or three blocks meeting at a corner were cut diagonally to fit like a jigsaw, and dove-tailed together. An additional line of architraves could be set on top to weigh them down. As the bearing surface was often insufficient, there are many examples of patched architrave-blocks. The decoration consisted usually of hiero-glyphic inscriptions or, during the 'clas-sical' phase of Egyptian architecture, the Middle Kingdom, of a row of 'Doric' dentils.

Vandier, J., *Manuel d'archéologie égyptienne* I (Paris 1952) 277ff

ashlar

Hewn rectangular blocks of masonry with dressed edges laid in horizontal courses. The Phoenicians, who were extremely skilled masons, introduced the use of ashlar in the Middle Bronze period (eg RAS SHAMRA). In Palestine, the use of ashlar masonry is associated with the period of the United Monarchy (*c*. 1010-935 BC) (see ARAD, GEZER, HAZOR, MEGIDDO).

Israelite masonry at Samaria (c. 9th C BC)
(after Albright)

Assur (modern Qalat Shergat)

Mesopotamia, see map p. xviii. Important residential city of Assyrian kings and religious centre dedicated to the national god Assur.

The oldest architectural remains date from about the middle of the 3rd millennium BC (Agade-period and earlier?) and consist of the archaic Ishtar temple with its shallow BREITRAUM-cella. At the beginning of the 2nd millennium, Assyria emerged as an independent political power. Under the energetic king Shamshi-Adad I (*c.* 1814-1782 BC), the town on its promontory overlooking the Tigris was fortified with ramparts and strong bastions in a semi-circular outline. The temple of Assur, which had been begun during the reigns of Ilushuma and Irishum, was completed by Shamshi-Adad. It was a large building (110m × 60m), adjacent to a steep hillside in the most prominent part of the town. The lack of space of this site influenced the layout of the temple. A double and triple (on the E side) wall surrounded an irregularly shaped forecourt with monumental gates. A second courtyard gave access to the vestibule and this led into the transverse cella, where a statue of the god was placed against the NW wall. The brickwork is of excellent quality, and the walls around the first courtyard were adorned with engaged half-columns. This temple retained the same plan until the end of the Assyrian period although the layout of the cella was changed three times (first bent-axis Breitraum, then the Assyrian long-room and lastly the Babylonian broad cella).

The great ziggurat probably originated at the time of Shamshi-Adad I but was dedicated during the Middle Assyrian period (14th-13th C BC) and restored by Shalmaneser III (858-824 BC). It measured 61m × 62m at the base; the original height and the mode of access are unknown. The facade was decorated with stepped recesses (76cm deep between pillars 1.80m wide).

East of the ziggurat, which stood alone in its own enclosure, is the site of the Middle Assyrian Old Palace with its almost square ground plan (*c.* 110.5m × 112m × 98.30m × 98m). It comprised one large and several smaller courtyards, surrounded by transverse shallow rooms.

A much larger New Palace was planned by Tukulti-Ninurta I (1244-1208 BC) but hardly anything remains of this structure. His reconstruction of the Ishtar temple is much better known. The archaic temple

21

Assur: ziggurat

was levelled and the orientation changed from NE to NW. Tall gate-towers flanked the entrance. The walls were decorated with rounded recesses. A broad ante-cella and another subsidiary chamber led to the oblong cult room (32.5m × 8.7m). Opposite the entrance stood a baldachin; from there one had to turn right in order to face the niche reserved for the divine statue which was reached by a wide stairway with sixteen steps. The niche (5.10m wide, 6.40m deep) may have been vaulted. There were three DOUBLE SANCTUARIES at Assur. The oldest, the Sin-Shamash temple, was built by Assur-nirari in the 15th C BC. The shrines stood facing each other across a single courtyard in a completely symmetrical disposition. The layout of the sanctuaries was from then on standardised shallow ante-cella and oblong cella ('Langraum').

The Anu-Adad temple (built by Tiglath-pileser I *c.* 1100 BC) is also a symmetrical structure as both gods were equally powerful. However, this complex incorporated two ziggurats (36.6m × 35.1m at the base) and the sanctuaries were set side by side between them. The courtyard just extended to the front of the shrines.

The Nabu-Ishtar temple was the last Assyrian temple to be built (by Sin-shar-ishkun, *c.* 629-612 BC). It had very carefully laid foundations of limestone. There are in fact three temples; a double-sanctuary with adjacent parallel shrines dedicated to Nabu and Tashmetum (his divine consort), fronted by an oblong courtyard and the single shrine of Ishtar, as well as various subsidiary chambers.

A BÎT-AKITU was linked by rails (to facilitate the transport of the holy statues) to the main temple. It consisted of first two and then three oblong halls surrounding a porticoed courtyard planted with trees.

The private HOUSES of Assur which belonged to the wealthy officials, were spacious dwellings of a tripartite plan with a reception room giving access to the private quarters behind. Corbel-vaulted brick tombs, and also some with true vaults, were built underneath the houses. The royal tombs are situated underneath the Old Palace. They were barrel-vaulted (since Ashur-nasirpal, 883-859 BC) and had heavy basalt doors and sarcophagi of the same material.

Andrae, W., 'Der Anu-Adad Tempel', *Wissenschaftliche Veröffentlichungen der Deutschen Orientgesellschaft (WVDOG)* 10 (Leipzig 1909)

Andrae, W., 'Die archaischen Ishtar-tempel in Assur', *WVDOG* 39 (Leipzig 1922)

Andrae, W., *Das wiedererstandene Assur* (2nd ed., Berlin 1977)

Haller, A., 'Die Gräber und Grüfte von Assur', *WVDOG* 65 (Berlin 1954)

Haller, A., Andrae, W., 'Die Heiligtümer des Gottes Assur und der Sin-Shamash-Tempel in Assur', *WVDOG* 67 (Berlin 1956)

Preusser, C., 'Die Paläste in Assur', *WVDOG* 66 (Berlin 1955)

Assyrian architecture

The name Assyria derives from the national god and his eponymous cult city Ashur. The countryside between the Tigris, the foothills of Kurdistan and the lesser Zab, which constituted the heartland of Assyria, was a fertile region. At the beginning of the 2nd millennium BC, Assyrian merchants were responsible for much of the trade in precious metals and other commodities conducted with Anatolia and southern Mesopotamia.

Around 1400 BC Assyria emerged as a major political power and gradually extended its territorial and military supremacy until it grew into an empire that dominated the whole of the Near East including Egypt, until it collapsed around 610 BC under the combined onslaught of Medes and Babylonians. Assyria's rise to glory was achieved by a highly efficient army, fighting countless wars, and an equally well-organised administration in the many dependent provinces. The king was not only the supreme commander of the forces, leading his troops personally into battle after battle, he was the head of his civil service, and stood in a special ritual relationship with the state god Ashur which entailed religious and cultic responsibilities.

In spite of the almost ceaseless activity that characterised the reign of an Assyrian monarch, he concerned himself personally with extensive architectural projects on a scale that rival those of the great pyramid-builders of the IV Dynasty. The restoration and building of temples had been a pious duty of Mesopotamian kings since the Early Dynastic period and Assyrian temples dedicated to their own god Ashur as well as all the other major Mesopotamian deities were built in every Assyrian town. The characteristic layout consists of a rectangular forecourt with lateral subsidiary chambers, monumental gateways flanked with portal sculptures and the combination of a shallow transverse ante-chamber with an oblong cella in which the image stood on an elevated pedestal in a vaulted niche. The Assyrian ZIGGURAT is traditionally more closely associated with a temple on the ground (as already at MARI and TELL AL-RIMAH) and was not accessible *via* ramps as in Babylonia, but probably from the roofs of these temples (see ASSUR).

Richly endowed and splendidly decorated as these temples may have been, the greatest Assyrian architectural creations

Nineveh: Shamash gate (restoration)

were the huge palaces. The capital was moved repeatedly during the neo-Assyrian period (*c.* 900-610 BC) (see NINEVEH, KHORSABAD, NIMRUD, ASSUR) and several palaces were built in all of them. To some extent, concern about the political stability at the beginning of a new reign may have prompted the kings to dislodge the whole court and embark on such grand building schemes. The workforce for these projects was recruited from the many re-settlement programmes instigated by the Assyrian kings, and the necessary funds were raised by tribute and taxation, as well as booty.

An Assyrian palace was more than a royal residence, state department, treasury, armoury and citadel. It was a visible expression of the power and indestructibility of the Assyrian empire, which was meant to impress itself on the tributaries and ambassadors, allies and merchants alike. Scenes of the triumphant

Assyrian army in action in every part of the empire were carved with vivid details on the alabaster orthostat-slabs that lined the walls of corridors and reception rooms. The layout of the palaces varies considerably, but there was usually a clear division into various functional units grouped around courtyards (see BABANU/BITANU). The state apartments centred around the throne room were in the centre of the palatial grounds, with a carefully guarded access, while the private residential suites were at the back. Monumental gateways with ramps for chariot traffic were guarded by colossal stone statues of human-headed bulls or lions (see LAMASSU). The decoration of courtyards and interiors consisted not only of sculpted orthostats which were probably painted, but also of glazed tiles, wall paintings and tapestries.

The methods of construction were

basically the same as those described in MESOPOTAMIAN ARCHITECTURE. Stone was more easily procurable than in the south and was applied for door-sockets, sills, floors and column-bases, but the walls were built in mudbrick. The private and royal tombs had simple rectangular chambers, roofed with corbel- or true vaults.

Assyrian architecture is essentially of Mesopotamian origin and the foreign influence is of minor importance in spite of the many different cultures incorporated into the empire. Any import came from the more immediate neighbourhood of North Syria, for instance the BÎT-HILANI-type structures built by Sennacherib at NINEVEH and probably the practice of lining the walls with orthostats.

Frankfort, H., *The Art and Architecture of the Ancient Orient* (4th ed., Harmondsworth 1970)

Moortgat, A., *The Art of Ancient Mesopotamia* (London, New York 1969)

axis

A building is described as being on an axis if one can draw a straight line through the middle of the plan vertically or horizontally. It usually coincides with the direction of access, although the axis of a space can also be determined by the most prominent feature or focus, such as a throne or a statue of a god in a temple. In such an instance, the position of the entrance is of secondary importance.

The term BENT-AXIS has become current usage in Mesopotamian archaeology to describe the mode of access in Sumerian temples, where the entrance is at 90 degrees to the main axis which is defined by the cultic focus and the longitudinal dimension of the building.

B

babanu

An Assyrian word that designates the private sector (courtyard and apartments) in an Assyrian palace, usually situated behind the throne room, as opposed to the BITANU, the public sector. The central unit of both is a large courtyard.

Babylon (modern Babil)

Mesopotamia, see map p. xviii. Very little remains of the ancient Mesopotamian metropolis except an extensive ruin-field in the vicinity of the Arab village of Hilla. The Euphrates, which used to run straight through the town, has shifted its course and almost all the remains of the early Babylon – it was the capital of the Amorite dynasty during the 2nd millennium BC – are below ground-water level and therefore out of reach for the predominantly German archaeologists who have been working on the site since 1899. They concentrated on the Babylon of the Neo-Babylonian period (*c.* 625-539 BC). It was Nebukadrezzar II (*c.* 605-562 BC) who was responsible for making the town into one of the most splendid cities of the ancient world. The site was inhabited until the 2nd C BC.

The royal and holy city of Babylon was surrounded by a rectangular, impressively strong double wall built of baked brick. A second, outer wall, some ten miles long, protected parts of the city's large suburbs, and its 'green belt' consisted mainly of date palm groves. The normal population was around 100,000 but it has been estimated that up to a quarter of a million people may have actually lived in 'greater Babylon'. Most of the public buildings were situated in the Inner City of roughly square plan, bisected by the Euphrates into two unequal parts. The famous double walls were pierced by eight gates, all named after gods, and the most splendidly decorated one was the Ishtar Gate since the ritual processions on the occasion of the Babylonian New Year festival had to pass through it. It was a double gate corresponding to the double wall with an arched doorway and projecting towers. The facade and the passage were decorated with symbolic emblems of the city's patron-god Marduk, fashioned of especially moulded, colourful glazed bricks set off against a deep blue background (now in the Berlin Museum).

A similar scheme of decoration was applied to the walls bordering the city's most magnificent street, the Processional Way which linked the Ishtar Gate to the festival-temple (see BÎT-AKITU) in the northern part of the town. The street was *c.* 20m wide and paved with limestone and red bracchia. A single large gate led from this road to the Southern Palace ('Südburg') which Nebukadrezzar erected over the smaller palace built by the Assyrian king Esarhaddon and his own father Nabupolassar. Afterwards it was extended by Nabonidus (*c.* 556-539 BC), and used as a royal residence under the Persians. The huge complex is composed of several palace-units disposed around a

Babylon: Processional Way

sequence of five courtyards. The middle unit contained the large throne room (56m × 17m). It had particularly thick walls which may have supported a barrel-vaulted ceiling. The interior decoration differed markedly from that found in Assyrian palaces; there were no carved orthostats, nor colossal LAMASSU-demons to guard the entrance. Instead, the walls were ornamented with wall paintings or murals of glazed bricks, featuring stylised plants and heraldic animals. At the NE corner of the palace which bordered the Euphrates, structures consisting of parallel vaulted corridors below ground level were discovered; these have sometimes been interpreted as the substructure of the famous 'Hanging Gardens' which the king was said to have built for his Median wife Amytis.

An immensely strong structure with very thick walls (21m), the so-called 'Vorwerk', served as a barrier against the strong current of the river at this point. It was constructed with baked bricks set in bitumen mortar.

There were other palaces in the NE part of the city (the smaller 'Nordburg' and outside the inner wall Nebukadrezzar's main citadel, the 'Hauptburg', and the Summer Palace), which formed part of the city's defences. Nebukadrezzar reports that the building of the Hauptburg took only fifteen days. In spite of this record speed, the workmanship is excellent throughout. The stamped mudbricks bearing the king's title were carefully set in lime-mortar mixed with powdered brick-dust, above lower courses of baked bricks laid in bitumen as a prevention against damp. The Summer Palace was situated on a hill and built on a terrace 20m high. It was oriented to take advantage of the cool north wind and

27

afforded a splendid view of the town.

The skyline of Babylon was dominated by the ziggurat, the famous 'Tower of Babel'. It was set within the vast sacred precinct on the southern end of the town, surrounded by the river, a canal, a double wall and the Processional Way. The Sumerian name of the ziggurat was *Etemenanki*, 'The Foundation of Heaven and Earth'. It stood in its own enclosure and is now badly denuded. Descriptions by Herodotus and a Babylonian scholar called Anu-bel-šunu describe it as having had seven stages of different colours with a temple at the top. Archaeologists discovered a core consisting of the ruins of previous ziggurats, which had been levelled and enlarged several times before Nebukadrezzar added a casing (15m thick) of burnt brick. Access to the second stage was probably by a perpendicular ramp.

The main temple and the sanctuary of the city-god Marduk, called *Esagila*, was on the S side of the ziggurat. It was a massive rectangular building (85.80m × 79.30m) with a facade heavily corrugated by niches and buttresses, accessible from all four sides. There was an annex grouped around two courts on the E. The ground plan of the temple conformed to the late Babylonian type: a broad transverse ante-room preceded the main sanctuary which contained the statue of the god in a deep niche opposite the doorway. Subsidiary rooms were grouped around three sides of the rectangular inner courtyard. Nothing of the fabulous wealth and luxurious fittings, which Nebukadrezzar described in his inscriptions, has survived the greed of plunderers.

Dombardt, T.H., *Der Babylonische Turm* (Berlin 1930)
Heinrich, E., *Wissenschaftliche Veröffentlichungen der deutschen Orientgesellschaft* (*WVDOG*) 99 (Berlin 1968) 36ff
Koldewey, R., *Das Istartor von Babylon* (Leipzig 1908)
Koldewey, R., *Die Temple von Babylon und Borsippa* (Leipzig 1911)
Koldewey, R., Wetzel, F., 'Die Königsburgen von Babylon', *WVDOG* 1, 2 (Leipzig 1931, 1932)
Reuther, O., 'Merkes, die Innenstadt von Babylon', *WVDOG* 47 (Leipzig 1926)
Unger, E., *Babylon: Die heilige Stadt nach der Beschreibung der Babylonier* (Berlin, Leipzig 1931)
Wetzel, F., Weissbach, F., 'Das Hauptheiligtum des Marduk in Babylon: Esagila und Etemenanki', *WVDOG* 59 (Leipzig 1938)

Babylonian architecture

After the fall of Nineveh in 612 BC which marked the end of the Assyrian empire, Babylon established itself as the last independent major Mesopotamian power until it was conquered by the Persian king Cyrus in 539 BC. In spite of increasing economic instability, the kings of Babylon spent fantastic sums on large-scale building projects throughout the land (eg in URUK: the so-called *Bît-reš*; in UR: palace and quay; the temple of Nabu in Borsippa etc). The capital city BABYLON, which had suffered considerably from the wholesale destruction inflicted by the Assyrian king Sennacherib in 689 BC, was almost completely rebuilt with vast palaces and temples, and was surrounded by enormous and well-fortified city walls. The architecture of this age is in keeping with the Mesopotamian tradition. Temples have heavily buttressed walls and favour the BREITRAUM-cella with a low platform for the divine statue, reached from the central courtyard by a shallow transverse ante-cella or vestibule.

The extensive PALACES were quite different from those of Assyria. They were composed of a large number of small units

Babylon: in the palace of Nebukadrezzar

(consisting of a few rooms, passages and a small courtyard) and a large main courtyard which gave access to the state apartments (in Babylon, several such units were axially arranged when the palace was extended). The throne-room was a Breitraum like the temple-cella, with the royal seat placed against the long wall. The decoration consisted mainly of polychrome glazed bricks. Heraldic compositions of plant ornaments (as in Nebukadrezzar's throne room: flowers and column elements in white, yellow and blue) and sacred animals were used instead of the narrative scenes of war and ritual found in the Assyrian palaces.

HOUSES were set close together in irregular building plots typical for crowded city conditions. The external facades had flat, zigzag-like recesses which formed a characteristic step-like pattern. The larger mansions had several courtyards; they were oriented to the north where the entrance lay, while the reception rooms (Breitraum-type as in the palaces) and private quarters were accommodated on the south behind the largest square courtyard.

Mudbrick was the basic building material, but kiln-baked bricks were used on an unprecedented scale, bonded with an extremely durable bitumen-and-lime mortar. The Babylonian bricks were of excellent quality and of a large square format, stamped with official inscription for public monuments. Massive vaults and arches were used in the palaces (best preserved in Babylon: NE corner of Südburg, but vaults were probably constructed for the roofing of the throne rooms too, judging from the thickness of the walls).

Andrae, W., in Otto, W.G.A. (ed.), *Handbuch der Archäologie* (Munich 1939)

Koldewey, R., *Das wiedererstehende Babylon* (4th ed., Leipzig 1925)

baked bricks

The bricks must be fired in a kiln until they become red-hot. For this, considerable heat is required (*c.* 900°-1000°C). A traditional method still employed in the Middle East today consists of stacking the raw bricks in a wide circle of diminishing diameter until a dome is formed, leaving just a small opening at the top for ventilation. Then a fire of brushwood bundles, thorns etc, is lit inside the structure which has to be fed continuously for up to forty-eight hours until the whole dome glows red, showing that the necessary temperature has been reached. Kilns with a furnace and fired with wood are also in use. Ancient methods must have been very similar, although it is not clear what kind of fuel was used (in southern Mesopotamia probably dried reeds). Such methods are relatively inefficient; the waste caused by over- and under-burning is high and the fuel consumption can be up to a quarter of the weight of the bricks. It is therefore not surprising that baked bricks were only used exceptionally in Ancient Near Eastern architecture; as a rule, only on such parts of a building that were likely to be exposed to damp (in courtyards, bathrooms, drains, the revetment of ziggurats, foundation walls near rivers etc). In Egypt, baked bricks were not employed before the Roman period at all. In Mesopotamia, they were used on an unprecedented scale during the Neo-Babylonian period (see BABYLON).

Kiln for the fabrication of baked bricks, Luxor (Egypt)

bamah

Hebrew word translated as 'High Place' in the English version of the Old Testament where it is mentioned unfavourably alongside the 'groves' as a pagan cult place. Archaeological evidence revealed that 'High Places' were not exclusively open-air sanctuaries on hills or mountain-sides. They could also be installed on lower ground and in cities. In this context, the term denotes the whole Canaanite cult area including altars, courtyards, store houses etc (see MEGIDDO, ARAD, HAZOR).

barque chapel

In Egyptian temples the barques used for the ritual journeys of the gods were stored in small peripteral chapels on a podium with a central stand for the barque. In the Graeco-Roman period they became more elaborate, like miniature buildings, complete with a NAOS and a covered ambulatory.

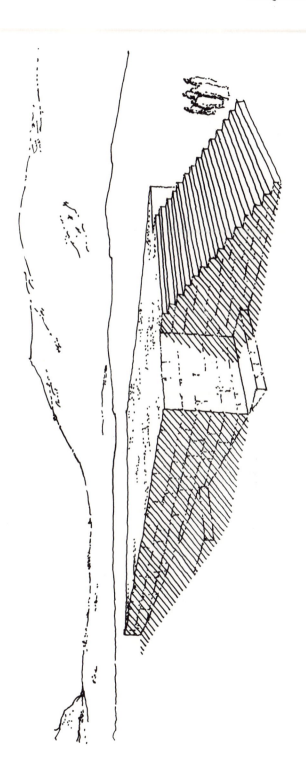

Bamah: isometric reconstruction (after Barrois)

Bastam (ancient Rusa Urutur)

Iran, see map p. xviii. Urartian town and citadel founded by King Rusa II (between 685 and 645 BC) and destroyed at the end of the 6th C BC. The citadel (850m × 400m) was entered by a great gateway with flanking towers and surrounded by a buttressed stone wall (5m high) which was surmounted by a mudbrick superstructure. Next to the gate was a large hall with fourteen columns holding up the roof. South of the citadel an unusual rectangular building was discovered with rooms surrounding an inner courtyard. It might have served as a royal guesthouse.

Kleiss, W., *Istanbuler Mitteilungen* 18 (1968)
Kleiss, W., *Iran* 9 (1973); 13 (1975)
Kleiss, W., *Archäologische Mitteilungen aus dem Iran Neue Folge* 6 (1975)
Kroll, S.E., *Archaeology* 25, 4 (1972)

bastion

Projection in the walls of fortifications, often at the corners which allowed the defenders to overlook and cover a wide area of ground. The shape of the bastions could be semi-circular, triangular (as on archaic Egyptian seal representations), square or, most frequently, rectangular. It is not always easy to distinguish bastions from towers or buttresses, as the upper parts of the walls are mostly too denuded. Bastions and towers were larger, and could accommodate one or more chambers. As these could be in the upper parts of the structures only, available from the battlements for instance, such provisions are not apparent on the excavated ground plan. As a result, the terms are used more or less synonymously in archaeological publications.

bathroom

The use of water for cleansing purposes was probably rather limited in relation to the use of oil, as in many hot countries even today. But archaeologists have interpreted certain rooms as bathrooms or ablution rooms, which had special in-built facilities such as water-proof walls, lined with baked brick, stone or a coat of bitumen; stone slabs for massage treatments, drainage, installations for containing and pouring water or oil, resting benches and the like. There is as yet no evidence for public baths.

Egyptian villas (eg at ILAHUN or TELL EL-AMARNA) feature *en suite* bathrooms next to bedrooms lined with stone, complete with latrines connected to underground vessels.

In Mesopotamia they were mainly found in palaces (eg MARI, KALAKH). They contained bench-like stone slabs and the floors were made impermeable by the application of a thick coat of bitumen over baked-brick floors.

Bath-tubs of bronze were in use in North Syria during the 1st millennium BC. At ZINJIRLI five suites of well-equipped bathrooms in conjunction with rest rooms and toilets were discovered.

battered

Said of a wall when its face is inclined in such a way that the angle between the base and the top of the wall is between 60° and 75°.

Battered walls are a characteristic feature of earth architecture, probably as the result of the moist plaster running down the vertical walls of a wattle and daub structure. This broadening of the base incidentally improved the stability of the building and thus the technique was also used in brick walls, especially for free-standing walls in defensive structures or those that were exposed to great lateral pressure as in ziggurats, where a great mass of crude brickwork had to be contained by a battered baked brick casing. In Egyptian stone architecture, battered walls seem to be an archaic feature, imitating earth walls (eg in PYLONS).

battlements

The upper parts of fortification walls with lateral cover in the form of stepped walls (CRENELLATIONS). Battlements were of considerable strategic importance during the Bronze and Iron Age and are shown on numerous ancient ARCHITECTURAL REPRESENTATIONS.

beam

Long, strong piece of timber placed horizontally to support the floor or ceiling joists in a room.

Many charred remains of ancient beams have been found in excavations from the Neolithic period onwards. They appear as soon as rectangular houses were being constructed. The trunks of date palms make adequate beams for a span up to 4m and were used in the southern, and generally tree-less, areas like southern Mesopotamia or Egypt. In the more northern parts, where timber was plentiful, a variety of trees were used. Much coveted were the cedars and similar conifers which grew in Northern Syria and Southern Anatolia. They were virtually indispensable for monumental buildings because they could span much larger spaces (8-12m), and exports to Egypt and Mesopotamia are attested from the 3rd millennium BC onwards.

Beni-Hasan

Egypt, see map p. xvi. Cemetery on a cliff-face on the E side of the Nile near Minya. It contains thirty-nine ROCK TOMBS dating from the XI and XII

Beni-Hasan: rock-cut tomb (Middle Kingdom)

Dynasties (c. 2133-1786 BC) which had been commissioned by wealthy administrators (nomarchs).

The oldest tombs at Beni-Hasan have a simple square tomb-chamber with a single or treble row of columns or pillars cut from the rock. Later examples have larger chambers with lotus columns and the late tombs are fronted by vaulted porticoes supported by eight- or sixteen-sided, gracefully tapered and fluted (Proto-Doric) pillars. The tomb-chambers behind have vaulted ceilings carved from the rocks and the walls are painted with lively scenes of pastoral and domestic life.

Newberry, P.E., Griffith, F.L. *et al.*, *Beni-Hasan* I-IV (London 1891-1910)

bent-axis approach

In Sumerian temples the cult room could

33

be entered by a doorway facing the image of the god and the altar. Alternatively, the cella was accessible by a doorway set in one of the long walls at the far end of the podium, which meant that the worshipper or priest had to turn right in order to approach the divine statue. The reasons for this preference are not known. During the Ur III period (*c.* 2112-2004 BC) it was generally replaced by a straight line approach. See also AXIS.

Beth-Shan (modern Beisan)

Palestine, see map p. xix. Eighteen levels of occupation, ranging from the Chalcolithic to Arab times, were discovered. The archaeological reports, especially those concerning architecture, only deal with levels IX to VII (*c.* 14th and 13th C BC).

Of interest are the so-called Canaanite Temples. The installation of level IX had a longitudinal and irregular layout. A long corridor on the S side led to a stepped altar. There were three offering tables in a large court behind the altar. At level VII this haphazard arrangement was replaced by a more regular layout. It consisted of a large hall (or portico and fore-court?) with two columns, and benches around the sides. A flight of steps led to the raised, shallow cella. The later temples (VI, V) show Egyptian influence in plan and decoration.

James, F.W., *The Iron-Age of Beth-Shan* (Pennsylvania 1966)
Rowe, A., *The Topography and History of Beth-Shan: The Four Canaanite Temples of Beth-Shan* I (Philadelphia 1930); *The Temples and Cult-objects* II (Philadelphia 1940)

Beycesultan

Anatolia, see map p. xv. Prehistoric site inhabited from the Chalcolithic Period to the 2nd millennium BC.

At level II (Early Bronze, beginning of the 3rd millennium BC), there is evidence for a small fortified town. The houses had stone foundations and timber-reinforced brick walls. MEGARON-type buildings were provisionally interpreted as sanctuaries, since many vessels and 'cult' objects were found in them.

Level V (*c.* 18th C BC) has remains of a palace. Rooms at different levels were grouped around a central courtyard (20m square). Some had raised floors to allow for heating passages running underneath. The principal reception area was on the E side of the court. An imposing painted hall, with wooden columns supporting the roof, was approached from this courtyard through an elaborate portico. There was an ablution room, another painted chamber, secondary courtyards and evidence for a second storey with a wooden balcony. Minoan or Cretan palaces were thought to have influenced this unusual design, but the excavators claim that this palace antedated the Mediterranean examples.

Lloyd, S., Mellaart, J., *Beycesultan* I, II (London 1962, 1965)
Mellink, M.J., *Bibliotheca Orientalis* 24 (1967) 3-6

Bît-Akitu

'House of the Festival' in Babylonian. At New Year, the statue of the Babylonian god Marduk was taken on a journey outside the city to dwell for a week in the Bît-Akitu, a small temple usually linked with the main urban sanctuary by a processional way (see BABYLON and ASSUR).

bitanu

In an Assyrian palace the public sector

comprising a large courtyard surrounded by official buildings.

Bît-Hilani

This word of doubtful etymology signifies a type of porticoed building popular in Northern Syria and Southern Anatolia during the final phase of the 2nd and the beginning of the 1st millennium BC.

It formed an isolated and self-contained architectural unit that could not be extended, consisting first of a portico with one to three wooden columns placed at the top of a flight of steps. The bases of these columns were sometimes supported by elaborately sculpted pedestals in the shape of striding, sitting or crouching animals. One or two doors led to a long room parallel to the facade with an optional small suite of rooms beyond. Next to the portico was a stairway which probably led to an upper storey accommodating living rooms. Such structures formed independent palatial units within a citadel and were probably used for official receptions etc (see TELL ATCHANA, ZINJIRLI and TELL HALAF). The Assyrians took a liking to this attractive kind of building and Sennacherib had a somewhat modified version of the Bît-Hilani built in his palace at KHORSABAD.

Frankfort, H., *Iraq* 14 (1952) 120-131
Hrouda, B., *Handbuch der Archäologie* I (Munich 1939) 180ff
Lloyd, S., *Early Anatolia* (Harmondsworth 1956) 163

bitumen

Latin word for naturally occurring semi-solid hydrocarbon (petroleum). According to the Vulgate translation of the Bible, the Babylonians used 'bitumen instead of mortar' (Genesis 11, 3). There are indeed

Baked bricks set in bitumen (Babylon, palace of Nebukadrezzar)

numerous bitumen springs in South Mesopotamia as well as on the Dead Sea. There is some evidence that the substance (called *ittu* or *kupru* in Akkadian) was indeed used as MORTAR: eg at ABU SHAHREIN or UR, where the plano-convex bricks during the Early Dynastic period were laid in bitumen. But generally its use was restricted to the purpose of water-proofing. Burnt bricks laid in bitumen form an efficient protection against dampness (see Nebukadrezzar's palace in BABYLON). Walls could also be coated with bitumen to form a water-tight surface.

Boghazköy (ancient Hattušaš)

Anatolia, see map p. xv. The site on a rocky plateau in central Anatolia had a long history of occupation, going back to the 3rd millennium BC. From a modest small settlement it grew into a densely populated city, with a strong citadel and several large and prosperous temples, during the 2nd millennium BC.

In the middle of the 15th C BC, a king who called himself Hattušiliš made Hattušaš the capital and administrative centre of the Hittite empire. His successors enlarged and strengthened the defences until the whole plateau was surrounded by a tremendous wall (estimated area of the town: *c.* 300 acres). The town was destroyed in *c.* 1180 BC.

The fortifications, consisting of ramparts, towers, bastions and fortified gates, are still the most impressive architectural achievement of the Hittite builders. The walls were built of rough cyclopean masonry to a height of 6m and then overlaid with a casemated mudbrick superstructure. Huge ramparts of earth raise the foundations of these walls to a consistent level, and an evenly sloped glacis of dressed stones, as well as a secondary lower wall down the slope at particularly exposed parts, made an attempted assault almost impossible. The walls were further strengthened by regularly spaced bastions and buttresses. The town walls were pierced by three monumental gates. Pairs of great monolithic, roughly dressed boulders were set upright at an angle in such a way that they formed a pointed arch. The jambs of the monoliths were carved with the heads of lions or sphinxes, or decorated with reliefs (as in the King's Gate with the figure of an armed man, now at the Ankara Museum). The central gateways were flanked by projecting stone walls which supported mudbrick towers. Postern-tunnels with corbelled vaults of triangular section led underneath the walls to allow for skirmishes during a siege.

There were several temples at Hattušaš, but the best-known and largest is

Boghazköy: King's Gate (reconstruction) (after Bittel)

Temple I, dedicated to the Weather-god Hatti and his consort, the Sun-goddess of Arinna. The entire complex measured 160m × 135m. Huge store houses, accommodation for the temple personnel, and various other buildings all with parallel, narrow rooms at ground level, enclosed the sanctuary on all four sides. These subsidiary buildings had thick walls and were probably several storeys high, thus hiding the inner temple completely from the outside. The temple (64m × 42m) consisted of a large rectangular courtyard surrounded by chambers and a corridor on two sides. A pillared portico on the N end gave access to the main sanctuary. It was accommodated in an annex protruding from the main body of the temple, and large windows allowed light to penetrate into the cella. Access to the cella was *via* a series of vestibules and the HILAMMAR. The segregation of the sanctuary from the rest of the temple is also emphasised by the use of granite instead of the limestone employed elsewhere. The masonry is composed of very large blocks, probably dressed *in situ*.

The citadel, Büyükkale, was erected on the highest part of the hillside and surrounded by a buttressed wall with a single fortified gate. Public and residential buildings were loosely grouped around several irregularly shaped courtyards on the rising ground, with the royal residence at the top, of which very little remains. The ground plan of most of these structures consists of parallel narrow rooms, doubtlessly supporting one or more upper storeys which must have contained the actual accommodation.

Bittel, K., *Die Ruinen von Boghazköy* (Berlin 1937)
Bittel, K., *et al.*, *Wissenschaftliche Veröffentlichungen der Deutschen Orientgesellschaft (WVDOG)* 60 (1937); 61 (1941); 63 (1952); 71 (1958); 74-76 (1963-1967); 81 (1969)
Güterbock, H., *Archiv für Orientforschung Beiheft* 5 (1940); 7 (1942)

brazier

Small stove filled with red-hot charcoal used to heat interiors during the winter months in the northern regions of the Near East. Brick braziers of cubic shape, pierced with holes on all sides, have been found in Anatolia (BOGHAZKÖY, KÜLTEPE) and a metal one on wheels at TELL HALAF.

Breitraum

'Broad-room'; a term introduced by German archaeologists to distinguish a room whose entrance on the long side is perpendicular to its axis, from a 'Langraum' where the entrance on the short side coincides with the main axis. The 'Breitraum-cella', an originally long and spacious cult room uniting worshippers and the statue of the deity in one space, was apparently divided into two distinct spheres sometime in the Early Dynastic period (*c.* 2700-2400 BC). The separation could be effected by piers, pillars or a wall. This divided the space into a relatively small cella containing the divine image, a podium or altar and a longitudinal ante-room.

This was the standard Southern Mesopotamian pattern, used in Sumerian and Babylonian temples. It was also used for Syro-Palestinian sanctuaries (MEGIDDO, BETH-SHAN, TELL MARDIKH etc). The longitudinal cella in combination with a shallow ante-cella or vestibule is characteristic for Assyrian temples. The standard layout for the Jewish temples, as described in the Old Testament Temple of Solomo, also had a Langraum-cella (see JERUSALEM).

'Broad-room', 'Steinerner Bau' (Stone Building) (Uruk IV)

bricks *see* BAKED BRICKS, GLAZED BRICK AND TILE, MUDBRICK

Buhen

Egypt, see map p. xvi. Egyptian fortress and stronghold on the southern border against Nubia. It was originally a XII Dynasty garrison, which was destroyed and eventually rebuilt during the XVIII Dynasty. From then on it was in constant use until the end of the XX Dynasty (11th C BC).

It was a large rectangular structure (170m × 150m), secured by a dry ditch and ramparts. The outer walls (10m high, 4.85m thick) were crowned with crenellations and strengthened by projecting square towers and round bastions. There were two gates. The main one had a wooden drawbridge and was flanked by massive spur-walls projecting from the facade. An interior staircase led to the battlements. The governor's residence in the NW corner of the fortress had direct access to the ramparts. There was also a pillared audience-hall surrounded by administrative quarters and private rooms.

Emergy, W.B., *Egypt in Nubia* (London 1965)

building inscription

The maintenance and restoration of existing monuments was one of the most costly responsibilities of ancient Oriental kings. As soon as the predominantly mudbrick structures fell into neglect they deteriorated rapidly, and the ancient cities must have had a fair number of ruined or semi-ruined buildings at all times. Rather than restore a former edifice, a new one could be built either on the levelled remains of the old structure (if it was on a particularly hallowed spot), or completely afresh at some other place. (It is of interest that the texts do not distinguish between restoring and building anew!) The chief responsibility for such a task always lay with the local ruler or the king and the completion of a monumental work of architecture, be it a palace, a temple, fortifications or other civic works, was an important event which was celebrated with the appropriate rites. In historical times, an account of the operation including the name and date of the king in charge, could be deposited within the building.

The bulk of such documents comes from Mesopotamia where a large number of building inscriptions, dating from the Early Dynastic period until the end of the Neo-Babylonian era, were recovered. A variety of materials (clay, stone, metals) were fashioned in diverse shapes (prismatic, nail-shaped, conical, or like a human figure carrying a basket on its head, the so-called Papsukkal-figure). The length and contents of these inscriptions, which were also transmitted as 'literature' in the Mesopotamian scholastic tradition, vary a good deal. They range from a few lines to the full-scale historical reports with several columns of densely written texts, issued by the Assyrian kings. The latter kind also include curses and blessings addressed to future generations who are exhorted to treat the building and its inscriptions well, lest the wrath of the gods be invoked upon them.

Mesopotamian influence was probably responsible for the custom of depositing building inscriptions in Elamite and Achaemenian buildings. On Egyptian temples large reliefs covered the outside walls (from the New Kingdom onwards) proclaiming the name and deeds of the royal builder.

Barton, G.A., *The Royal Inscriptions of Sumer and Akkad* (New Haven 1919)
Lackenbacher, S., *Le roi bâtisseur, les récits de construction Assyriens dès origines à Teglathphalasar III* (Paris 1982)

buttress

Vertical element in the shape of a flat pillar, projecting from a brick or stone wall. The structural purposes of buttresses are manifold: they act as a retaining force against the lateral thrust of a heavy wall; their tops, if flush with the walls, can be used to support the load of beams and rafters; they can serve as drains (especially if lined with baked bricks or stone as in some ziggurats). Furthermore, regularly spaced buttresses have a distinct aesthetic quality, enhanced by the strong light of the Middle East, which enlivens the otherwise monotonous facade of a mud-brick building.

In Mesopotamian temples, the vertical articulation of walls by means of buttresses and recesses is one of their main characteristics from prehistoric times (see TEPE GAWRA) onwards.

Byblos

Levant, see map p. xix. Byblos was the Greek name for the Phoenician city of Gubla. It had a long and varied history of occupation, from Neolithic times to the Byzantine era.

It is a site where the development of domestic architecture can be traced in a continuous process, beginning with simple branch-shelters in the 5th millennium BC. These were eventually made more solid by stone foundations. The houses of the Chalcolithic village (*c.* 3500-3200 BC)

Buttresses on the retaining walls of the ziggurat at Choga Zanbil (restored)

were round at first, then rectangular with an apse at one end. At the beginning of the Early Bronze period, the rectangular houses had gabled roofs held up by wooden posts. At the beginning of the 3rd millennium BC, Byblos grew into a densely populated town protected by a rampart. A prosperous period followed (level VI, *c.* 2800-2350 BC) based on a flourishing timber trade with Egypt.

The Temple of Baalat Gebal (The Lady of Byblos, identified with Isis/Hathor) of level VI (Early bronze, *c.* 2800-2350 BC) had two courtyards, one surrounded by three large rooms and a second that gave access to the cella flanked by two chapels. Five seated colossi

at the entrance are local imitations of Egyptian architectural sculpture.

The Temple of the Obelisks (19th-18th C BC) was erected on the same spot. The precinct was entered by a gateway on the E side which led into an irregularly shaped courtyard. A transverse vestibule led into the sanctuary proper, which had a court that contained numerous obelisk-shaped stelae. The cella in the centre, preceded by an ante-chamber, was on an elevated position and open to the sky. A great number of cult objects were found interred at the foot of the walls.

Dunand, M., *Fouilles de Byblos* I (Paris 1926-32); II (Paris 1933-38); V (Paris 1973)

C

capital

The top part of a column, at the end of the shaft and below the ABACUS, which provides an enlarged surface for the horizontal elements carried by the support. A support does not by necessity have a capital, and it is doubtful whether the simple tree trunk used as a post had any ornate form of termination.

Only capitals made of stone have survived. In Mesopotamia, capitals were sometimes made of metal, but none has been found. Most of the capitals preserved belonged to Egyptian columns. The Egyptians did not develop a coherent aesthetic canon or order as did the Greeks, who perfected the structural logic of trabeated architecture. The Egyptian attitude towards design was additive rather than coherent; therefore the capital formed an independent element and did not influence the form and measurements of the architrave or the base.

Egyptian columns in all but monumental stone structures were made of tree trunks, and we know from architectural representations that the top parts of such columns could be adorned with bunches of leaves and flowers. The plant capitals of the Egyptian stone column may derive from such perishable decorations, in keeping with Egyptian practice of 'eternalising' transitory ornaments (see KHEKHER ORNAMENT or DJED ORNAMENT). The choice of plants to be rendered in stone, however, was probably determined by their symbolical associations. The many forms of the lotus flower (or lily), for instance, corresponded to the hieroglyph for Upper Egypt; the single-stemmed papyrus with an open flower was symbolic for Lower Egypt, but there were religious connotations as well. The most elaborate floral capitals date from the Graeco-Roman period. Exquisitely carved, and composed of many different layers of foliage, they resemble festive bouquets (see PHILAE, EDFU).

The so-called 'Hathor capitals' may go back to the practice of tying ritual objects to the posts of archaic temples. The whole column has the shape of a sistrum (a sort of ritual rattle), with the shaft representing the handle, while the capital bears the face of Hathor with her characteristic locks and cow's ears, on one or each of the four sides of the capital. Such columns are known from the Middle Kingdom onwards, in temples dedicated to this goddess (see DENDERA). A late variation of this type is the Bes capital, who as the god of fertility appears on some Ptolemaic MAMISSIS (eg Philae, Dendera).

Probably the strangest capital ever invented was the Achaemenian animal-protome capital (PERSEPOLIS), which fuses various decorative and sculptural elements from diverse sources into a typically Persian composite.

The Proto-Aeolic capital was employed on top of pilasters and columns in the Levant and Syro-Palestine (eg SAMARIA, MEGIDDO). It consists of a double volute scroll on either end of a triangular leaf, probably associated with the Tree of Life, a recurrent theme in the decorative arts of these civilisations. It might have reached Greece by intermission from Cyprus.

Hathor capital, Dendera (Graeco-Roman period)

Carchemish (modern Djerablus)

North Syria, see map p. xix. Large site NE of Aleppo, on a great limestone plateau overlooking a fertile plain. This favourable position ensured that the site was in almost continuous occupation from Neolithic times to the Roman period. The majority of architectural remains date from Early and Middle Bronze Age (Old Hittite kingdom and Hittite empire, 2nd millennium BC) but those of the Syro-Hittite period (beginning of 1st millennium BC) are preserved best. The site is known mainly for its fine relief sculpture.

The defences of the town were very similar to those in ZINJIRLI, and consisted of two parallel heavy walls on mudbrick foundations with rectangular bastions. The gateways were flanked by towers and decorated with sculpted reliefs. The public buildings were disposed around an irregularly shaped space, and approached by a processional way which was ornamented with carved orthostat slabs on either side. So was the Great Staircase which led from the Lower Palace to the one on the acropolis. The facade of the Temple of the Weather-god was decorated with glazed bricks. There were two

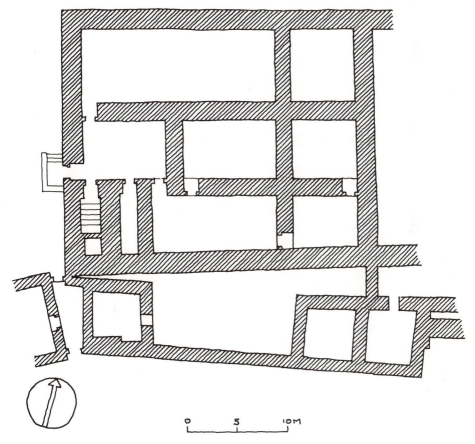

Carchemish: houses D and E (level II) (after Woolley)

courtyards; the inner had an altar for burnt offerings and gave access to the relatively small (8m × 7.10m) cella. Close to the edge of the terrace stood a BÎT-HILANI with a single chamber and a staircase inside. Its facade was composed of two solid piers of sculpted figures between which was a deep portico held up by two large columns. The walls were very thick (7m) and must have reached a considerable height.

Woolley, C.L., *et al.*, *Carchemish* I-III (London 1914, 1921, 1952)

casemate

A room built into the thickness of a wall or between two parallel walls. Mainly found in fortifications.

casemate wall

A type of wall which consists of two parallel walls, which are linked by perpendicular walls on the inside, while the space between them is filled with rubble, or left empty to serve as casemates. Such structures (in mudbrick or stone), could be built more quickly than a solid wall of comparable thickness. They were used primarily for perimeter walls, either for sanctuaries (eg Early Dynastic URUK, UR, KHAFAJE) or for fortresses (BOGHAZKÖY). Most casemate walls were built in areas where earthquakes occurred (Anatolia, Syro-Palestine). The Early Bronze Age town walls at JERICHO contained hollow spaces like small chambers and K. Kenyon suggested that they might have been constructed that way to stop the whole length of the wall from collapsing during a tremor (in *Archaeology in the Holy Land*, London 1979, p. 91).

Çatal Hüyük

Anatolia, see map p. xv. Neolithic settlement with urban characteristics, incorporating eleven successive building levels (0-X) from *c.* 6500-5650 BC. The houses were built of mudbrick, were rectangular in plan and had an added store room. Each house had only a single storey and no doorway. The only means of access was from the roof by wooden ladders. Light came through small windows high up in the wall, and there were ventilation shafts (see MULQAF) as well. Each room had at least two wooden platforms and raised benches. The bones of the dead were buried underneath these platforms. About forty structures were found which the excavator considered to be sanctuaries because of their lavish ritual decorations and the many objects he found in them. Their ground plans and interior arrangements were identical to those of the houses. Some of these 'shrines' were decorated with wall paintings for specific rituals only (they were then covered with plaster), others with three-dimensional reliefs that incorporated the horned heads of bulls or rams. Numerous figurines representing nude females have led to the assumption that the site had been a centre of worship for the cult of the mother-goddess.

Mellaart, J., *Çatal Hüyük: A Neolithic Town in Anatolia* (London 1967)

causeway

In Egyptian funerary installations, a simple ramp could lead from the river to the site, to facilitate the transport of building material and the heavy sarcophagus. Eventually the ramp could be screened off by lateral walls, or even covered over by slabs of stone with slits to provide light. The walls of the causeway could be decorated with painted reliefs (eg SAQQARA, causeway of Pepi II; see PYRAMID).

cavetto

A hollow moulding (see CORNICE).

ceiling

The flat upper surface of a room which can be the underside of an upper storey floor or of a roof-construction. It can be panelled in wood or plastered over and painted. Archaeological evidence for ceilings is limited to those of Egyptian tombs and temples. Some of these ceilings (eg in rock-cut tombs) were carved to represent a vault, which might indicate a similar practice in domestic interiors. The paintings on the ceilings in Egyptian tombs either represent the starry night-sky, or repeat the simple patterns used to decorate the rooms of houses. In stone temples, the ceiling was simply the underside of the roofing slabs, which was carved with reliefs and painted over a thin layer of plaster.

Painted ceiling in a tomb at Western Thebes (New Kingdom)

cella

A term borrowed from the terminology of Greek architecture to describe the inner sanctuary of a temple. In Ancient Near Eastern archaeology, one finds it used synonymously with 'Holy of Holies', 'inner shrine' and ADYTON.

In temples dedicated to the cult of a particular deity who was worshipped through a sacred image or statue, this effigy resided in the cella, which corresponds to the private quarters in a house or palace. It usually also contained an altar and other cult furniture, such as benches, emplacements for vessels, niches etc. The room immediately preceding the cella is called an ante-cella.

Nimrud: cella and podium in the sanctuary of Tashmetum (Nabu temple)

cellar

Subterranean rooms underneath or near a house used for storage purposes are virtually unknown in the Ancient Near East as this space was often reserved to bury the deceased of the household. There are some Late Egyptian temples, which had subterranean treasure-chambers reached by narrow downward sloping corridors (eg DENDERA, EDFU).

cenotaph

A funerary monument erected for a person actually buried at a different place. In Egypt, the practice of providing two tombs, only one of which was eventually used, was initiated soon after the unification of the Upper and Lower Egyptian kingdoms. Several archaic cemeteries had contained royal tombs before Memphis became the capital with SAQQARA as its necropolis. Most important was probably ABYDOS as the cult centre of the Under-world God (Osiris). Several kings of the I and II Dynasties have tombs in Abydos as well as Saqqara. As actual bodily remains were found in neither, it is not absolutely certain which tombs contained the deceased kings. In analogy to the later practice (especially since the Middle Kingdom when the cult of Osiris reached great popularity) of building dummy tombs or cenotaphs at Abydos, it may be surmised that the archaic graves were similar monuments. The largest structure, the so-called Osireion, dating from the 14th C BC, belonged to Seti I and is situated behind the great temple (see ABYDOS).

centring

A provisional timber framework, supporting an arch or vault during construction. Due to the scarcity of strong timber in most parts of the Ancient Near East,

alternative methods of building arch-like structures were used, such as corbelling, or the method of letting the inclined courses of brick lean against a solid wall (see VAULT).

Choga Zanbil (ancient Dur Untash)

Iran, see map p. xvii. Elamite town and religious centre founded by king Untash-Napirisha (c. 1260-1235 BC) in a previously uninhabited area. It was eventually destroyed by Assurbanipal in the 7th C BC. The town which also had numerous industrial installations for the fabrication of glazed tiles etc was surrounded by a wall (c. 100ha). The major excavated complex is the ziggurat, surrounded by temples, courts and shrines within its own *temenos* (1200m × 800m). It is better preserved than any comparable monument in Mesopotamia and its present height is c. 25m. The plan is a square (105m at the base) and it is built of mudbricks set in bitumen and cement, with a facing of glazed bricks in blue and green. The structure, though doubtlessly inspired by Mesopotamian ziggurats, had several peculiarities. It did not consist of super-imposed, solid terraces but of five large 'boxes' of increasing height, one placed inside the other and all starting at ground level. The highest was also the innermost ($28m^2$ in plan and 50m high). Three storeys are preserved, five are assumed to have existed originally. Four monumental, vaulted, brick doorways, each over 7m high, led into a complex arrangement of tombs, tunnels and chambers. Two temples dedicated to the god Inshushinak were built into the thickness of the second storey, among many other chambers on each side of the terrace. Access to the first stage was by a triple ramp: one perpendicular to the face ziggurat, and two

Choga Zanbil: ziggurat

parallel to it (as in UR: Urnammu's ziggurat).

In the eastern corner of the city, three monumental buildings with large courts surrounded by long halls and store rooms were discovered. One of them, known as the HYPOGEUM, included five underground tombs. They were similar to those at HAFT TEPE which were also built of baked bricks set in bitumen. All but one of the bodies had been cremated.

Ghirshman, R., *Mémoires de la mission archéologique en Iran (MDAI)* 39 (Paris 1966); 40 (Paris 1968)

citadel

A military stronghold within a town or settlement where it provides a refuge for the population in times of war. In the 3rd millennium BC, temple enclosures might have served a similar purpose, comparable to the walled churchyards in the Middle Ages. With the emergence of a secular leadership, strongly built palaces with their fortified gateways commanded the defensive system of the town (eg KISH, TELL BRAK, TELL ASMAR). Egyptian wall paintings in the tombs of BENI-HASAN (*c.* 21st C BC) depict small towns or villages guarded over by brick structures with battered outside walls and battlements. It was the Hittites in Anatolia who first built large citadels. They contained the lodgings of the local ruler, administrative quarters and sanctuaries, and are in fact characteristic for Hittite towns, not only during the Imperial period (15th-12th C BC) but also in the Syro-Hittite time (beginning of the 1st millennium BC). These citadels were always located on the most advantageous spot of the site, usually the highest, commanding the best view, and offering natural defences such as steep hillsides. The surrounding walls therefore often followed the contours of the ridge or plateau on which the citadel was built (see BOGHAZKÖY: Büyükkale; CARCHEMISH).

During the Iron Age (1st millennium BC), citadels were built in Palestine (TELL EL-FUL, BETH-SHAN, ARAD), North Syria (Syro-Hittite towns), East Anatolia (see URARTIAN ARCHITECTURE) and Assyria (eg KHORSABAD: there was a citadel within a citadel, since the main palace and temple were situated on a platform surrounded by its own wall within the precinct of the town-citadel).

Urartian citadel at Van (Anatolia)

clerestory

A method of lighting rooms by raising their walls above those of the neighbouring roofs and inserting openings or windows in these elevated walls. Ancient Near Eastern interiors were much darker than the artificially lit buildings of our age. The most obvious way of letting in light was through the doors. In larger buildings, the important rooms would therefore be grouped around an open courtyard. Secondary, or even tertiary lighting (rooms being illuminated only from an adjacent room), was quite common in larger conglomerations. The clerestory form of lighting became necessary when an important space was situated in the centre of the building, away from an open courtyard. Although archaeological evidence does not bear this out for want of walls preserved to a sufficient height, it must have been very common in large complexes such as palaces, temples and fortifications throughout the Ancient Near East.

Architectural representations from the Amarna period in Egypt show that the large villas had clerestories for their main reception hall (see TELL EL-AMARNA). The huge hypostyle hall in KARNAK had a central 'nave', which was lit by a clerestory provided by stone grilles.

colonnade

A row of columns, either free-standing or linked by an architrave. They were much used in Egyptian architecture (especially during the XVIII Dynasty) where graceful colonnades surrounded open courts or provided a link from one part of the temple to the next (eg LUXOR).

The term is also sometimes used erroneously to describe PORTICOES which were attached to buildings and roofed over.

column

Vertical supports, simple wooden posts for instance, can hold up coverings of shelters (branch huts, tents etc) and constitute the only solid structural element. When permanent houses in brick or stone began to be built, the roofing structure was mainly supported by the walls. Additional support, however, was needed as soon as rooms exceeded the given size dictated by the length of the roofing beams. Straight tree-trunks placed on a flat slab could support heavier loads than the simple pole, and were used in more monumental buildings. The geographical position would determine what kind of wood was used; date palm in Southern Mesopotamia and Egypt, and hardwoods in the Levant and Anatolia. Stone columns were extensively used only in Egyptian and Achaemenian

Clerestory in the Great Hypostyle Hall at Karnak (XIX Dynasty)

Colonnade of Amenophis III, temple of Luxor (XVIII Dynasty)

monumental architecture. Archaeological evidence for wooden columns is mostly indirect; imprints of holes left in the soil, or stone bases. Architectural representations and descriptions in contemporary records occasionally supplement the scarce information.

The Egyptian column developed like all other columns from a wooden post. In fact, all the columns used in domestic architecture, including palaces, were made of wood, as building in stone was a privilege reserved for the gods and the dead. Models of houses and paintings of Egyptian interiors show that these wooden supports were covered with plaster, which could be moulded and painted in various patterns (horizontal or vertical stripes etc). In addition, the top part of the columns could be decorated with ribbons or flowers and branches of greenery. The reason for

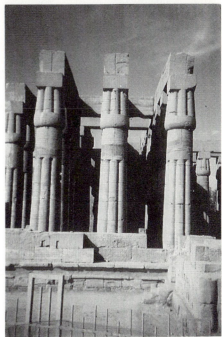

Papyrus-bud columns, court of Amenophis III, temple of Luxor (XVIII Dynasty)

51

*Plant columns, Isis temple at Philae (Graeco-
   Roman period)*

this lavish ornamentation was probably the fact that the trunks of date palms, when stripped of their scaly bark, are not very attractive, but they provide a rough surface to which plaster adheres easily.

The stone columns of monumental buildings recall to some extent the wooden prototype. But because they were employed in an architecture in which every feature had some other than merely utilitarian purpose, the columns were not just supports in stone, but emblems or ciphers of a now largely forgotten code. This double function is evident right from the beginning (see SAQQARA: Djoser's complex) and has resulted in much speculation concerning the origin and symbolic meaning of the Egyptian column. Almost all Egyptian stone columns are of vegetal shape; their capitals are formed to look like a single open or closed flower, a tightly bundled bouquet of buds, fronds of palm branches etc; some refer to cult objects. Structurally, the column, the capital and the abacus formed a single unit, either all cut from a single block or composed from different segments of the same kind of stone. The proportions of the columns, especially the relation of the height to the thickness of the shaft, varied in different periods. During the Old and Middle Kingdoms the height was approximately 5½ or 6 times the diameter. During the New Kingdom (especially the Ramesside period) columns were much stumpier (4 or less times the width of the shaft); but during the Ptolemaic epoch, the more graceful proportions of the Old Kingdom were introduced again. The dressing of the whole column followed its erection. The base was considered a separate part, consisting on the whole of a simple round slab. For a detailed enumeration of all types of Egyptian stone columns:

Arnold, D., in Helck, W., Otto, E. (eds),

Lexikon der Ägyptologie V (Wiesbaden 1984) 343-347

Jéquier, G., *L'architecture et la décoration dans l'ancienne Egypte* I (Paris 1920) 897ff

Columns in Mesopotamia are much less in evidence, since most of the load-bearing was done by the thick mudbrick walls. As additional supports they were mainly of the wooden type, either using the native palm or an imported wood. The shafts were sometimes covered in sheet metal (eg AL-UBAID). In Assyrian PALACES, probably under the influence of North Syrian architecture (see below), columns were a special feature made of bronze or cedarwood. In Sennacherib's palace at NINEVEH, the columns of the BÎT-HILANI stood on cushion-shaped bases, which in turn were supported by the figures of striding lions, as depicted on a relief-slab now in the British Museum, London. The stone column is virtually unknown in Mesopotamia, but parts of brick columns were found which were composed of specially shaped segmental or triangular bricks (eg UR, KISH, MARI). Large, semi-engaged cylindrical brick columns decorated with coloured clay cones were found at URUK: level IV.

The North Syrian columns found in the various local palaces of the 15th to the 9th C BC, left elaborately carved stone bases; either simple rounded cushion-shaped bases with a decoration of palmettes or volutes (ZINJIRLI), or sculpted to represent animals (CARCHEMISH: crouching lions; Tell Tayanat: pairs of lions carrying a platform for the column). The wooden shafts did not survive, but architectural representations show that the upper parts were ornamented by carved leaf-decorations. Free-standing columns were also depicted in Assyrian reliefs. They supported sculptures of mythological beasts, some of which were found at TELL HALAF for instance.

Egyptian influence made itself felt in

Assyrian columns and lion supports (palace relief, Nineveh)

Achaemenian capital from Persepolis (after Schmidt)

many aspects of Levantine art and architecture and various provincial variations of the Egyptian plant columns can be deducted. The Proto-Aeolian pilasters (see CAPITAL) may have had round columnar versions. The Achaemenian columns were very tall (up to 20m), with smooth or fluted shafts resting on bell-shaped bases. The capitals were set upon a ring of petals recalling Egyptian models, and upon it a piece composed of two vertical 'Ionian' scrolls became the base for the sculpted IMPOSTS, which acted like the forked supports. The imposts are therefore always in pairs (foreparts of bulls, bull-men, dragons). The whole structure could be painted (see PERSEPOLIS).

corbel

A block of stone or brick, projecting from a wall in order to support the weight of another horizontal element laid across (beams, rafters etc). A stepped series of corbels can be used as stairs in the upper parts of a house. This practice is still widely used in the Near East today.

Aurenche, O., *Dictionnaire de l'architecture du Proche-Orient ancien* (Lyon 1977)

Corbel-vaults were produced by gradually overlapping the bricks of the walls until they met at an apex. Stout and solid brickwork was needed to act as a canti-lever to stop the overhanging bricks from collapsing (this is not necessary when a circular structure is corbelled). As this technique allows a space to be vaulted without a timber centring, it was much used throughout the Ancient Near East (see VAULT).

cornice or gorge

A projecting, ornamental moulding along the top of a door, window, wall etc. In Egypt, the cornice is an ubiquitous feature of monumental stone architecture. It is slightly curved at the upper part and bounded at the bottom by a semi-circular TORUS (the curve was introduced around the V Dynasty, the early cornice was straight). It has been suggested that the Egyptian cornice represented the protruding reed-stems of archaic 'reed-and-daub' structures, weighed down and outwards by the pressure of plaster on the flat roof. The vertical stripes with which the cornice is mainly decorated look like the individual reed-stems.

courtyard

An open space enclosed by fences or walls of buildings. In regions with very hot

Cornice above temple doorway, Kom Ombo (Graeco-Roman period)

55

summers interior courtyards are an integral part of any architectural complex as they greatly improve the micro-climate of the habitation. The warm air of the courtyard, which is open to direct radiation of the sun towards the evening, rises to be replaced by the cool air of the night and is gradually distributed to the surrounding rooms. It can produce a drop in the air temperature of 10-20°C. This reservoir of coolness lasts for most of the day and accounts for the pleasant atmosphere of the courtyard which can be further enhanced by basins of water or simple fountains.

The courtyard also provides air and light for the adjacent rooms. It is the scene of most household activities as well as recreation. Large houses, palaces and temples can have several courtyards within the various architectural blocks.

The floor of a courtyard can be protected by paving in brick or stone to render it weather-proof, either across the whole surface or just along the main paths. Drains and raised doorsills prevented rain-water from penetrating into the surrounding rooms. However, not all central spaces on an ancient ground plan should automatically be interpreted as open to the sky as other means of ventilation and 'air-conditioning', notably the MULQAF, were developed. Up to 12m could be roofed with good-quality beams without any structural problems and larger spans could be covered by more light-weight timber constructions supported by projecting corbels high up on the wall. The lighting could have been provided by a clerestory and light-shafts penetrating into the surrounding chambers or corridors. One of the reasons for substituting a

Courtyard in a fellah's house, Luxor (Egypt)

courtyard with a covered space in Mesopotamia was probably the damage incurred by the often heavy rainfall.

Dunham, D., 'The Courtyard House as a Temperature Regulator', *New Scientist* (8 September 1960) 659-666

Margueron, J., 'Remarques sur l'organisation de l'espace architectural en Mésopotamie', *Archéologie de l'Iraq du début de l'époque néolithique à 333 avant notre ère*, Colloque CNRS 580 (1980) 157-169

crenellation or merlon

Step-like termination in brick or stone at the top of battlements to provide shelter without obstructing the view for patrolling guards. Architectural representations depict crenellated fortifications in Egypt, Anatolia, Syro-Palestine and Assyria.

cult temple

Egyptian temple dedicated to the worship of a particular deity represented by a divine statue residing in the innermost part, the NAOS. Most existing structures date from the New Kingdom and the late (Graeco-Roman) period.

The plan is rectangular and symmetrical. The constituent elements are distributed around a longitudinal axis with a tripartite division into PYLON and courtyard, HYPOSTYLE HALL and the inner sanctuary. The ground level rises gradually the further one proceeds towards the interior, and the height of the ceiling decreases simultaneously. There is a corresponding loss of light and brightness, from the sun-lit courtyard to the naos in utter darkness. The largest cult temple in

Cult temple of Isis, Philae (Graeco-Roman period)

Egypt is at KARNAK, the sanctuary of Amun. It grew by accretion, as successive kings added courtyards and pylons to the existing structures.

Badawy, A., *Architecture in Ancient Egypt and the Near East* (Cambridge, Massachusetts, London 1966)

curtine wall

In fortifications, the wall between two projecting towers.

cyclopean masonry

Composed of very large, irregular, and only roughly dressed stone blocks. It was used mainly in Anatolia and West Iran for fortifications.

Cyclopean masonry, Boghazköy (Anatolia)

D

dais

A raised platform inside or outside a building, made of wooden planks or of solid mudbrick, which serves as seating or sleeping accommodation. In a palace, the throne can be elevated on a dais.

Dashur

Egypt, see map p. xvi. Royal necropolis south of Cairo, with two pyramids of the IV Dynasty and three of the Middle Kingdom (two of them are mudbrick structures and now very eroded). The Northern or 'Red Pyramid' and the Southern or 'Bent Pyramid' (see below) were built by Sneferu, the first pharaoh of the IV Dynasty (c. 2613-2494 BC).

The Northern Pyramid, built on a square base entirely in stone, is the first 'true' pyramid. Unlike the later 'classical' pyramids of GIZA, the inclination of its faces is considerably flatter (43°36′) which might be due to the experimental character of this structure. The burial chamber with a high corbelled roof was situated in the bedrock underneath the apex of the pyramid and was reached through a corridor on the N face.

The Southern or 'Bent Pyramid' is larger (c. 200m at the base) and probably later than the Northern Pyramid. It is remarkably well preserved, much of its original limestone casing is intact, and the subsidiary pyramid is also less denuded than at other sites. The name derives from the present appearance of the pyramid:

the inclination of the outer faces change abruptly from a steep 54°31′ to the flatter 43°21′ about half way up to the top. The reasons for this change, whether deliberate or accidental, are still unknown. There are two separate entrances (on the S and W side) which lead to two superimposed chambers with corbelled roofs. The W corridor was found barricaded with portcullis blocks. No sarcophagus remained in either chamber. South of the pyramid, within its enclosure wall, stands a small subsidiary pyramid, also containing a burial chamber and a corridor.

The cult area next to the pyramid consisted of a very simple courtyard with an altar and two round-topped stelae inscribed with the name and figure of the king. An open causeway on the W linked the pyramid with the mortuary temple lower down the slope. This was a rectangular structure surrounded by a wall accessible through a narrow court on the S side. The central courtyard was closed at the N end by a pillared portico consisting of a double row of monolithic pillars. Behind them were six niches which probably contained the seated statues of the king. The simplicity and axiality of the whole arrangement is very different from Djoser's funerary complex at SAQQARA. It contains, however, all the basic elements of the Old Kingdom mortuary temple. It has been argued that this change at the beginning of the IV Dynasty might have been inspired by new rituals required for a royal burial.

Arnold, D., *Mitteilungen des Deutschen*

Archäologischen Instituts Abteilung Kairo 31 (1975); 33 (1977)
Fakhry, A., *The Bent Pyramid of Dashur* (Cairo 1954)
Fakhry, A., *The Monuments of Sneferu at Dashur* I, II (Cairo 1959, 1961)

Deir-el-Bahari

Egypt, see map p. xvi. Situated on the W bank of ancient Thebes (now Luxor), this site is famous for the two MORTUARY TEMPLES, which side by side are set against the sheer limestone cliffs of the hillside – one of the most dramatic settings of any Egyptian monument.

as his burial place. Recently it has been theoretically reconstructed as a monumental and elegant superimposition of various architectural units which may have been inspired by contemporary two-storeyed houses, if not by the immediate natural surroundings with its horizontal layers of rock. (Conservative reconstructions assumed a pyramidical superstructure.)

The complex was reached by a causeway flanked by royal statues. The rectangular and walled forecourt was planted with regular rows of trees. At the back arose the royal funerary monument with its flat-topped (or pyramidical) termination, surrounded by pillared porticoes. A

Deir-el-Bahari, Western Thebes: mortuary temples of Mentuhotep (Middle Kingdom) and Hatshepsut (New Kingdom)

The older structure, of which relatively little remains today, belonged to the XI Dynasty king Nebhepetre-Mentuhotep II (*c.* 2060-2010 BC). Unlike later New Kingdom mortuary temples it also served

central ramp led from the forecourt to the second stage. At the back of the structure was a colonnaded small courtyard, concealing the entrance to the royal tomb under the pavement. Hewn out of the

*Deir-el-Bahari: mortuary temple of
Hatshepsut (XVIII Dynasty), colonnade on
second court*

rock-face at the back were the funerary cult-chamber for the king and similar arrangements and tombs for his wives.

Arnold, D., *Der Tempel des Königs Mentuhotep von Deir-el-Bahari* I (Cairo, Mainz 1974)

The temple right next to Mentuhotep's was built more than half a millennium later for Hatshepsut, queen of the VIII Dynasty (*c.* 1503-1482 BC), by her adviser and ARCHITECT SENMUT. It is currently being reconstructed by a team of Polish archaeologists. The temple of Hatshepsut has a similar layout to Mentuhotep's, but the exigencies of this particular site (the danger of falling rocks as well as the dominating visual presence of the cliff-face) were dealt with in a more assured and successful manner. The whole funerary complex was arranged in three successive stages, gradually rising towards the rocky background where the chapels

and cult chambers were accommodated. A broad central ramp from the open forecourt led straight up to the three superimposed terraces with their deep pillared porticoes on either side. They are beautifully decorated with delicate painted reliefs. Colossal OSIRIDE PILLARS of the queen marked each end of the lower porticoes. The whole monument is deceptively simple with its clear outlines and the rhythmical effect of light and shade of the vertical supports. But closer inspection reveals a wealth of architectural subtlety, such as the use of alternating rectangular and polygonal pillars, harmonic proportions, etc.

Naville, E., *The Temple of Deir-el-Bahari* V (London 1909)
Werbrouck, M., *Le Temple d'Hatshepsut à Deir-el-Bahari* (Brussels 1949)

A third monument was built at Deir-el-Bahari by Hatshepsut's successor,

Tuthmosis III (*c.* 1504-1450 BC). It was originally more than three metres higher than the third terrace of her temple, but practically nothing of this monument has survived.

Lipinska, J., *Deir-el-Bahari II: The Temple of Tuthmosis III Architecture* (Warsaw 1977)

Deir-el-Ballas

Egypt, see map p. xvi. The site has remains of two XVIII Dynasty palaces. Usually the mudbrick palaces of Egypt leave little more than their foundations, but the Northern Palace has walls preserved to a considerable height as well as traces of a wooden roof. Elements of a solidly built upper storey have been found, as well as a substantially preserved stairway.

The Southern Palace is more fragmentary, and only part of the ground plan could be established which like the Northern Palace contained large, columned halls surrounding a central block divided into oblong compartments.

Smith, W.S., *The Art and Architecture of Ancient Egypt* (2nd ed., Harmondsworth 1981) 279f

Deir-el-Medineh

Egypt, see map p. xvi. Site of a workmen's village on the west bank of Thebes (modern Luxor). Founded by Tuthmosis I (*c.* 1525-1512 BC), it remained occupied until the XX Dynasty (*c.* 1200-1085 BC). The present ruins date from the Ramesside period (*c.* 13th-12th C BC).

*Deir-el-Medineh: workmen's village and
   Ptolemaic temple*

The village was built to accommodate the workmen employed for the excavation and decoration of the royal tombs in the 'Valley of the Kings'. The location of these tombs was a strictly kept secret and the workers were therefore kept in isolation in a guarded and purpose-built settlement, including sanctuaries and a necropolis. The residential part was enclosed by a rectangular wall with two gates. One main thoroughfare ran from N to S and was crossed by perpendicular side-streets. The houses were small and comprised only a few rooms on the ground floor (ante-room, reception room, subsidiary rooms and kitchen). Some houses, however, might have had upper storeys; steps leading to the roof have been found. To the W and N of this part were the public and official sanctuaries (now occupied by the Ptolemaic temple of Hathor).

The XVIII Dynasty tombs of the necropolis have small pyramidical superstructures, while the later Ramesside ones resemble small chapels.

Bruyère, B., *Fouilles de l'Institut d'Archéologie Orientale du Caire* 1-8, 10, 14-16, 20, 21, 26 (1924-53)

Dendera

Egypt, see map p. xvi. Although this site has been inhabited from the Old Kingdom onwards, the main building there, the Temple of Hathor, belongs to the late period of Egyptian history, the Ptolemaic and Roman era (*c.* 4th C BC-3rd C AD).

The whole complex is surrounded by a vast mudbrick enclosure, and contains the temple itself, remnants of a sacred lake, two MAMISSIS and the ruins of a mudbrick structure interpreted as a 'sanatorium for sick pilgrims'.

The present facade of the temple belongs to the Roman (1st C BC) extension which also comprises the first hypostyle hall. Screen-walls between the massive pillars leave the upper part open in order to let light penetrate the interior. The hypostyle hall has twenty-four columns with four-sided Hathor capitals. A central doorway through the original Ptolemaic pylon-shaped facade leads to a much smaller hypostyle hall, with six Hathor columns supporting the flat, painted stone ceiling, which is completely preserved. This hall is flanked by three oblong service rooms on either side. The floor rises gradually as one proceeds along two parallel transverse halls to the sanctuary of the goddess – a shrine within the temple, which originally contained the naos and the cult-statue. A narrow corridor around the shrine gives access to eleven chapels arranged side by side. Another corridor leads to the subterranean cellar or crypt, where the temple's most valuable objects were kept safe.

The flat roof of the temple, accessible through a stairway on the E side of the first transverse hall, was the scene for important seasonal rites known as the Ritual of Dendera. The roof therefore accommodated several small chapels, with fine relief decoration illustrating the ritual.

The southern facade of the temple has a large niche, decorated with the Hathor emblem which marked the position of her shrine within the temple for those who were not admitted to the direct presence of the goddess.

Of the two *mamissis*, the larger and better preserved dates from the Roman period. There are two courts and an open ambulatory around the sanctuary. The supports have composite floral capitals, and the crouching figure of the god Bes decorates the abacus. The interior arrangements of the sanctuary consist of side chambers, a transverse hall and three parallel shrines.

Mariette, A., *Denderah: Description générale du grand temple de cette ville* (Paris 1869-75)

Dendera: temple of Hathor (Graeco-Roman period)

djed-ornament

An Egyptian element of decoration imitating a bundle of reeds graded at the top. The hieroglyphic sign means 'stability'. The ornament was often used on the stone-cut window screens or partitions.

dome

Contrary to their widespread use in the Islamic civilisation, domes did not play an important role in the monumental architecture of the Ancient Near East. Large spaces could be successfully spanned by a dome only in Roman times. Small domes, however, have a very long tradition, going back to Neolithic times, when the very first solid houses had a round plan and were covered initially with branches, and eventually with a corbelled dome in stone or brick. Such oval and circular huts with domes were the dwellings of poorer people throughout the Middle East, until historical times.

The rectangular or square plan is more difficult to cover with a dome, as the transition of the four straight sides to the round perimeter of the dome has to be negotiated by pendentives in the corners. Excavated examples come mainly from underground tombs (eg UR: Royal tombs; GIZA: mastabas of Seneb and Neferi). Some monumental buildings in Mesopotamia are supposed to have been roofed with a brick dome, especially during the KASSITE period (eg UR: Edublalmah; 'AQAR QUF) but none of the structures was preserved to a sufficient height to settle the issue.

Mallowan, M., *Iraq* 2 (1934) 11ff
Piéron, M., *Bulletin de l'Institut français*

Domed ovens at Kültepe (Anatolia): mudbrick and stone

d'archéologie orientale, Caire 6 (1908) 173-177
Spencer, A.J., *Brick Architecture in Ancient Egypt* (Warminster 1979) 126ff

door and doorway

The archaeological evidence concerning doors and doorways is generally limited to the indication of an opening in a wall (if it is preserved above the foundations), the emplacement of pivot-stones (or their imprint left in the soil), lintels, or the occasional stone threshold. Traditional builders in the modern Near East, especially in rural areas, however, still use similar devices as in the ancient times and on the basis of this combined evidence, some observations and generalisations can be made.

In Neolithic times, houses did not always have a doorway. At ÇATAL HÜYÜK for instance, access was by ladders through an opening in the roof. This made the buildings easily defensible and obviously did not pose any problems to bricklayers. There were certain structural considerations to be taken into account when providing comparatively large openings for mudbrick structures. The possible weakening of the walls had to be overcome either by making the openings as small as conveniently possible (in Neolithic times room enough just for crawling was acceptable, later this changed to more human proportions), or by enforcing the resulting opening on all sides by vertical and horizontal posts or beams (lintels, jambs), and by strengthening the brickwork on either side by projecting flat pillars or buttresses (see GATEWAY). As the street level in a built-up area was ever rising due to accumulated dust and waste, the sills in

Monolithic jamb and door-socket, Boghazköy (Anatolia)

65

urban areas were often below street level, while in more isolated areas sills could be up to a foot above it in order to stop the dust and sand from blowing into the house.

The door-leaf was usually fashioned from wooden planks. Hinges were not used to fasten the door to the house, but a system of pivots; one rising upwards and fitting into a socket in the lintel, and the other going downwards to revolve in a recess in the sill, or a special pivot-stone or just a hole in the ground. The entrance was barred by various systems of horizontal bolts of wood or metal which could be drawn across the doorways from the inside.

In a simple mudbrick house, the door and the roof were the most costly items as they were fashioned of wood, which in most areas of the Ancient Near East was an expensive commodity. Sumerian con-tracts for the sale of properties, for instance, specify whether a house was to be sold 'with or without a door or a roof'.

Egyptian doorways from the Amarna period onward (15th C BC) have no true lintels and the pivots revolve in the masonry projecting from the jamb all around. During the New Kingdom, this stone frame was invariably decorated by a cornice.

The FALSE DOORS found in tombs probably imitate a wooden prototype, but as part of a monumental and very traditional architecture they may have developed into a genre without much reference to contemporary doors.

The 'broken lintel doorway' apparently originated in the Amarna villas (see TELL EL-AMARNA). It looks like a small pylon and the door-jambs capped with cornices on either side almost meet in the middle. In Ptolemaic and Roman temples they

Doors in a mudbrick house, Esna (Egypt)

'Broken-lintel' doorway, Isis temple at Philae (Graeco-Roman period)

became the standard form of doorway.

A reconstructed example of a monumental palace door from Mesopotamia is the 'Bronze gates of Balawat', exhibited in the British Museum. They consist of a two-leaved door made from wooden planks, fastened to vertical posts at the side and decorated with horizontal strips of embossed bronze (9th C BC).

Badawy, A., *A History of Egyptian Architecture* I (Cairo 1954) 185ff
Damerji, M., *Die Entwicklung der Tür und Torarchitektur in Mesopotamien* (Dissertation, Universität München 1973)

double sanctuary

When a temple was built to accommodate more than one deity, this is usually reflected in the architectural design by the provision of a second (or more) cella (eg ABYDOS in Egypt, where seven gods were worshipped, each in his own cult room; NIPPUR: Early Dynastic Inanna temple with two cellae next to each other). Alternatively, two or more complete temple units could be built in close proximity within the same precinct. Early examples from Anatolia are the double-*megaron* installations at BEYCESULTAN.

Double sanctuaries with parallel temples were popular during the Neo-Assyrian period and later (first half of 1st millennium BC) in Mesopotamia. Such a complex was often built for a male deity and his consort (eg TELL HARMAL; NIMRUD: Ezida for Nabu and Tashmetum; URUK: Seleucid An and Antu temple). The sanctuary dedicated to the female partner is somewhat smaller than the male god's to reflect her inferior status. In the double sanctuary dedicated to two male gods (eg ASSUR: Anu-Adad temple and Sin and Shamash temple) or to a male and a female deity of equal importance (ASSUR: Nabu-Ishtar temple), the dimensions are the same.

A parallel double sanctuary in Egypt dates from the Ptolemaic period (KOM OMBO), but the division affected only the internal arrangement of the temple since there is only one pylon and courtyard for each god.

Dur Kurigalzu *see* 'AQAR QUF

Dur Sharrukin *see* KHORSABAD

Ebla *see* TELL MARDIKH

Edfu

Egypt, see map p. xvi. The present town of Edfu is built on top of a *tell*, the multiple accumulated layers of earlier settlements, going back to the beginning of Egyptian history. The only conspicuous ancient monument, however, is the Temple of Horus, which was built during the Ptolemaic period (in this case exactly dateable because of building inscriptions; the first phase lasted from 237 to 212 BC and it was completed in 142 BC).

The temple is entered through a massive pylon decorated with sunken reliefs, which depict the pharaoh slaying his enemies. A perimeter wall of stone surrounds the whole temple complex and a narrow ambulatory separates the temple from this wall. The large rectangular first courtyard is surrounded on three sides by covered colonnades with composite floral capitals. The first hypostyle hall has a screen wall facade typical for the Late Period. The layout of the inner sanctuary resembles that of other Ptolemaic CULT TEMPLES (eg DENDERA), with its succession of two hypostyle halls (the second gives access to the temple roof, which here too was used for ritual functions), flanked by service chambers, two transverse vestibules and the oblong inner shrine which still contains the original naos of polished granite. A narrow corridor behind it leads to small lateral chapels reserved for various other deities.

The 'Birth house' (see MAMISSI) is from the same period and consists of the single chamber or 'birth room', decorated with the traditional reliefs. The ambulatory has low screen-walls between the columns.

Lacau, P., *Annales du Service des Antiquités de l'Egypte* 52 (Cairo 1952) 215-221

Egyptian architecture

Egyptian, like Mesopotamian architecture, developed over some 3,000 years. Egypt's geographical position across the Red Sea, protected by the barriers of mountain-ridges and deserts, made the country comparatively secure from external aggression which was such a constant threat to most other Ancient Near Eastern countries. This isolation helped to consolidate a civilisation which had its roots as much in the African continent as in the Fertile Crescent that surrounds the Arabian desert.

The country was united into the 'Kingdom of Upper and Lower Egypt' at an early stage in its history (around 3100 BC). The pharaoh was considered to be of such importance, being ultimately responsible for the prosperity of the country and its people, that his efficacy could not cease with his death. There arose the belief in the immortality of the

Plant column at Edfu (Graeco-Roman period)

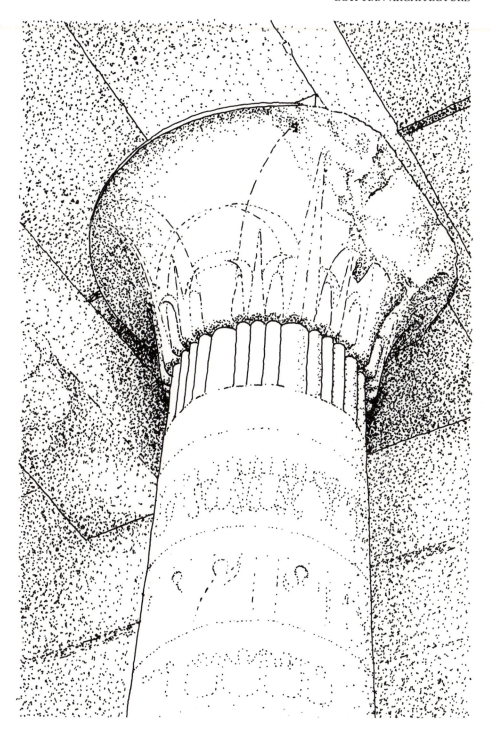

royal soul, which could be procured by complex rites and rituals. Egyptian funerary architecture provided the eternal dwelling-place for the king's mortal body and the soul, which could be kept alive by actual or magical sustenance. Gradually, the privilege of tomb-building was extended to non-royal persons. Without a proper tomb and without the necessary ties, there was no afterlife. The paintings and reliefs inside the tombs give a vivid portrayal of the pleasures awaiting the soul once it had successfully entered the 'Country of the West'. These positive expectations concerning the dead are quite unlike those held by other ancient Oriental peoples and gave rise to a tremendous architectural and artistic productivity directed towards the tomb.

The building of the 'eternal house' was always considered to be much more important than the building of a house for mere mortals. For the kings, their first concern was the provision of a suitable royal tomb, complete with all the necessary cultic installations. The theological ideas and ritual practices pertaining to the afterlife changed several times, but the urge to build himself a decent tomb if he could afford it remained a major force in every Egyptian until the end of their civilisation (see TOMB).

The funerary complex of king Djoser at SAQQARA (c. 2667-2648 BC) is the first monumentally conceived work of Egyptian architecture. It has an experimental character which disappeared in later periods. The interpretation of the various dummy buildings and courts is largely conjectural because there are no pertinent texts which refer to their use. It was the first project to be entirely built of stone although in a manner which clearly shows that the structural and aesthetic possibilities of this material were not yet fully understood. Stone in Egypt was used to render 'immortal' what was transient, and only the 'houses' of the dead and the gods were

executed in this material. It also immortalised or fossilised features of the impermanent structures used for daily living; shelters of wood and reeds, daubed palm-branch huts and mudbrick houses. This architectural dichotomy between 'eternal' and 'perishable' remained characteristic for Egyptian buildings until the Graeco-Roman period; even palaces and fortifications were built in mudbrick.

The age of the IV Dynasty (c. 2613-2494 BC) was the greatest time for Egyptian funerary architecture and was also the great age of masonry. The pyramids and mortuary temples of GIZA were built with unequalled precision and on a scale that was never attempted again. The stark and polished stone surfaces allowed the beauty of the stone to be the only ornament.

From the V Dynasty onwards, the pure monumentality and strict geometry gave way to a more sensual aesthetic. The walls of the royal tombs at ABUSIR were decorated with painted reliefs which document the reality of Egyptian life. It was also at Abusir, in the porticoes of the sun temples, where the first plant-columns appear as structural supports rather than sculpted facade decoration as at Djoser's complex. The plant-column is a uniquely Egyptian structural element. The prismatic pillars of the IV Dynasty were replaced by the more graceful, taller supports, which could evoke the living plants and flowers beloved by the Egyptians, apart from more esoteric associations with specific deities and religious usages. The repertoire of forms and of the various combinations was considerable, although certain types were preferred at various times (see COLUMNS).

The architecture of the Middle Kingdom is little known. Most royal pyramids were built in brick (eg LISHT, ILAHUN), and the private rock-cut tombs were modelled on contemporary domestic buildings, with their shady porticoes and vaulted ceilings.

Valley temple of Chephren, Giza (IV Dynasty)

With the political expansion of Egypt under its energetic pharaohs of the New Kingdom, large building projects, especially CULT TEMPLES, were initiated. The example of the sanctuary of Amun at KARNAK is representative for New Kingdom architecture and for the approach to temple-building in particular. Mesopotamian temples, for instance, were levelled once they were beyond repair and a new structure, very often following the same ground plan, was erected on top of the old building. The Egyptian temple of this age grew by accretion along one axis (the central longitudinal axis had always been of great importance to Egyptian architects), although previous structures could be altered, incorporated in new ones, or obliterated. The basic tripartite unit of pylon with courtyard, hypostyle hall

and cella recalled the similar division in private houses, where entrance/lobby were followed by the reception rooms and the private quarters were at the rear. Reliefs and painting covered every inch of wall-space and even the ceilings and columns of the temple interior. The large-scale reliefs on the outer facades told of the exploits and conquests of the royal builder and the divine patronage he enjoyed, whereas the scenes on the inside walls magically perpetuated the religious ceremonies performed in the sanctuary. The huge palaces at Thebes have more or less sunk into the subsoil and the only well-documented examples of New Kingdom palace architecture come from the short-lived TELL EL-AMARNA. They comprised large porticoes with palmiform columns, a succession of lofty state apartments and gardens. The apartments were lavishly decorated with painted reliefs.

The last important phase of Egyptian architecture dates from the Graeco-Roman period, when huge temples were built according to the old Egyptian tradition but with the advantages of solid workmanship and structural innovations (DENDERA, EDFU, PHILAE, KOM OMBO). The columns of these late temples have delicately carved floral capitals, some of the most beautiful elements of Egyptian design ever produced.

Badawy, A., *A History of Egyptian Architecture* I (Cairo 1954); II (Berkeley, Los Angeles 1966); III (Berkeley, Los Angeles 1968)

Baldwin Smith, E., *Egyptian Architecture as Cultural Expression* (New York 1938)

Cenival, J.L. de, *Living Architecture: Egyptian* (Fribourg 1966)

Jéquier, J., *L'architecture et la décoration dans l'ancienne Egypte* 2 vols (Paris 1920, 1922)

Lange, K., Hirmer, M., *Egypt: Architecture, Sculpture, Painting* (4th ed., New York 1968)

*Composite floral columns, Isis temple at Philae
(Graeco-Roman period)*

Ricke, H., *Bemerkungen zur ägyptischen Baukunst des Alten Reiches* I (Zurich 1944); II (Cairo 1950)
Smith, W.S., *The Art and Architecture of Ancient Egypt* (2nd ed., Harmondsworth 1981)

Elamite architecture

The civilisation of Elam in south-west Iran (referred to as the Susiana by classical authors) developed around the middle of the 3rd millennium BC. SUSA, the main city, was already a fortified town when it was conquered by the Akkadian king Naramsin (23rd C BC). The country remained under Mesopotamian supremacy except for brief periods of political independence in the beginning and the middle of the 2nd millennium BC until it became incorporated into the Achaemenian empire (7th C BC). As a result of this long association, Elam's culture was strongly influenced by Mesopotamia.

Elamite architecture is known only from relatively few sites. Susa was completely rebuilt during the Persian period; HAFT TEPE has remains of several ziggurats, royal graves, temples and palaces, dating from the middle of the 2nd millennium BC. CHOGA ZANBIL was built some 200 years later, during the most illustrious period of the Elamite kingdom. The great ziggurat differed in several important

Elamite vaults, Iran-i Kharka (reconstruction after Ghirshman)

points from the contemporary Mesopotamian structures. It was not built of solid layers of mudbrick, but was composed of five concentric structures of decreasing height, which incorporated a complex of tunnels, tombs and chambers.

As in Mesopotamia, the basic material of construction was mudbrick; bitumen and cement were used as mortar. The Elamites were very skilled in building vaults and arches. The tombs at Haft Tepe and Choga Zanbil were roofed with massive barrel-vaults, and so were many rooms in the palaces of Susa. The private houses resembled those in Mesopotamia. The rooms were distributed around one or several courtyards. They were distinguished, however, by a special, transversely situated reception room open to the central courtyard, which could be vaulted and had a central (arched?) doorway (similar rooms are still in use in the modern Middle East and called *iwan* or *liwan*). The techniques of glazing bricks may have originated in Elam rather than in Babylonia; they were used to decorate the facade of the ziggurat at Choga Zanbil, and an 'industrial area' outside the *temenos* wall at Haft Tepe was a possible site for their manufacture.

Berghe, L.V., *Archéologie de l'Iran ancien* (Leiden 1959)
Ghirshman, R., 'L'architecture élamite et ses traditions', *Iranica Antiqua* 5 (1965) 93-102

elevation

Elevations in the sense of technical drawings representing the facade of a building are obviously unknown in the Ancient Near East. But drawings, reliefs or paintings exist which show the exterior appearance of contemporary houses, fortresses and temples (see ARCHITECTURAL REPRESENTATION).

As only a fraction of Ancient Near Eastern buildings have survived with their walls and roofs intact, the reconstruction of an ancient elevation, ie the relative height of the walls, the arrangement and distribution of doorways, windows, upper storeys etc, remains hypothetical and is therefore rarely found in modern archaeological publications.

Eridu *see* ABU SHAHREIN

Esna

Egypt, see map p. xvi. The modern town covers a large TELL and the major architectural remains are situated in a deep pit containing parts of the Temple of Khnum. The screen-walled facade, typical for the Late Period, leads to the hypostyle hall built in Roman times. The roof is still intact and the massive columns have finely carved floral columns.

Downes, D., *The Excavations at Esna 1905-1906* (2nd ed., Warminster 1975)

Et Tell = ancient 'Ai

Palestine, see map p. xix. This site was occupied during the Early Bronze period (Early Bronze I C, *c.* 3000-2860 BC) when it was a well-planned, walled city divided into religious and civic quarters. After an interval, following total destruction (an earthquake?), it was again inhabited during the 1st millennium BC. The religious centre was transferred to another building and had a tripartite plan with a Breitraum cella similar to the twin temples in ARAD.

Callaway, J.A., *The Early Bronze Age Sanctuaries at 'Ai (et-Tell)* (London 1972)
Marquet-Krause, J., *Les fouilles de 'Ay (Et-Tell) 1933-35* I-II (Beirut 1949)

False door, from a VI Dynasty tomb at Saqqara

F

facade *see ELEVATION*

false door

A dummy door in stone found in Egyptian tombs. The soul of the deceased was believed to emerge through this door, in order to partake of the funerary offerings placed in the burial chamber.

The design of the false door underwent certain changes. During the Old Kingdom, the panel of the door was recessed in rectangular flat surrounds with plain lintels and jambs which were sometimes inscribed. A cylindrical roll underneath the lintel was placed on top of the innermost panel (it has been interpreted as the rolled up mat which could be let down to be used as a sunscreen in real doors). From the Middle Kingdom on, the false doors have a torus frame and are surmounted by a cornice. Some false doors are in fact connected with small chambers (see SERDAB) which contain a statue of the deceased person. In other cases the image of the dead owner of the tomb is standing or sitting in front of the false door.

Festival house *see* BÎT-AKITU

fireplace

The repeated burning of fires on any one place leaves permanent marks in the soil, and the emplacement of the fire can therefore be ascertained fairly easily by excavation. In private houses, this was mainly in the courtyard – most of the cooking was done in the open, as there was no provision for the escape of smoke, except in Anatolia where the winters are much colder and encourage indoor living. Fireplaces can have different shapes (round, oval, rectangular, horseshoe), and can either be sunk into the ground and smeared with clay or built up in order to offer added protection from the flames, as well as improving the ventilation and providing support for the cooking utensils. As most activities in the kitchen were done by people crouching on the floor, the high built-up fireplace was very rare.

fire temple and fire altar

Indo-European groups began to settle in Iran at the beginning of the 1st millennium BC. Although the question of their religion is far from being clarified, it seems that at least the court and the aristocracy of the Medes and Achaemenians, like their later successors, the Parthians and the Sassanians, adhered to a belief in a single divine creator and god, Ahuramazda, which was formalised by the prophet Zoroaster at a still uncertain date. No elaborate temples were needed as the cult was performed under the open sky in front of fire altars, which could be portable, as shown on the reliefs ornamenting the facades of the royal rock-cut tombs (eg Naqsh-i-Rustam). There is also no evidence that the fire had to be kept permanently alight during the 1st millennium BC.

Fire temples, actual monumental containers of the sacred flame, are known with certainty from the post-Achaemenian period. The Sassanians (224-642 AD) built monumental fire temples, known as Chahar-Taq, characterised by a central room with four pillars supporting a domed roof.

The earliest extant example comes from NUSH-I-JAN, a Median site, dating from the middle of the 8th C BC. The originally free-standing temple had a stepped, lozenge-shaped ground plan. A single door led into a low barrel-vaulted antechamber, equipped with a bench, a basin and a niche. One door led to a spiral staircase that gave access to the roof; another led to the main room, a triangular shaft (11m × 7m; 8m high) which contained the square, white-plastered brick fire altar set behind a low protective wall.

It seems that the Achaemenians did not build such solid structures for the sacred fire. Large well-built terraces, accessible by monumental stairways, which served as platforms for the celebration of the cult which was performed by the king in front of an assembled audience, are known from PASARGADAE, PERSEPOLIS and other sites. The superimposed terraces near the Iranian oilfield at Masjid-i-Suleiman, for instance, probably supported fire altars which may have been fed by natural gases.

Boucharlat, R., 'Monuments religieux de la Perse achémenide, état des questions', *Temples et Sanctuaires: Séminaire de recherche 1981-1983* (Lyon 1984) 119-137
Erdmann, K., 'Das Iranische Feuerheiligtum', *Sendschriften der Deutschen Orientgesellschaft* 11 (1941)
Schippmann, K., *Die Iranischen Feuerheiligtümer* (Berlin, New York 1971)

Fire temple (?) at Naqsh-i Rustam

flagstaff

Carrying colourful flags, these were part of an Egyptian temple facade, especially during the New Kingdom and later periods. The tall wooden poles, which were probably fashioned from imported timber such as cedar, were set in specially prepared hollow grooves in the walls of the pylon, secured by metal fastenings and put on stone bases. Contemporary architectural representations show that the flagstaffs towered high above the pylon.

floor

The most common method of flooring interiors in the Ancient Near East was to use rammed earth, which dries to a very hard surface. It was then coated with one or several layers of mud-plaster which could be renewed whenever necessary. An admixture of clay and powdered lime or gypsum could render such floors very hard and virtually impermeable. The plastering usually covers the lower parts of the walls as well, forming a kind of skirting. Wooden floors were used only for upper storeys (especially in the timber-rich areas of North Syria and Anatolia). Brick floors were found in official buildings and more luxuriously appointed private houses. These, too, could be covered with a coat of plaster. Baked-brick floors were reserved for representative rooms in palaces, or bathrooms. Stone was used in palaces and temples (especially in Egypt). As the example of a sandstone sill, carved with a pattern of a carpet, from an Assyrian palace (now in the British Museum) suggests, various woven mats or rugs, made of straw, reeds or wool, must have provided additional covering for floors and platforms (imprints of matting on the soil of an excavated building are found not infrequently).

Niches for flagstaffs, first pylon, temple of Amun, Karnak

fluted

A column is said to be fluted when it has vertical, slightly concave grooves along the length of its shaft. In Egypt, fluted columns, the so-called Proto-Doric columns, were popular during the Middle Kingdom (eg BENI-HASAN, DEIR-EL-BAHARI: temple of Mentuhotep). Sometimes polygonal pillars (eight- or sixteen-sided) are described as fluted columns (XVIII Dynasty: Deir-el-Bahari: temple of Hatshepsut), but they seem to have more affinity to square sectioned beams with their edges planed off.

The tall columns in Achaemenian palaces were fluted with a very high number of grooves (eg PERSEPOLIS).

77

fortification

This became a necessity almost as soon as people began to settle permanently in one place and accumulate goods, which had to be secured against organised raids, the most elementary form of war.

The basic requirement was a reasonably strong wall surrounding the settlement. It had to be able to withstand the assault techniques of the time. A rubble-filled mudbrick wall was sufficient to cope with Neolithic or Early Bronze Age methods of attack but in the later 2nd and the 1st millennia BC, when battering rams and iron tools were used by highly organised armies, a system of multiple ramparts, ditches and heavy walls on stone foundations became necessary.

Fluted support, Beni-Hasan, Egypt (Middle Kingdom)

Fortifications at Nineveh (restored)

Gates are the weak point in any wall and their number was kept to a minimum. The walls surrounding the gate needed strengthening by buttresses, which eventually became gate-towers to maximise the defensive potential. Equipped with accommodation for armed guards and with battlements, they were a common feature of Bronze and Iron Age fortifications throughout the Ancient Near East.

Additional defences were earth ramparts, moats (especially in the Nubian forts on the Nile, eg BUHEN), dry ditches, stone glacis (common in Anatolia, eg BOGHAZKÖY), secondary walls and bastions along the main defensive wall. The aim was to keep the besieging enemy under easy surveillance (hence the towers and battlements), at a safe distance out of reach of arrows, and to make an attempted assault of the walls as difficult as possible. The Hittites and the people inhabiting the war-torn areas of Syro-Palestine (2nd and 1st millennia BC) built some of the best-appointed fortifications, making the most of the rocky and difficult terrain of their towns. They also provided facilities for aggressive defence, such as postern-tunnels and sally-ports.

Burney, C.A., *Anatolian Studies* 16 (1966) 55ff
Lawrence, A.W., *Journal of Egyptian Archaeology* 51 (1965) 69-94
Naumann, K., *Die Architektur Kleinasiens* (2nd ed., Tübingen 1971)

foundation

The kind of foundation suitable depends not only on the size and function of the building but also on the geographical and climatic conditions of the area. In many archaeological excavations, the successive layers of foundations form the only available record of a site's architectural history and therefore they are usually well documented in the final publications.

Egypt has a desert climate and a dry, rocky soil with the exception of the alluvial strip bordering the Nile, where the water level changed annually and the ground was relatively soft and unstable. It was not necessary to provide substantial foundations on the desert ground, and the Egyptian builders seemed to take the stability of their soil for granted even in areas near the waterways, and failed to provide proper groundings for buildings near the river. Masonry or heavy brick walls were set on top of a shallow trench filled with sand. This basically sound method was sometimes spoilt by adding layers of flat stones, which were eventually crushed by the weight of the walls. The massive columns in the Great Hypostyle Hall at KARNAK for instance, or the New Kingdom obelisks, were set in a hole partly filled with sand, and rested on small rectangular stones. Elsewhere (eg MEDINET-HABU), mudbrick was used for the foundations of large stone columns. As a result, the majority of Egypt's monuments in the vicinity of the Nile have disappeared and those that still exist have had to be underpinned and are still threatened by rising damp which causes the stone to crumble under the effect of salination etc. A change of method occurred only after the XXV Dynasty, when instead of a few trenches underneath the walls, the whole area of the temple was covered with carefully laid blocks three or four courses deep. The well-preserved structures of the late period (KOM OMBO, DENDERA, EDFU) make one regret that this expedient had not been applied earlier.

Clarke, S., Engelback, R., *Ancient Egyptian Masonry* (London 1930) 69ff

The situation is reversed in Mesopotamia, where the southern part is alluvial, and where the rivers were forever liable to radically change their course and flood unpredictably. Also, stone was rare and mudbrick the universally employed building material which does not take kindly to rising damp. Proper, deep foundations were a necessity and, at some periods, foundations received just as much if not more attention than the actual building above. The most economical method was to build directly on the levelled courses of walls from a previous building, while the rest of the defunct brickwork was used as an infill. This was done in urban areas for private houses, but also in temples and palaces. One result of this practice was the conservative nature of Mesopotamian architecture which changed but little over long periods of time. Another outcome was the gradually rising level of the habitations, which eventually formed TELLS. The larger the building, the higher the layers, one of the reasons why the temples were apparently on platforms above the street level. Where stone was at all available, it was used for the foundations of important buildings. (For example, the city walls of ABU SHAHREIN were partly built on gypsum; the Early Dynastic temple at AL-UBAID had limestone foundations; so had most of the sanctuaries in the Neo-Assyrian towns (eg NIMRUD), while the Neo-Babylonians used costly baked bricks for their palaces near the Euphrates (BABYLON).)

During the Early Dynastic period, temples were sometimes built on virgin ground above specially prepared substructures, which practically duplicated the complete plan of the building and could take up to a third of the height of the superstructure (eg KHAFAJE).

Foundations in rocky and earthquake prone Anatolia were also a matter of concern. Depending on the terrain, either vertical shafts were dug until a stable surface was reached, or the bedrock was cut into step-like graduations to allow for a solid integration of brick wall and ground surface, with wooden planks between. Foundations were often built up in layers of different materials, eg mudbrick and stone, especially in Southern Anatolia (ZINJIRLI). On sloping ground, platforms of earth or mudbrick were built to establish an even and sufficiently large surface.

Naumann, K., *Die Architektur Kleinasiens* (2nd ed, Tübingen 1971)

In Syro-Palestine, stone foundations set in trenches a few courses deep had been in use since Proto-Neolithic times (eg JERICHO). Sand-filled trenches underneath brick walls were also found (eg Tell al-Hasi).

foundation deposit

The custom of making some sacrifice in order to ensure the felicitous completion of the building and the good luck of its inhabitants, is well known from many ancient or modern societies. In many cases, objects or slaughtered animals were interred beneath the foundations.

Archaeologists have found numerous such foundation deposits in Ancient Near Eastern sites, usually at the corners of buildings. The rites connected with the foundation of a building were doubtless different in each culture and also depended on the sort of building, a temple, a palace or a private house.

In Egypt the deposits could consist just of animal sacrifices, or of plaques inscribed with the name of the king, various pottery vessels (probably containing food offerings) and charming miniature tool-sets made of clay or even copper (one such set was found at DEIR-EL-BAHARI in Hatshepsut's temple). Elsewhere, the most common objects were clay jugs and platters, jars and bowls of pottery or metal, sometimes in real size, sometimes *en miniature*. In Mesopotamia, BUILDING INSCRIPTIONS were deposited alongside the usual objects or instead of them. Sumerian temples were given magical protection by inscribed figurines with elongated nail-shaped bodies embedded into the walls at the four corners.

Clarke, S., Engelbach, R., *Ancient Egyptian Masonry* (London 1930) 60ff

Douglas van Buren, E., *Foundation Figures and Offerings* (Berlin 1931)

Ellis, R.S., *Foundation Deposits in Ancient Mesopotamia* (New Haven, London 1968)

G

garden

Apart from the kitchen garden and the orchard, which must have been part of many homesteads since the beginning of organised agriculture, ornamental gardens with flowers, trees and ponds were planted for comfort and pleasure. Ancient Near Eastern literature abounds with allusions to the delights found in fragrant and cool gardens, and paintings preserved in Egyptian tombs (eg Nebamun's, XVIII Dynasty, British Museum) show formally laid out flower-beds, trees and shrubs surrounding a pond stocked with fish and water-fowl. Such were the gardens surrounding the luxurious villas and palaces at TELL EL-AMARNA. Archaeologists have occasionally found traces of gardens within temples (eg DEIR-EL-BAHARI: Mentuhotep's temple) or palaces (eg MARI, RAS SHAMRA, BABYLON), but they were doubtlessly much more in evidence in antiquity than excavations suggest.

gateway

The entrances of city walls and monumental buildings were the focal points of the whole facade. Decorative elements were often used to enhance the appearance of the gateways (eg by relief orthostats in the Syro-Hittite palaces; see CARCHEMISH, ALAÇA HÜYÜK, or by glazed bricks as in BABYLON etc).

As gateways are basically large openings they can weaken the incumbent masonry, and from the strategic point of view they provide obvious targets of assault. They therefore have to match the strength of the walls, do minimal damage to the structure of the brickwork, and provide a defendable means of access and exit. The jambs were strengthened by vertical pilasters or buttresses, and the wooden lintel of an ordinary doorway was usually replaced by an arch, which distributes the pressure from the wall above more evenly and allows for a wider span. The flanking buttresses could develop into gate-towers protruding above the wall, which could in turn be surmounted by battlements and contain chambers and stairways for the use of the guardsmen (eg Ishtar gate at BABYLON).

The actual doorway of the gate was made of heavy timber planks and secured by bolts on the inside. It was often set back into a funnel-shaped opening formed by the projecting lateral bastions or buttresses. This made an attack difficult and provided additional space for peaceful activities which habitually centred around the city gates in ancient Oriental towns.

When the city walls were double, the arrangement of the gateway naturally repeated this feature by providing a double gate with an interior longitudinal or transverse hall.

In Assyria, Anatolia (Hittites) and Persia, gateways were magically protected against evil spirits and malevolent demons by sculpted 'guardians of the gate' in the shape of sphinxes, lions or winged creatures with animal bodies and human heads (see LAMASSU). Egyptian stone

Gate at Medinet-Habu, Western Thebes (XIX Dynasty)

gateways were without arches, and only their FORTIFICATION featured projecting gate-bastions (BUHEN and MEDINET-HABU). The monumental pylons had portals flush with the walls, which were crowned by a cornice. Mesopotamian gateways had projecting pilasters or buttresses flanking the arched opening which were articulated by multiple recesses and niches. The monolithic parabolic arches were a development peculiar to Hittite gateways, and were surrounded by high mudbrick walls.

Gezer

Palestine, see map p. xix. A site which was almost continuously inhabited from Chalcolithic times to the Byzantine period. The first town belonged to the Middle Bronze Age (*c.* 17th C BC) and had strong fortifications, which consisted of a glacis, a wall and a strong, tower-like gate structure with three entries. The local sanctuary, a BAMAH, contained a row of ten monoliths up to 3m high.

In the 10th C BC, Gezer became one of the Royal Cities of Solomo, and a casemate wall and a gateway flush with the wall – of the same type as those in MEGIDDO and HAZOR – were found. They were executed in the fine ASHLAR masonry characteristic for this period.

Dever, W.G., *et al.*, *Gezer* I-II (Hebrew Union College, Jerusalem 1970, 1974)
Macalister, R.A.S., *Excavations of Gezer* I-III (London 1912)

Giza

Egypt, see map p. xvi. Cemetery and pyramid-field of the IV and V Dynasties (middle of the 3rd millennium BC) that belonged to the Old Kingdom capital of Memphis.

The rocky plateau of Giza is dominated by the famous Pyramids set to the precise point of the compass, diagonally behind each other. These huge monuments were originally surrounded by their enclosures, which contained mortuary temples and the burials of other members of the royal family, as well as distinguished servants of the crown.

All three pyramids have a square base. They were constructed of locally quarried limestone (maybe incorporating solid rock in the centre), cut into large dressed blocks. The outer casing was of a better

Pyramid of Chephren, Giza (IV Dynasty)

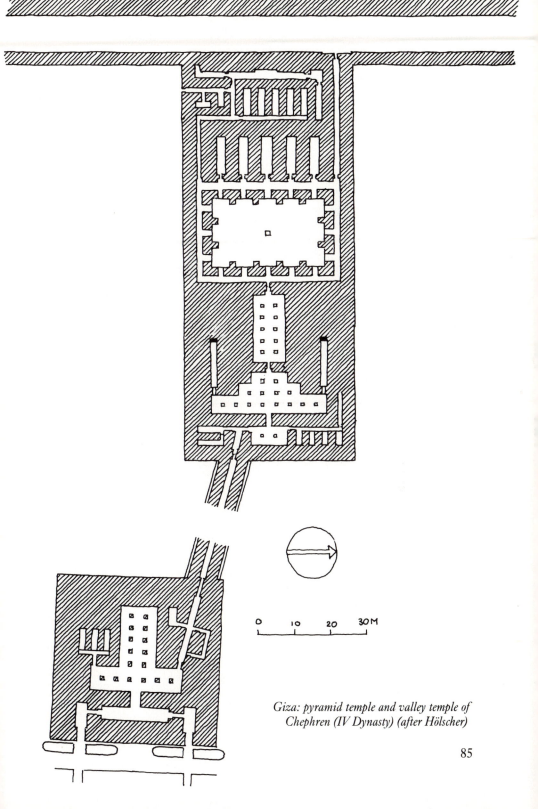

0   10   20   30M

Giza: pyramid temple and valley temple of
Chephren (IV Dynasty) (after Hölscher)

85

quality limestone shipped from Tura, and the cap-stone at the top was a huge monolith of Aswan granite. The superbly dressed, smooth blocks of the outer casing have been gradually dismantled since the Middle Ages, to be incorporated in countless houses and structures of Cairo and Giza.

The pyramid of Cheops, or the Great Pyramid, is the largest and most perfectly executed of all pyramids (440 cubits square and 280 cubits high; *c.* 230m^2 and 146.6m, with an inclination of 51°52' to the ground). The interior arrangements as they are understood at present (new investigations are being carried out almost constantly) indicate that the location of the burial chamber was transferred in the course of building, probably as the work progressed beyond its originally set limits. This resulted in various shafts and corridors with dead ends. An ascending corridor branching off the original access shaft led downwards. A continuing corridor, the Grand Gallery (*c.* 50m long and 9m high), has a corbel vault in the upper seven courses to distribute the pressure evenly. According to Petrie, it was used to store the massive monolithic plugs that sealed up the ascending corridor. The gallery ends in a low and narrow passage which widens into an ante-room that originally contained the portcullis blocks securing the burial chamber. This is called the King's Chamber as it contains the now lid-less sarcophagus. It is built entirely of granite; from this simple and unadorned chamber, two shafts penetrate the core of the pyramid to the outside. Their exact purpose is still debated. Above the flat roof of the King's Chamber are five separate compartments, ending in a gabled roof. They were apparently built as a safeguard against the considerable pressure of the incumbent masonry. The entrance was sealed up and no traces were left to indicate the access to the burial chamber, which was furthermore blocked by plugs and portcullis blocks. In spite of these precautions, the contents of this grandest of all tombs have been robbed.

The pyramid of Chephren (210.5m at the base) is less steeply inclined (52°20'), and preserves some of the original limestone casing at the top and some courses of granite at the base. The burial chamber lies at ground level and has been cut out of the rock. It has a pointed gable roof. There were two corridors, one underneath the pavement slabs and one set higher up in the face of the pyramid.

The supplementary structures of the original pyramid complexes are best known from Chephren's monuments. The Valley temple is in fact substantially preserved and a beautiful example for the stark simplicity of IV Dynasty architecture – a solid building in stone, logically assembled in huge blocks of limestone and granite, devoid of any adornments save for some finely chiselled lines of inscription. Two entrances flanked by sphinxes lead to a narrow transverse corridor with a central passage giving access to a T-shaped hall supported by rectangular granite pillars. A narrow passage leads to the exit at the N corner, which was connected with the causeway linking this building with the mortuary temple on the plateau. It passed the sculpted rock in the shape of a sphinx bearing the likeness of king Chephren who thus kept perpetual watch over the royal cemetery.

The mortuary temple of Cheops is known only from the ground plan. It was a simple structure, a rectangular enclosed courtyard surrounded by a portico and accommodating the king's statues in niches on the E side. N and S of the temple, two large boat-pits were hewn out of the rock. One of these vessels, built of cedarwood, has been found excellently preserved. It had probably been used as a state barge before it was interred to serve the king in the afterlife.

The mortuary temple of Chephren

*Pyramid of Mykerinos and subsidiary
pyramid, Giza (IV Dynasty)*

seems to reflect the more complex ritual
requirements of his time. It provided
chapels for the two crowns and canopic
jars (containing the inner organs of the
dead king), and a succession of transverse
and oblong columned halls in a strict
symmetrical layout which led to a large
court surrounded by a portico and the
usual deep niches for the royal statues at
the back. Behind them were further
chambers and the FALSE DOOR.

The pyramid of Mykerinos is the
smallest of the three large pyramids (108m
at the base, 51° inclination). The final
burial chamber was below ground level. It
was lined with granite and had a pent roof
cut underside into a pointed vault. A
separate chamber with niches was
intended for the canopic jars and the
crowns. The mortuary temple of
Mykerinos resembles the courtyard-type
of Cheops'.

87

The private cemeteries first grew up around the eastern and western side of the Cheops pyramids. Plain-faced stone MASTABAS with elaborate interior arrangements, comprising chapels and offering rooms, were roofed with barrel-vaults and domes. Giza also provides the first examples of rock-tombs, cut out of the quarries around the pyramids. They were used to bury the royal relatives of Chephren and Mykerinos.

The tomb of Khentkawes marks a departure from the architectural practices associated with the sun cult that seems to have inspired the conception of the pyramids. Like the tomb of Shepsekaf at SAQQARA, it is a huge sarcophagus-shaped structure fashioned of limestone blocks, with its own funerary complex comprising a lower temple, a causeway and an upper temple made of brick. The interior arrangement of the tomb itself contained magazines, chapels and the burial chamber.

Borchardt, L., *Einiges zur dritten Bauperiode der grossen Pyramide bei Gize* (Berlin 1932)
Hassam, S., *Excavations at Giza* (Oxford, Cairo 1942)
Hölscher, U., *Das Grabdenkmal des Königs Chephren* (Leipzig 1912)
Junker, H., *Grabungen auf dem Friedhof des Alten Reiches bei den Pyramiden von Giza* I-IV (Vienna 1929-41)
Petrie, W.M.F., *Pyramids and Temples of Gizeh* (2nd ed., London 1883)
Reisner, G., *A History of the Giza Necropolis* I (Cambridge, Massachusetts 1942)

glacis

In a system of fortifications, a natural or artificial slope running from the ramparts or walls to the open country. It can be cased in stones set in mortar (eg

Glacis from Boghazköy (Anatolia)

BOGHAZKÖY, TELL HALAF) or made of PISÉ with a mud-plaster covering (common in Palestine, eg MEGIDDO). The purpose of the glacis was twofold: to allow archers on the battlements maximum range of fire and to make the employment of siege-engines and ladders more difficult.

glazed brick and tile

The techniques of glazing were first discovered when ceramic pottery was coated with a glaze that was made permanent by high temperature firing. Made of powdered quartz and alkali, it was coloured turquoise by copper-salts to produce quantities of beads and small objects. There was a growing demand for

Glazed brick relief from Susa (Louvre)

these artifacts; in Egypt since the 3rd millennium BC but particularly during the 2nd millennium. The blue colour was believed to have magical properties which could avert malicious or demonic influences.

As they were costly to produce, glazed bricks were used sparingly, to form patterns at the top of walls, on crenellations, around doorways etc (eg in the Steppyramid at SAQQARA, in the Assyrian palaces of KHORSABAD, NINEVEH and NIMRUD etc).

The Elamites in Iran were producing glazed bricks or tiles during the 2nd millennium BC (see HAFT TEPE and the temples and ziggurat at CHOGA ZANBIL). In BABYLON, glazed bricks were used on an unprecedented scale, covering the complete facade of the Ishtar gate and part of the Processional Way. This formed a water-proof highly decorative surface which was further embellished by raised relief made of moulded bricks in the shape of mythological creatures. The craftsmen may have been emigrants from Elam, who left their country on account of the Assyrian wars. The Achaemenians, especially at SUSA, employed the same type of three-dimensional glazed-brick decoration as the Babylonians.

Godin-Tepe

Iran, see map p. xvii. The vicinity of this site (Seh Gabi) was inhabited during the Neolithic period (from about 6000 BC). At level VII (mid-4th millennium BC), a large building was discovered, with substantially preserved walls, complete with doorways and lintels, and in one room, the floors of the second and third storey were still *in situ*.

Levine, L.D., *Iran* 12 (1974)

Six phases of architecture were counted in the Outer Town area from period IV (2950-2400 BC) to period VI (3500-3200 BC). Level II dates from the Median period (8th C BC) and contains the remains of a fortified Median manor, surrounded by strong walls (*c.* 4m thick) and several towers at the corners which were accessible by a narrow passage from the interior of the manor. To the W was a double row of parallel, oblong store rooms linked by two corridors. In the E were two columned halls (one with 30 columns) and there was a small 'throne room' with benches on four sides and a mudbrick

throne seat at its SE corner. Kitchens with ovens and a drain were also discovered.

Cuyler Young Jr, T., *Iran* 13 (1975)

Gordium

Anatolia, see map p. xv. Iron Age city (6th-4th C BC) which became the capital of the Phrygian kingdom (also called 'Midas City' after the proverbially wealthy king).

The most conspicuous monument is the so-called tomb of Midas, carved out of the rock-face in the shape of a gabled house facade and formally decorated with geometrical patterns in light relief. There is a subterranean chamber reached by a long corridor. Other similar facades nearby have imitation shuttered windows and

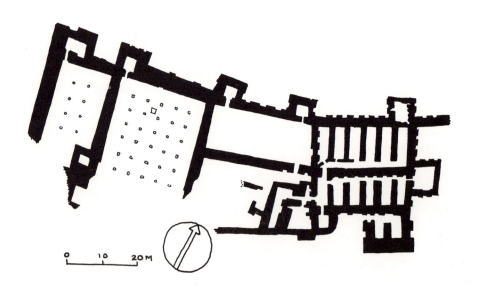

Godin-Tepe (after Cuyler Young Jr)

doorways and the internal arrangements of the chambers have the same features as domestic interiors, such as benches along the walls, beds etc.

Architectural terracottas discovered at Pazarli and Gordium show that the gabled roof was indeed a Phrygian characteristic. The purpose of these structures is not exactly clear; it has been suggested that they were in fact open-air sanctuaries with carved rock-faces as in many other Anatolian mountain-sites in the vicinity of a clear-water source.

Barnett, R.D., 'The Phrygian Rock Monuments', *Bibliotheca Orientalis* X, 3 and 4 (1953) 53ff
Young, R., 'Gordium', *Anatolian Studies* 1 (1951) 11ff; 2 (1952) 20ff

Guzana *see* TELL HALAF

H

Hacilar

Anatolia, see map p. xv. Important Neolithic site with nine levels of occupation (*c.* 7000-5000 BC).

The remains of buildings at level VI (*c.* 5600 BC) show that they were exceptionally well built. Nine large houses were found (up to 10.5m × 6m) around two sides of a rectangular court, the walls of which consisted of rectangular mudbricks on stone foundations (1m thick). Some of these houses had upper storeys made of wood, and timber posts supported the ceiling. Access to the houses was by centrally placed double doorways.

At level II (*c.* 5435-5250 BC), the settlement was surrounded by a rampart (36m × 57m) of mudbrick on stone foundations with small towers or bastions. Various clusters of buildings (workshops, houses, granaries etc) were grouped around a central open space. Some houses had huge internal buttresses supporting upper storeys built of wood and mudbrick. The main room had a raised hearth in the middle. The so-called 'NE shrine' had a large alcove, a raised platform between two short walls, a hearth in front and two rows of wooden columns along the main axis. This building may also have been the house of an important individual.

The fortress of level IIB was built by a new population above the levelled remains of earlier buildings. Massive walls (up to 4m thick) surrounded the whole mound. Blocks of rooms were grouped into complexes separated by small courtyards. Upper storeys made of light timber with daub fillings were burned to charcoal when the fortress was stormed and burnt down.

Mellaart, J., *Excavations at Hacilar* I-II (Edinburgh 1971)

Haft Tepe

Iran, see map p. xvii. The site was occupied from the 6th millennium BC but is best known for its important Elamite ruins dating from *c.* 1500-1300 BC. The remains of about a dozen ziggurats, royal tombs, temples and palaces were discovered. The whole area of the city must have covered at least 30ha, but only a small part has been excavated.

The temple complex was surrounded by mudbrick walls (4-9m thick). It consisted of a courtyard (25m × 15m) paved with baked bricks, which contained a central low platform (an altar?) and a transverse portico in front of two parallel long halls (9m × 7m). Below each were vaulted burial chambers, built of baked brick set in gypsum mortar, reached by a passage from the eastern hall. A baked-brick platform was divided into three unequal sections by partition walls. These subterranean rooms appear to have been family vaults, like those found at CHOGA ZANBIL and SUSA.

Negahban, E.O., *Iran 7* (1969) 173–177
Negahban, E.O., *Akten des VII Internationalen Kongresses für Iranische Kunst*

und Archäologie: Archäologische Mitteilungen aus Iran Ergänzungsband 6 (Munich 1979)

Hasanlu

Iran, see map p. xvii. A prehistoric settlement (6th-3rd millennium BC) grew up on the central mound and later spread to the foot of the hill. At the beginning of the 1st millennium BC, the unwalled town was protected by a fortified citadel built above the existing ruins. The buildings within the citadel were erected on a stone pavement in mudbrick. The plan of the enclosed area belonging to period IV (10th C BC) is well preserved. Two imposing structures stood on either end of a rectangular court. Building II on the S side was larger. It was entered through a deep portico with wooden pillars which led into a transverse ante-room, and secondary chambers on either side equipped with fireplaces and a staircase.

The spacious main hall (18m × 24m) had two rows of four wooden columns (7m high, 50cm thick) on stone bases. Round the walls hung with textiles were mudbrick platforms. A single column stood in front of a small platform and a paved area with a drain, where offerings could have been performed, if the interpretation of this building as a sanctuary is correct. 'Burnt Building I' also consisted of a deep porch and a columned hall and this type of structure may have indirectly been influenced by the Syro-Hittite BÎT-HILANI (Cuyler Young). Connections have also been made with the later(?) Urartian columned halls and hence the Achaemenian APADANA.

The houses had two or three stories and gabled roofs of poplar wood covered with twigs and mud. Some had framed windows and arched doorways. The interiors were occasionally decorated with glazed tiles.

Cuyler Young Jr., T., *Iranica Antiqua* 6 (1966) 48-71

Dyson, R.H., *Expedition* I, 3 (1959) 4ff; II, 3 (1960) 2ff

Dyson, R.H., *Archaeology* 16 (1961) 63ff; 18 (1965) 257ff

Dyson, R.H., *American Journal of Archaeology* 67 (1963) 210ff

Hattušaš *see* BOGHAZKÖY

Hawara

Egypt, see map p. xvi. Site of the pyramid complex of Amenemhet III (*c.* 1842-1797 BC), which with its numerous chapels and buildings was so extensive and complex that it was known to the ancient Greeks as the 'Labyrinth'.

The pyramid itself was built in mudbrick with a casing of limestone. The burial chamber was a shaft hewn out of the bedrock before the pyramid was constructed and it contained a tightly fitted box-like monolith of granite which was to receive the sarcophagus through a concealed shaft. Many ingenious devices such as blind alleys, trap-doors, false chambers etc, were constructed in an attempt to foil the grave-robbers.

Arnold, D., 'Das Labyrinth und seine Vorbilder', *Mitteilungen des Deutschen Archäologischen Instituts Abteilung Kairo* 35 (1979) 1-9

Lloyd, A.B., 'The Egyptian Labyrinth', *Journal of Egyptian Archaeology* 56 (1970) 81-106

Michalowski, K., 'The Labyrinth Enigma: Archaeological Suggestions', *Journal of Egyptian Archaeology* 54 (1968) 219-222

Petrie, W.M.F., *Kahun, Gurob and Hawara* (London 1890)

Hazor

Palestine, see map p. xix. Large and important site occupied from the Early Bronze Age (*c.* 2600 BC) to Hellenistic times. Five different temple or cult areas were discovered, which all show great diversity of plans. At level XVII (17th C BC) there was a double sanctuary in the Lower City, a symmetrical arrangement with a courtyard for each temple

Level XIV (Late Bronze, 14th C BC) in area H had a large temple (IB) with a cella measuring 13.5m × 9m. A rectangular niche was set into the wall opposite the entrance. Two stone pillars supported the roof, and basalt orthostats lined the walls. In earlier stages, this room was approached through a transverse vestibule; later an inner hall was inserted with two staircases (probably inside a tower-like structure). A rich collection of cult objects was found in the main room of this temple, which was probably dedicated to the storm-god Hadad. Around the 10th C BC, Hazor was redeveloped after the destruction of the Middle Bronze city. It was surrounded by a casemate wall of the

Hazor: plan of citadel (after Kenyon)

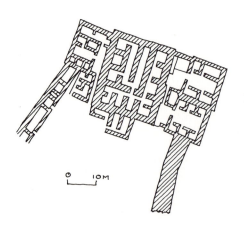

Solomonic type (see also MEGIDDO, GEZER) and there was a fine three-chambered gateway with lateral towers.

Yadin, Y., *et al.*, *Hazor* I-IV (Jerusalem 1958, 1960, 1961)

High Place *see* BAMAH

hilammar

A rectangular vestibule before the cella of a Hittite TEMPLE. Access from the temple courtyard was through three doorways between two pillars which were sometimes decorated with reliefs (eg BOGHAZKÖY, Temple I).

Hittite architecture

Between *c.* 1740 and 1190 BC, the Hittite kings, based at their central Anatolian capital Hattusas (BOGHAZKÖY), ruled over an expanding empire which became one of the major military forces of the 2nd millennium BC. It clashed with Babylon and Egypt and controlled most of Asia Minor, Syria and North Mesopotamia. The empire was finally defeated during the upheavals connected with the so-called 'Sea-Peoples'. Hittite culture survived for some centuries in small kingdoms south of the Taurus range, such as CARCHEMISH, Karatepe and ZINJIRLI.

Like the Assyrians, the Hittites were a warlike race and their major architectural projects were fortifications. They developed a technique of building formidable defences around the numerous Anatolian towns often sited in difficult mountainous terrain. The city walls were mainly made of stone, sometimes in two parallel courses joined on the inside and filled with rubble (see CASEMATE WALL).

They followed the contours of the site. The walls were armed with projecting bastions and towers. The crenellated battlements were depicted on Egyptian and Assyrian reliefs. Corbelled posterns, protected by lateral towers, formed tunnel-shaped passages beneath the ramparts. The gates, with their megalithic parabolic arches, had sculpted relief-decorations on the jambs (BOGHAZKÖY; ALAÇA HÜYÜK). The masonry, especially around the city gates, was often composed of large undressed boulders (CYCLOPEAN MASONRY).

The ground plans of many domestic as well as monumental buildings in Hittite architecture have oblique or irregular outlines. Axiality was generally avoided and the individual units were freely juxtaposed or concentrically distributed around an element in the middle (as for instance the magazines around Temple I at Boghazköy). Sculpted orthostats lined the lower courses of exterior walls in important buildings, and became particularly popular during the Neo-Hittite period.

Windows set near to the floor level in the external temple walls are another Hittite characteristic (eg Temple I at Boghazköy). Many Hittite holy places are known, particularly near springs. They were marked by large carvings of divine figures without any permanent architectural structures. An exception was the national open-air shrine at YAZILIKAYA which featured propylaea and other buildings.

Akurgal, E., *The Art of the Hittites* (London 1962)

Lloyd, S., *Early Anatolia* (Harmondsworth 1956)

Naumann, K., *Die Architektur Kleinasiens* (2nd ed., Tübingen 1971)

house

The Ancient Near East is often referred to as 'the cradle of civilisation', for it was there that agriculture, urbanisation and writing originated. The development of the house as a permanent shelter for man and his belongings is closely related to the processes of cultural evolution. The subject of domestic architecture, which has been of secondary interest for the first generations of archaeologists, is now receiving a great deal of attention in accordance with the recent trend towards a more anthropological approach in archaeology (especially by the French school). The continuity of traditional building methods in the Near East, particularly in rural areas, has helped to interpret the often scant remains of ancient domestic structures. Architectural representations and small-scale, three-dimensional objects in the form of houses (see SOUL HOUSE) are particularly interesting with regard to the articulation of facades, the reconstruction of roofs etc.

The earliest remains of solid and permanent man-made shelters were found in Palestine, from the Natufian period (9th millennium BC; eg at 'Ain Mallaha and Beidha). These huts were round, semi-subterranean, and had dry-stone walls up to 1.20m high. In the following Pre-Neolithic period (8th millennium BC), the huts were larger (3-4m in diameter) and built of hand-shaped mudbricks with a superstructure of lightweight materials (eg JERICHO, Mureybet). In order to subdivide a round house, internal straight walls crossing each other at right angles were used (Mureybet IIIB) and the flat mud-roof could be supported by wooden poles. The limitation of the circular plan is its inflexibility and henceforth this shape was employed only for small, single-room dwellings (see DOME). The rectilinear plan, however, can be extended or subdivided simply by adding further walls and

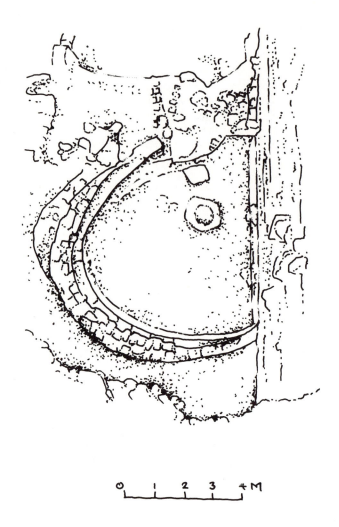

0   1   2   3   4 M

*Remains of a house of pre-Pottery Neolithic A
   at Jericho*

this orthogonal 'multi-cellular' house plan became the standard type of Ancient Near Eastern domestic architecture. Court-yards, open terraces, porticoes etc can be regarded as open-air extensions of the living space, taking into consideration the predominantly hot climate. Upper storeys were in use from Neolithic times (eg ÇATAL HÜYÜK) but they leave few traces recoverable through excavation. In analogy to contemporary Near Eastern houses, they would have contained the actual living accommodation, with the ground floor being used primarily for storage.

A considerable number of people could be accommodated in one complex and their accumulation eventually produced the dense settlement patterns of Ancient Near Eastern conurbations. A large number of the population, however, especially in the great cities of the Bronze and Iron Age, must have lived in much simpler and more primitive shelters – constructed of reeds or wattle and daub – which have left hardly any traces of the once certainly extensive slums of the Ancient Near East.

Aurenche, O., *La maison orientale* (Paris 1981)
Cauvin, J., *Les premiers villages de Syrie-Palestine du IXième au VIIIième millénaire avant JC* (Lyon 1978)

Anatolian houses often had stone foundations which could protrude above ground, forming a socle around the base of the mudbrick walls. Wooden reinforcements inside the brick walls were added as a precaution in the earthquake-prone areas. The longitudinal *Megaron* house-type developed in the western regions (TROY), while rectangular two-room houses with oblique corners and a forecourt were typical for Central Anatolia (with or without a second storey of mudbrick and wood taking up part of the flat roof-terrace) (eg KÜLTEPE).

In North Syria, houses could be of the Anatolian type (obliquely shaped rooms massed under one roof as in Alalakh) or the Mesopotamian type (with an interior courtyard as in TELL HALAF). Wood-enforced mudbrick was commonly used for exterior walls.

Naumann, K., *Die Architektur Kleinasiens* (2nd ed., Tübingen 1971)

Domestic architecture in Mesopotamia is traditionally associated with the central courtyard, around which one or more suites of parallel rooms were distributed. This central courtyard can also be roofed over, partly or wholly (especially in the Diyala region and Assyria, where the winters are much cooler than in the South) and then formed the central recep-

tion area, probably lit by a clerestory. The ubiquitous building material for the walls was mudbrick. A single entrance was the prevalent type of access. Planned residences of wealthy individuals were recovered from a number of locations (eg UR, MARI, TELL ASMAR). Their plans vary a good deal, and the likely existence of upper storeys make a definite attribution of functions for the various recovered rooms on the ground floor questionable. Special fittings like paved courtyards, private chapels, bathrooms with drains, reception rooms, stone door-sockets or sills and private grave-vaults could be found in the more luxuriously appointed dwellings.

Delougaz, P., Hill, H.D., *Private Houses and Graves in the Diyala Region* (Chicago 1967)
Heinrich, E. in de Gruyter, A. (ed.), *Reallexikon der Assyriologie und Vorderasiatischer Archäologie* IV (Berlin, New York 1972) 176ff
Preusser, C., *Die Wohnhäuser in Assur* (Berlin 1954)

In Egypt, the numerous soul houses in clay represent the simple homesteads of the poorer population, ranging from open shelters with an inclined roof held up by wooden posts, to more substantial rectangular brick houses, with a flat roof-terrace reached by an outside ladder and some small dark chambers on the ground floor. A forecourt or yard in front or around the house was essential as the preparation of food etc was done in the open air. The model houses of the Middle Kingdom, and the tomb paintings of the New Kingdom depict the much more comfortable houses of the notables and officials of the crown. A shady portico with painted columns formed the entrance to the house which could have one or two storeys. The main hall was in the centre of the house, its roof supported by plastered

HOUSE

Tell Harmal: town plan (after Lloyd)

wooden columns, lit by a clerestory and furnished with platforms, benches and wall paintings. The tripartite plan, which divides the house into several functional zones (entrance/vestibule – reception area – private/bedrooms), became the standard layout for the well-appointed middle-class house. This type of dwelling is best exemplified by the free-standing country mansions, surrounded by an enclosed space accommodating open-air kitchens, stables, granaries and gardens, which belonged to the XVIII Dynasty courtiers and officials at TELL EL-AMARNA. In the crowded urban areas, houses were built closely together and sometimes had several upper storeys. Light was provided by windows in the side walls and ventilation by air-shafts (MULQAF). The flat roof-terrace protected by a parapet provided open-air quarters much frequented during the cool hours of the evening.

Davies, N. de G., 'The Town House in Ancient Egypt', *Metropolitan Museum Studies* I (1929)
Peet, T.E., Woolley, C.L., *The City of Akhenaten: I. Domestic Architecture* (London 1923)
Ricke, H., *Der Grundriss des Amarna Wohnhauses* (Leipzig 1932)

Ur: a private house
  (Ur III period) (after Woolley)

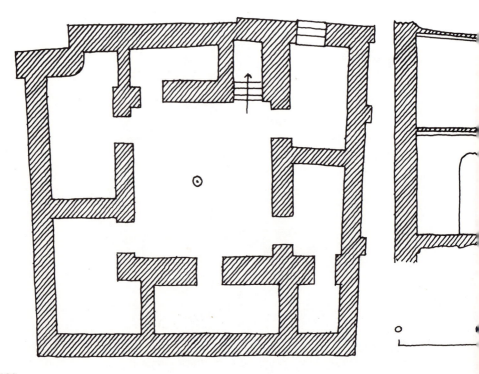

hypogeum

Term borrowed from classical architecture to describe underground rooms or vaults used as burial chambers underneath houses or palaces (eg HAFT TEPE, CHOGA ZANBIL, ASSUR, UR; see TOMB).

hypostyle hall

The Greek word means 'under columns'. Hypostyle halls can therefore be any large space the ceiling of which is supported by columns, but in Ancient Near Eastern archaeology it denotes the large halls in Egyptian temples (especially of the New Kingdom) which preceded the inner sanctuary and had a considerable number of stone columns to support the roof. In the large hypostyle hall of the Amun temple at KARNAK (13th C BC), a central higher aisle had columns with open papyriform capitals, while the lower flanking columns on each side had 'closed bud' capitals. In the architectural symbolism of the Egyptian temple, the hypostyle hall is thought to represent the 'primeval marsh' which surrounded the first bit of dry land at the creation of the world.

Hypostyle hall, temple of Khnum, Esna (Graeco-Roman period)

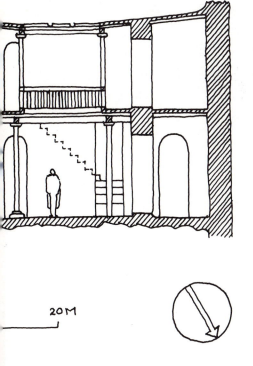

20M

Ilahun or Kahun

Egypt, see map p. xvi. An area at the edge of the Fayyum, which had been made arable during the Middle Kingdom as part of a scheme for the creation of new farmland. Sesostris II (*c.* 1897-1878 BC) had his mudbrick pyramid built there, and next to the valley temple the walled town of Ilahun (or Kahun) was discovered. It had been purpose-built to house the workmen and priests involved in the building and maintenance of the royal tomb, and is the most important excavated example of Middle Kingdom domestic architecture and town-planning.

The town was enclosed within a square formed by brick walls (387m per side) and oriented to the points of the compass. An

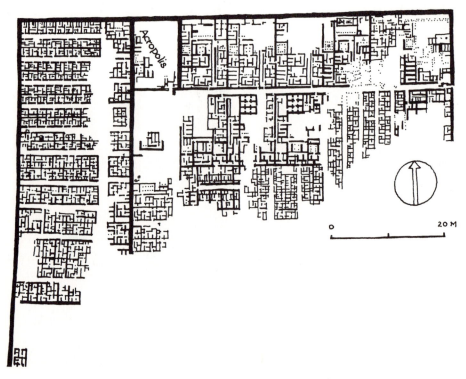

Ilahun: town plan (XII Dynasty) (after Petrie)

internal wall divided the town into two unequal parts, the smaller western part being reserved for the artisans. Straight roads running N-S were crossed at right angles by secondary streets. They enclosed regular blocks of double rows of houses built side by side. An estimated 10,000 people were living in the city. The houses in the workmen's quarter were smaller and more densely grouped together than the mansions in the northern part. These had columned halls, interior courtyards, a great number of rooms and corridors and separate women's quarters. Yet throughout the town, buildings seem to conform to an architectural master-plan (eg the tripartite ground plan was used throughout) and great care was taken in the actual building. Certain features are typical for Middle Kingdom architecture, such as the general use of brick barrel vaults (in houses and in the pyramid), arched doorways and octagonal columns.

Petrie, W.M.F., *Kahun, Gurob and Hawara* (London 1889-90)
Petrie, W.M.F., *Ilahun, Kahun and Gurob* (London 1891)

Imhotep

High priest, physician, architect and important official under several III Dynasty kings of Egypt, notably Djoser (*c.* 2667-2648 BC). He is traditionally associated with the first monumental work in Egypt to be executed in stone (see SAQQARA: funerary complex of Djoser). During the XXVI Dynasty he became subject of a special cult, and the Greeks eventually identified Imhotep with Asklepion.

Wildung, D., 'Imhotep und Amenhotep: Gottwerdung im alten Ägypten', *Münchener Ägyptologische Studien* 36 (1977)

impost

The architectural element between the capital and the abacus (or architrave) in a column. Forked imposts were used on Achaemenian columns (PERSEPOLIS, PASARGADAE), which may ultimately derive from the split trunks of young trees which used to support the nomad's tent. The stone imposts were sculpted in the shape of antithetically grouped recumbent bulls, bull-men and griffons.

Ishchali (ancient Neribtum)

Mesopotamia, see map p. xviii. A city belonging to the 2nd-millennium kingdom of Eshnunna. The foundation of a large (*c.* 100m × 67m) temple dedicated to Ishtar-Kititum in the west of the city goes back to Ibiq-Adad II of Eshnunna (*c.* second half of the 19th C BC). The temple rose above the densely built-up surrounding area on an elevated platform. The main shrine stood on its own socle within the surrounding walls. The important buildings were grouped around one large and several smaller courtyards. There were three entrances with steps leading up to a gateway flanked by gate-towers. The enclosure of the main sanctuary could be approached directly from the street, on the opposite side of the shrine. This shrine consisted of a transverse ante-cella and a broad BREITRAUM-CELLA with a niche for the sacred image. Behind the central court and at right angles to the main sanctuary were two more temples, one behind the other. They could be entered either through a gate from the street or *via* the central court at the long sides (see BENT-AXIS APPROACH).

Frankfort, H., *Oriental Institute Publications* 72 (Chicago 1955)

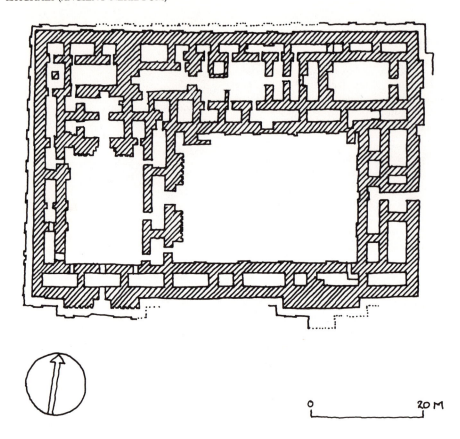

Ishchali: temple of Ishtar-Kititum (after Hill)

J

jamb

The upright vertical face of a doorway which supports the lintel and protects the wall-opening. In Egyptian and Achaemenian monumental architecture, the whole door-frame could be built of stone (sometimes cut from a single block). Elsewhere, bricks or wood or a combination of both were in use. Jambs with figurative relief ornamentation, especially on important gateways, ensured the magical protection of the building or city. Pairs of human-headed colossal bulls or lions (see LAMASSU) flanked the gateways in Assyrian and Achaemenian palaces; the Hittites carved images of lions, warriors and sphinxes on their monolithic gates.

Jarmo

Mesopotamia, see map p. xviii. Neolithic farming-settlement (c. 6700-6000 BC). The twenty-five excavated houses had rectangular ground plans with a courtyard in the middle. The walls were built of PISÉ on stone foundations. The clay floors were laid over a bed of reeds. The roofs were probably pitched and covered with mud-plastered reeds.

Braidwood, R.J., *Antiquity* 24 (1950) 189-195
Braidwood, R.J., *Bulletin of the American Schools of Oriental Research* 124 (1951) 12-18
Braidwood, R.J., Howe, B., *Prehistoric Investigations in Iraqi Kurdistan* (Chicago 1960)

Jericho (modern Tell es-Sultan)

Palestine, see map p. xix. This site had a very long sequence of habitation. It had a good position at the foot of hills, near clear water wells and lay on a frequented route along the Jordan Valley into the Judean Hills and the Dead Sea. The present stratigraphy was established by K. Kenyon.

The earliest Mesolithic levels (10th millennium BC) are associated with a population of hunters and food-gatherers living in simple hut-like shelters. The remains of one solid building, generally interpreted as a sanctuary, were found near the springs. It was a rectangular structure (3.50m × 6.50m) with stone walls enforced by wooden posts. Three large stone blocks had holes bored right through them, perhaps in order to support some upright object of ritual significance.

The succeeding period (Proto-Neolithic; 9th millennium BC) marks the transition from a semi-nomadic, hunting way of life to a settled community based on agriculture. The impermanent huts became solid houses made of hand-shaped bricks, circular and semi-interred.

The settlement prospered and assumed urban character in the following Pre-Pottery Neolithic A period (8th millennium BC). A free-standing stone wall (1.98m wide) surrounded the town. One great circular watch-tower survived to a height of 9.14m. It was also built of stone (8.50m diameter) and had an internal staircase leading to the top.

The site was repopulated after a period of abandonment and the architectural innovations made elsewhere (eg Beidha) were applied at Jericho (Pre-Pottery Neolithic B, 7th millennium BC). The houses now have a rectangular plan, with a courtyard flanked by rooms on either side. The walls were made of cigar-shaped, hand-made mudbricks and hard lime-plaster covered the floors. Two structures were interpreted as 'shrines'. One had a separate room equipped with a niche and a pedestal, that might have contained an upright stone pillar that was found nearby, and another had a rectangular room in the centre of which was a plastered rectangular basin.

After a long period of architectural regression, the Early Bronze (3rd millennium BC) town was again surrounded by a defensive wall made of mudbrick on stone foundations and enforced with timber. During the Middle Bronze Age (2nd millennium BC) the town reached its greatest expansion. New fortifications consisted of a plaster-faced artificial glacis (c. 25° from the horizontal), strong ramparts and mudbrick walls. A considerable portion of the town plan has been recovered. Two streets with wide cobbled steps led up the slope of the mound. There were drains underneath them. Houses built of mudbrick were closely packed together, with workshops and booths taking up the ground floor while the living accommodation was on the upper storeys. Wooden furniture and other household equipment which had been part of the funerary gifts, were discovered in the collective rock tombs.

Bertlett, J.R., *Jericho* (Guildford 1982)
Kenyon, K.M., *Digging Up Jericho* (London 1957)
Kenyon, K.M., *Excavations at Jericho* I-II (London 1960, 1965)

Jerusalem

Palestine, see map p. xix. The site seems to have been first occupied in the 4th millennium BC, but due to the many series of destruction and persistent quarrying, hardly any architectural structures survive from this or any subsequent period until the Roman age. The Temple of Solomo has been tentatively reconstructed from the Biblical account and Phoenician prototypes, although no architectural structures survived. It was probably an oblong and tripartite structure (100 cubits × 50 cubits), elevated on a platform and entered through a porch (*oolam*). The legendary pillars Joachin and Boaz flanked the entrance to the main hall (*heikhal*), which was lighted by windows high up in the wall (or a clerestory). A few steps at the back gave access to the Holy of Holies (*debir*), which served as Tabernacle for the Ark of the Covenant. This room is described as square (20 × 20 cubits) and lower than the main hall, but it might in fact have been a large, box-like structure made entirely of precious woods, within the *heikhal*. Next to the temple and surrounding it on all sides except the front, was a structure some three storeys high, which served the dual purposes of buttressing the widely spanned temple itself and offering storage for ritual utensils. The Old Testament accounts (I Kings 6, 1-35, II Chronicles 3, 1-14) explicitly state that Phoenician masons were engaged to build the temples. There are no contemporary Syrian temples which would serve as a comparison but the building methods described in the Bible recall Phoenician masonry (courses of dressed stone with imbedded timber beams; see RAS SHAMRA; SAMARIA). The tripartite organisation (which does not necessarily imply three different, independent rooms; a niche or internal division of the second space provided an equal amount of secluded sanctity) corresponds to the general Syro-Palestinian tradition. The rich interior decorations of ivory carvings have parallels in other sites, notably NIMRUD, where they had been imported and looted from the Syro-Palestinian area.

Busink, T.A., *Der Tempel von Jerusalem* (Leiden 1970)

Kenyon, K.M., *Digging Up Jerusalem* (London 1974)

Orrieux, C., 'Le temple de Salomon', *Temples et Sanctuaires: Séminaire de recherche 1981-1983* (Lyon 1984) 81-96

Weidhaas, H., review of Busink's article, in *Anatolia* 4 (1971-72) 184-192

K

Kahun *see* ILAHUN

Kalakh *see* NIMRUD

Kar Tukulti-Ninurta (modern Tulul Akir)

Mesopotamia, see map p. xviii. Residential city built by the Assyrian king Tukulti-Ninurta I (1244-1208 BC).

The town, which is only partly excavated, was surrounded by a rectangular wall. The palace was built on an artificial platform, and although no complete ground plan remains, fragments of wall paintings were discovered which feature stylised antithetically grouped animals and plant elements.

The Assur temple abutted against one side of the ziggurat (31m square) with its cella recessed into the core of this structure. The plan of the temple is essentially Babylonian: a square central courtyard was surrounded by two broad and shallow vestibules (on the N and E side), which were both entered through buttressed doorways. The entrance to the sanctuary itself had vertical recesses on either side, and led to the broad, transverse cella, with the image of the deity facing the door.

Andrae, W., *Das wiedererstehende Assur* (Leipzig 1938)
Eickhoff, T., *Kar Tukulti Ninurta* (Abhandlungen der Deutschen Orientgesellschaft 21, Berlin 1985)

Karmir-Blur

Anatolia, see map p. xv. Urartian citadel (9th C BC). It was one of the well-fortified provincial centres, built on a spur of limestone rock. At the SW corner of the site, a spiral staircase cut out of the mountain, lighted with three windows, led down to a huge hall. There was an open space in the centre which was surrounded by the major buildings. The 'palace' or administrative headquarters was housed in a single block of irregular outlines, comprising some 120-150 rooms. There were no interior courtyards, but the staggered floor levels of the rooms suggest that the roofs were of different height, which would improve the lighting conditions. There were probably two storeys over most of the rooms, with the ground floor accommodating mainly storage areas, workshops etc. The houses of the older type had a rectangular courtyard (*c.* 5m × 10m), one side of which was partly roofed over to form a porch supported by wooden columns or posts. One square living room and a store room of the same dimensions (*c.* 5m × 5m) opened onto the court. The lower part of the exterior walls were faced with vertical slabs (1.10m high); the windows had stone lintels. At a later date, several such house-units were combined to form regular blocks of houses. All buildings were built entirely of stone and the rocky ground made foundations superfluous. The temple of Haldi was a SUSI-type building with very thick walls (13m) of mudbrick on a stone substructure.

Barnett, R.D., Watson, W., *Iraq* 21 (1959) 1ff

Van Loon, M.N., *Urartian Art: Its Distinctive Traits in the Light of New Excavations* (Istanbul 1966) 55ff, 110ff

Karnak

Egypt, see map p. xvi. Vast temple-complex outside modern Luxor with substantially preserved and restored monuments dating from the Middle Kingdom to the Graeco-Roman period.

The largest of the several temple-precincts of Karnak is the temple of Amun. The present remains represent the final stages of continuous building activity which spanned more than a thousand years, extending and sometimes rebuilding the existing older structures.

The now vanished limestone temple of Sesostris I (*c.* 1971-1928 BC) was the first and original sanctuary at Karnak. It seems to have comprised a Royal Festival or *hebsed*-hall and a sequence of three small rooms, culminating in the shrine of Amun. A small barque-chapel, a delicate structure on a raised platform, its roof supported by square pillars, is the only building by Sesostris to be preserved. The growing importance of the Amun cult during the New Kingdom is reflected at Karnak by ever more ambitious building projects of successive pharaohs. During the XVIII Dynasty, Tuthmosis I (*c.* 1525-1512 BC) erected two pylons and extended the sanctuaries crosswise to the main axis. Hatshepsut (*c.* 1503-1482 BC) added her temple to the Middle Kingdom structures

Karnak: 'Brilliant Monument' or Festival House, Tuthmosis III (XVIII Dynasty)

and placed two obelisks (one of which is still standing) in front of it. Her successor, Tuthmosis III (*c.* 1504-1450 BC), converted or dismantled the previous sanctuaries, walled up the obelisks of Hatshepsut and built three pylons (6th, 7th, 8th). An interesting structure, known as the Festival Hall or the 'Brilliant Monument', also survives from this time. It served to celebrate the royal jubilee festival but it also incorporated chapels destined for the royal cult and suites for underworld and solar deities such as occur in the later New Kingdom mortuary temples. The entrance at the SE corner is flanked by statues of the king in the jubilee robe and leads to an ante-chamber from which a passage connects with the row of magazines on the S end of the building. The hypostyle hall is supported by unique downward-tapering columns (thought to be the stone equivalent of wooden tent-poles holding up the roof of the customary jubilee pavilion). The central aisle is wider than the side aisles and gives the impression of being higher because the walls and pillars on the side are lower than the columns, and are surmounted by a continuous architrave. The roofing slabs above project outwards and also cover the outer galleries, forming a simultaneous protrusion of slabs to the inside and outside. This considerable structural ingenuity has apparently never been repeated.

The monuments of the succeeding rulers of the XVIII Dynasty (the 3rd pylon of Amenophis III, the colossal statues in front of it, the court of Tutankhamun) are in more or less fragmentary condition, and have been moved from their original positions in the course of later building activities. During the Amarna period, the temple of Amun was vandalised, and Akhenaten built a separate sanctuary dedicated to Aten outside the precinct of Amun. Following the restoration of the Amun cult, Horemheb (*c.* 1348-1320 BC)

extended the transverse axis by two further pylons.

During the XIX Dynasty, the temple was enlarged considerably and the great hypostyle hall was begun by Seti I (*c.* 1318-1304 BC) and completed by Ramesses II (*c.* 1304-1237 BC). It contained 134 massive columns (22m high), standing very closely together like a thicket of gigantic stone plants. Twelve columns with open papyriform capitals formed the higher central aisle and the remaining 122 had papyrus-bud capitals. The central aisle was topped by a stone grille providing clerestory lighting along the main axis. Columns and walls were covered with painted reliefs. The first court contains a number of chapels and 'way-stations' of the Ramesside and later periods and was enclosed by the 1st pylon during the XII Dynasty (*c.* 10th C BC). In front of this monumental facade lies an avenue flanked by crio-sphinxes with rams' heads (an animal sacred to Amun), leading down to the river.

Other temples of the late pharaonic and Graeco-Roman periods include the small temple of Konsu, the Opet temple, the Ptah temple, and the precincts of Montu and Mut (New Kingdom foundation, largely rebuilt in the Late Period).

Barguet, P., *Le temple d'Amoun-Re à Karnak* (Cairo 1962)

Borchardt, L., in Sethe, K. (ed.), *Zur Baugeschichte des Amun-tempels von Karnak* (Leipzig 1905) 3ff

Lacau, P., Chevrier, H., *Une chapelle d'Hatshepsut à Karnak* I-II (Cairo 1977, 1979)

Legrain, G., *Les Temples de Karnak* (Brussels 1929)

Michalowski, K., *Karnak* (New York, Washington, London 1970)

Karnak: inside the Great Hypostyle Hall
   (XIX Dynasty)

karum

Akkadian for 'quay'. Also denotes the commercial quarter of a Mesopotamian city or the merchant colonies outside the homeland (see KÜLTEPE).

Kassite architecture

The Kassites were one of several groups of peoples with Indo-European affinities but uncertain origin who, after a long period of settlement in Iran, challenged the political establishment in Mesopotamia during the first half of the 2nd millennium BC. Following the Hittite raid on Babylon in 1595 BC, the Kassite dynasty became firmly ensconced as the rulers of Southern Mesopotamia (1519-1162 BC). It was a generally peaceful period and the foreign kings encouraged the local cultural traditions; arts and literature flourished. They rebuilt sanctuaries of all the important religious centres and built a new capital, Dur-Kurigalzu ('AQAR QUF).

In this city, the architectural innovations of the Kassites are well documented. While the ziggurat seems to follow the Mesopotamian pattern exemplified by Urnammu's ziggurat at UR, the royal palace is more original. It contained a pillared portico surrounding the central courtyard and fresco decorations featuring a procession of officials.

In c. 1440 BC, king Karaindash built a temple of Inanna at URUK, which is also very different from contemporary Southern Mesopotamian sanctuaries. It had an oblong axial and entirely symmetrical ground plan, with a longitudinal cella and stepped corner-bastions. The

Palace of Kurigalzu and ziggurat at 'Aqar Quf (Kassite period)

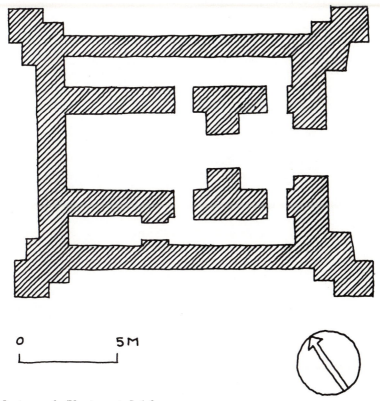

*Uruk: Innin temple (Kassite period) (after
UVB I, 10)*

entrance was axially aligned with the inner
doorway leading into the cella. Parts of the
exterior facade have survived; it consists of
a number of niches accommodating large
figures of male and female deities made of
moulded bricks. From water vessels which
they hold in their hands, symbolic jets of
water flow in serpentine curves over the
buttresses between the niches.

Large brick vaults were supposed to
have roofed this temple; as also in the
palace of Kurigalzu, the thickness of the
walls suggest that they were vaulted, a
technique much used in neighbouring
Elam during the same period.

Frankfort, H., *The Art and Architecture of
the Ancient Orient* (4th ed., Harmonds-
worth 1970) 126-129
Jaritz, K., 'Die Kulturreste der Kassiten',
Anthropos 55 (1960) 17-84
Woolley, C.L., *Ur Excavations* VIII
(London 1965)

Khafaje (ancient Tutub ?)

Mesopotamia, see map p. xviii. One of the
best documented sites for the development of early Mesopotamian temple
architecture.

The first five levels of the 'Sin' temple belong to the Jemdet-Nasr or Proto-literate Period (end of the 4th millennium BC). The sanctuary consisted of an oblong room with a triple stepped platform set against the short NW side. The interior space was subdivided into subsidiary chambers along both sides and a staircase that gave access to the roof. The only entrance was in one of the long walls leading into an open area which was eventually enclosed to form a courtyard. From the fourth level onwards, the temples were rebuilt by carefully filling up the levelled earlier structures, and putting the new walls on the stumps of the previous ones. In order to achieve even firmer foundations, these walls were again filled up when they had reached a height of 1m. In this way the temple retained its old plan but gradually rose high above the surrounding town and had to be reached by a flight of steps. The facade of the sanctuary at level V was decorated with narrow, doubly recessed niches carved out of the thick mud-plaster. The mudbricks used were the long and narrow 'RIEMCHEN' type.

The following five levels date from the Pre-Sargonic (or Early Dynastic) period (c. 2700-2400 BC). At level VI, the surrounding utilitarian buildings (magazines, workshops etc) and the courtyard were integrated into a coherent and self-contained space, set upon a platform deriving from previous ruins and enclosed by an irregular wall (30m long). The cella was still a long rectangle entered on the long side as far away from the divine statue as possible. The whole building with its single entrance in the strong enclosure wall is a segregated and self-contained unit, clearly separate from the rest of the city. The new feature of level VII were monumental gate-towers flanking the entrance to the temple precinct (the foundations extended 2.5m in front of the wall to form a small platform on which the two towers were erected). An impressive stairway led up from the street below. The following levels VIII to X show a progressive organisation of the subsidiary buildings around three sides of the courtyard. The outside walls of the precinct were strengthened and decorated by brick buttresses; the entrance was further enlarged and additional small sanctuaries were incorporated. The cells became increasingly less accessible. The bricks employed were PLANO-CONVEX BRICKS (level VI-X).

The temple of Nintu was contemporary with the temple of Sin. It grew from a small one-room shrine (level I) to a complex temple precinct comprising a double-sanctuary (two cellae and a rectangular courtyard) and a single shrine within its own court (level VI).

Apart from these slowly evolving temples within the city, a new temple was built in the Early Dynastic period in the SW part of the town. This Temple Oval was built on virgin soil above a layer of clean sand and double foundations of packed clay between the 4.5m thick foundation walls of the perimeter wall. In this way an artificial terrace was created which rose c. 1.5m above the surrounding area. The plan of the precinct was oval with a flattened base, getting narrower towards the SW. The whole complex was planned as one architectural unit complete with utilitarian buildings, priests' quarters, courtyards and the sanctuary itself. The interior space of the enclosure was ingeniously divided by three successive platforms which neatly separated the various areas accessible to the public or reserved for the priesthood. The sanctuary proper was set on its own platform towards the rear of the precinct and must have dominated the skyline of the whole complex. A single entrance reached by a flight of steps led to the first court where the priests' quarters were probably accommodated. The inner courtyard was

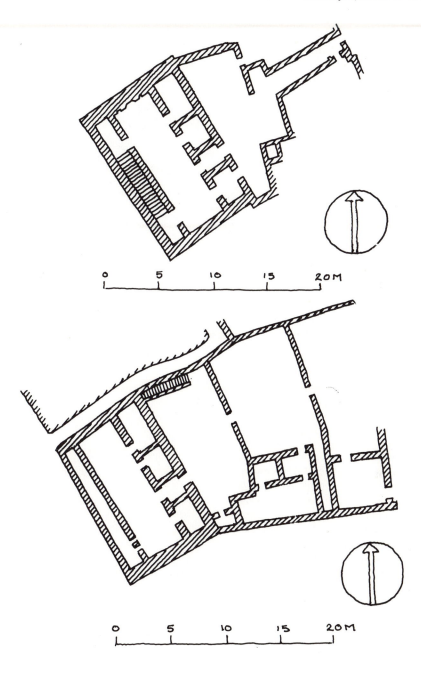

Khafaje: Sin temple II, V (Early Dynastic period) (after Delougaz, Lloyd)

115

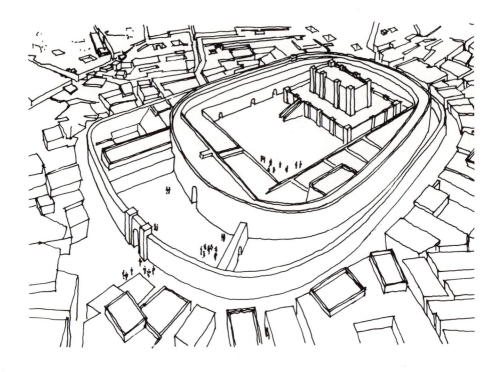

Khafaje: Temple Oval (Early Dynastic period)
  (after Darby)

enclosed by a concentric wall, encircling the next platform along which various store houses, magazines and workshops were grouped so as to form a rectangular space accessible through a gateway set into the massive interior wall. The sanctuary was placed right against the narrow back of the enclosure leaving only a narrow passage along three sides. The temple platform (25m × 30m) was ornamented with shallow buttresses all around and a stairway placed off-centre gave access to the temple on top of which no architectural remains have been found. This building was also constructed with plano-convex bricks.

Delougaz, P., 'The Temple Oval at Khafajah', *Oriental Institute Publications* 53 (Chicago 1940)

Delougaz, P., Lloyd, S., 'Presargonic Temples in the Diyala Region', *Oriental Institute Publications* 58 (Chicago 1942)

khekher ornament

The Egyptian sign *khekher* has the connotation of 'adorned, ornament' and represents upright plant-stems, bundled twice at the top and bottom and with a slight swelling in the middle. As an ornament in itself, it was used to decorate the top of walls or cornices in monumental buildings and probably derived from light-weight shelters made of plant-materials.

Egyptian hieroglyph: khekher

Khorsabad (ancient Dur Sharrukin)

Mesopotamia, see map p. xviii. As the ancient name indicates, this was the Citadel of Sargon, the Assyrian king, who built here between 713 and 707 BC. It was dedicated in 706 BC and soon afterwards abandoned by Sennacherib, the king's successor, who moved back to the old capital NINEVEH. This short occupation has left the buildings relatively undisturbed and it is therefore a prime example for Assyrian palace architecture.

The Citadel was only a comparatively small part in the NW of the planned town, which was surrounded by a huge wall (1750m × 1685m) pierced by seven gates. It had its own perimeter wall and two double gates which led to the lower town. While the royal quarters and the administrative and religious buildings were sited on an elevated platform projecting from the enclosure wall on the NE, the various buildings on the lower level were grouped around irregular open spaces and consisted of agglomerations of courtyards, corridors and adjoining rooms.

The temple of Nabu stood on a platform and was built along a vertical axis. Two successive courtyards led to the main temple conceived as a DOUBLE SANCTUARY with one transverse vestibule.

A broad ramp suitable for the royal chariots connected the lower citadel (surface 10 ha) with the Royal Palace on the SE rampart. A triple portal elaborately buttressed and flanked by LAMASSU-colossi led to a large courtyard (103m × 91m). Administrative and service quarters occupied a regularly planned block to the N, while on the opposite side was the temple area consisting of three large and two smaller temples around two courtyards to which abutted the ziggurat in the W. The royal quarters were reached through a portal set in the NW corner giving onto the second longitudinal inner courtyard. As in the first court, its wall surfaces were decorated with relief-orthostats showing the triumphs of the king's army. To the W, a triple gate guarded by winged bulls gave access to the throne room, a brilliantly painted long hall with the throne set against the narrow far end of the room on an elaborately carved stone platform. A staircase at the opposite end must have led to an upper storey.

The splendid decorations included the use of painted relief orthostats in the palace, and colourful ornamental strips of glazed bricks or tiles, white-washed plaster and enamelled large decorative 'nails' in the temples. The whole complex was designed to impress by its sheer size and the lavishness of its furnishings and ornaments and to inspire fear and admiration in the vassals and emissaries approaching the mighty Assyrian king.

Busink, T.A., 'La Zikkurat de Dûr-Šarrukin', *Comptes rendus de la troisième rencontre Assyriologique Internationale* (Leiden 1954) 105-122
Loud, G., 'An Architectural Formula for Assyrian Planning based on the Results of Excavations at Khorsabad', *Revue d'Assyriologie* 33 (1936) 153-160
Loud, G., 'Khorsabad' I-II, *Oriental Institute Publications* 38, 40 (Chicago 1936, 1938)

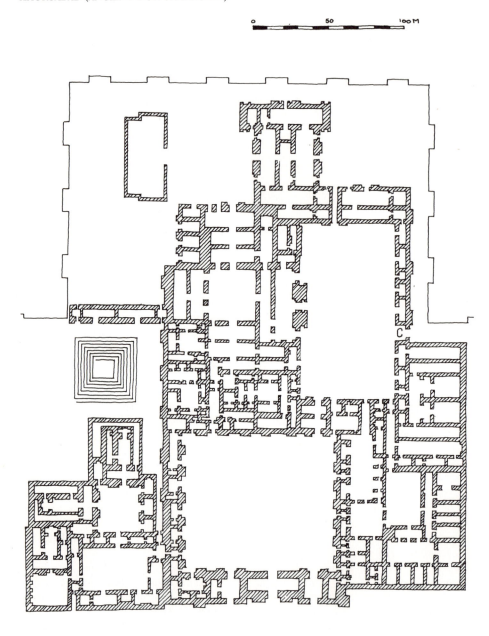

Khorsabad: Sargon's palace (after Place)   *Kish: palace (Early Dynastic period) (after Christian)*

Kish (modern Tell el-Ohemir)

Mesopotamia, see map p. xviii. Sumerian town and seat of several dynasties in the 3rd millennium BC.

The palace of Kish is a good example for a fortified royal residence. The surrounding wall (41m long, 13.5m wide, 4m thick) was strengthened by buttresses every six metres and battlemented towers were linked together by a curtain wall. A secondary wall left only a narrow corridor between the two lines of defence. The great courtyard (14.5m × 15m) was paved with three layers of baked bricks. In the eastern part, remains of columns made of brick were found (70cm in diameter) which may have supported some kind of portico. Doorways in the four sides of the courtyard led to various chambers on the ground floor which were probably used mainly for storage and workshops. The single entrance to the palace was approached by a flight of steps and the particularly massive walls on either side suggest projecting gate-towers. A large annex was built on the S side of this building, which was also strongly fortified, though relying more on aggressive defence by archers on battlements and towers than on the thickness of its walls (only 2m thick). An interesting feature inside is the columned hall (26.7m × 7.6m): the columns were composed of rhomboidal mudbrick segments arranged around a circular brick in the middle. The plan of the palace could not be recovered completely. It must also be borne in mind that upper storeys probably contained most of the representative and residential apartments, which would have had more access to light and air than the crowded and dark ground-floor accommodation. A system of flat roofs and terraces may have linked the

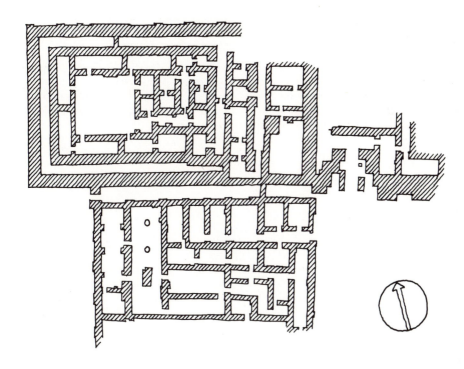

seemingly separate halves of the building.

Mackay, E., *A Sumerian Palace and the 'A' Cemetery at Kish, Mesopotamia* (Chicago 1929)
Margueron, J., *Recherches sur les palais mésopotamiens de l'âge du bronze* (Paris 1982) 69ff
Moorey, P.R.S., 'The "Plano-convex Building" at Kish and Early Mesopotamian Palaces', *Iraq* 26 (1964) 83-98

kisu

Akkadian term signifying the low socle or abutment along the external walls of Mesopotamian temples.

Kom Ombo

Egypt, see map p. xvi. Ptolemaic and Graeco-Roman temple dedicated to two gods (Harwer and the crocodile-god Sobek). The result is a DOUBLE SANCTUARY with a screen-walled facade pierced by two entrances which give access to the interior sequence of two hypostyle halls, three broad vestibules and the inner sanctuary featuring the two shrines surrounded radially by service rooms and cult chambers. As in other late temples, there are subterranean passages and access to the roof.

Badawy, A., *Kom Ombo, Sanctuaries* (Cairo 1952)

Kültepe (ancient Karum Kanesh)

Anatolia, see map p. xv. The first occupation of this site goes back to the 3rd millennium BC, but the most interesting remains date from the 19th C BC when Kanesh was an Assyrian KARUM, or trading colony. A great number of cuneiform tablets have been found, recording the business transactions of the local and Assyrian merchants. The town itself had a circular rampart, a small palace (11m × 12.5m) of the MEGARON type, and a citadel featuring colonnades. The *karum* was outside the town walls. The Assyrian trading community lived in well-built and spacious houses with little forecourts and upper storeys following the local tradition of domestic architecture.

Mellink, A., *American Journal of Archaeology* 69-73 (1965-69)
Özgüç, T., *Kültepe-Kanis* (Ankara 1959)
Özgüç, T., *Anatolia* 7 (1963) 16-66; 8 (1964) 46ff

Lachish = Tell Duweir

Palestine, see map p. xix. Bronze Age settlement, later strongly fortified (1st millennium BC) and finally destroyed by Nebukadrezzar II in 587 BC.

The Bronze Age sanctuary (15th-late 13th C BC), the so-called Fosse temple, was rebuilt several times. The oldest version consisted of a cella (*c.* 5m × 10m) with two wooden columns, a podium at the back and two small chambers behind.

Upper temple   Middle temple   Lowest temple

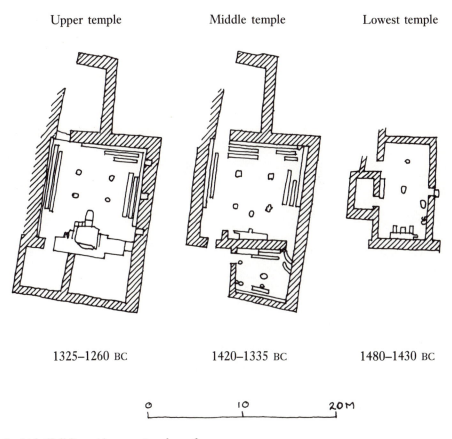

1325–1260 BC   1420–1335 BC   1480–1430 BC

Lachish (Tell Duweir): successive plans of Fosse temple (after Kenyon)

121

It was enlarged to twice its original size in the 14th C; an ante-chamber was added, and niches in the wall as well as three benches were probably destined for offerings. The fosses (trenches) dug outside the temple contained rich temple equipment and votive gifts.

The Canaanite sanctuary of the 1st millennium BC was much smaller (cella 3m × 4m). It also had benches along the walls inside and there was an open-air installation (BAMAH) complete with cult stelae (*massebot* and *asheroth*).

Tufnell, O., *et al.*, *Lachish II: The Fosse Temple* (London 1940); *Lachish III: The Iron Age* (London 1953); *Lachish IV: The Bronze Age* (London 1958)

lamassu-colossi

Šedu and *lamassu* were the names of benevolent demons in Mesopotamia. In Assyrian palaces, some of the more important gates and doorways had monolithic sculpted jambs representing striding winged bulls or lions with a human face. While the image of the human-headed bull is common in the Assyrian iconography, the architectural application may derive from Anatolia, where carved jambs had been used by the Hittites (see BOGHAZKÖY, ALAÇA HÜYÜK). Their purpose in the words of the Assyrian king Esarhaddon was 'to turn back an evil person, guard the steps and secure the path of the king who fashioned them' (Ash.62f). The Achaemenians took over the theme of the winged guardians, interpreted in the more dynamic manner of their art (see Gate of Xerxes, PERSEPOLIS).

Edzard, D.O. (ed.), *Reallexikon der Assyriologie und Vorderasiatischen Archäologie* VI (Berlin, New York 1980-83) 447

Lamassu in the palace of Nimrud

Larsa (modern Senkereh)

Mesopotamia, see map p. xviii. Capital of a small kingdom which enjoyed some importance in Southern Mesopotamia after the collapse of the III Dynasty of UR (*c.* 2004 BC).

The site is only partially excavated. The Palace of Nur-Adad (1865-1850 BC) was apparently never inhabited and was abandoned before completion. Although only parts of the ground plan have been recovered, it is a rare example of Mesopotamian palace design unimpeded by later alterations. It recalls other similar complexes at MARI, UR and ASSUR, but it is distinguished by a clear and purposeful juxtaposition of spaces around a large courtyard surrounded by narrow rooms and corridors. The thick walls (2m) and deep foundations strengthened with baked bricks, probably supported a high superstructure with upper storeys.

The Shamash temple, the *Ebabbar*, is also only superficially known. Building activities there can be traced from the 18th C BC to the Neo-Babylonian period (7th C BC). Three large courtyards were built along one axis which was emphasised by centrally placed, elaborately buttressed doorways, to form an elongated complex (*c.* 227m long). Narrow chambers were set into the thickness of the surrounding walls on all four sides. The outside faces were articulated with stepped niches.

There is now some evidence (see Calvert) that there were two sanctuaries at Larsa during the 3rd millennium BC: a ziggurat in the city centre and a temple on the summit of the mound (now below the Neo-Babylonian ruins). When Hammurabi began his scheme to rebuild the *Ebabbar*, he undertook to link the two sanctuaries, favouring the orientation of the ziggurat and arranging the *Ebabbar* along this axis.

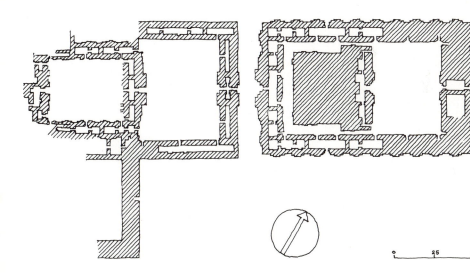

Larsa: ziggurat and courts of the Ebabbar (temple of Shamash) (after Braun)

Certain remnants of the older temple, however, were apparently preserved on purpose (eg annex, piers in room 9).

Calvert, Y., 'Le temple Babylonienne de Larsa', in *Temples et Sanctuaires: Séminaire de recherche 1981-1983* (Lyon 1984) 9-22
Huot, J.L., *Syria* 53 (1976) 2-45; 55 (1978) 195-196
Margueron, J., *Syria* 47 (1970) 261-277; 48 (1971) 271-287
Parrot, A., *Revue d'Assyriologie* 30 (1933) 175-182
Parrot, A., *Syria* 45 (1968) 205-239

libn, liben *see* MUDBRICK

lintel *see* JAMB

Lisht

Egypt, see map p. xvi. Necropolis and pyramid-field of the XII Dynasty.

The pyramid of Ammenemes I (*c.* 1992-1963 BC) closely follows the traditional Old Kingdom pyramid design. In fact, a large number of dressed limestone blocks were taken from older tombs at DASHUR, GIZA and SAQQARA. An offering chapel lay before the entrance to the tomb-shaft on the N face. The mortuary temple and tombs of courtiers and other members of the royal family were situated on two terraces and enclosed by a rectangular brick wall. The interior arrangements of the pyramid are unexamined due to the high level of ground-water.

The pyramid of Sesostris I (*c.* 1971-1928 BC) and its mortuary temple still copy the VI Dynasty pattern. The pyramid

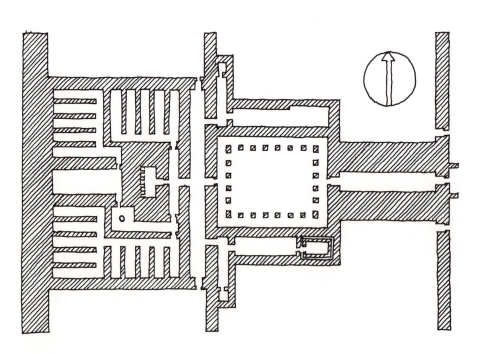

Lisht: pyramid complex of Sesostris I (XII Dynasty) (after Edwards)

(105m square) was 61m high and had an inclination of 49°. The inside was constructed in a new manner to save time and building materials and to frustrate the efforts of the ever active grave-robbers. After the base was laid, heavy stone walls were erected, radiating from the centre to the four corners and the middle of each side. Eight more parallel walls were built between them, thus creating sixteen chambers of irregular size and shape which were filled with rubble and sand. The whole was then encased by stones. This practice, also using bricks only, remained standard for most Middle Kingdom pyramids (e.g. DASHUR, HAWARA, ILAHUN). An inner wall of stone enclosed the pyramid, the inner apartments of the mortuary temple and a subsidiary pyramid on the E side. Between this and an outer brick enclosure lay a colonnaded court, the entrance to the mortuary temple and nine small pyramids belonging to members of the royal family.

Gautier, J., Jéquier, M., *Bulletin of the Metropolitan Museum of Art*, April 1907, October 1908, October 1914, November 1921, December 1922

Lansing, A., *Bulletin of the Metropolitan Museum of Art* 15 (1920) 3-11; 21 (1926) section 2, 33-40; 29 (1934) section 2, 4-9

Lythgoe, A.M., *Bulletin of the Metropolitan Museum of Art*, September 1908, July 1909, February 1915

Luxor

Egypt, see map p. xvi. Temple of Amun was founded by Amenophis III (*c.* 1417-1379 BC) and extended by various later kings of the XIX Dynasty. The cult-statue of the god was taken on frequent journeys in connection with rituals performed in western Thebes, and the layout of this temple seems to cater for ceremonial processions as well as the storage of the barques on which the god crossed the

Luxor: court of Amenophis III (XVIII Dynasty)

125

Nile. The largest part of the temple is taken up by a succession of colonnaded courtyards and processional ways along one main axis (which is in fact somewhat bent due to some realignment which became necessary at a later stage when the temple was linked with the avenue from the Amun sanctuary at KARNAK). The inner sanctuary contains two shrines, one for the divine statue and one for the barque, one behind the other. Rows of store rooms and cult rooms are disposed along the side walls of the inner sanctuary.

The architectural impression of this temple is dominated by the skilful arrangement of the supports in the porticoes of the courtyards. The towering colonnade of open papyriform columns by Amenophis III contrasts with the tightly massed papyrus-bud type columns surrounding the court in double rows. The present entrance pylon was built by Ramesses II (c. 1304-1237 BC) and there were originally two obelisks in front of the temple, one of which has been removed to Paris.

Borchardt, L., *Zeitschrift für ägyptische Sprache und Altertumskunde* 34 (1896) 122-138

Gayet, A.J., 'Le temple de Louxor', *Mémoires de la Mission Archéologique Française* 15 (1894)

Malkatta

Egypt (Western Thebes), see map p. xvi. Palace of Amenophis III (c. 1417-1379 BC), which used to be linked by a causeway to the now vanished mortuary temple of the same king.

Various separate buildings (a temple of Amun, an audience pavilion, residential quarters etc) were grouped parallel to each other, except for the more loosely spaced buildings in the so-called 'West city', where irregularities in the terrain had to be taken account of. Blocks of smaller buildings for workmen or personnel stood between them and the Western Gate. The palaces (eg the Southern Palace) feature rectangular columned halls used as throne rooms or reception rooms, which were surrounded on each side by a suite of three rooms thought to be reserved for the royal ladies. The decoration of the interior palace walls is preserved in some places; the plastered mudbrick walls and ceilings were painted with ornamental borders which surrounded larger compositions of animals, plants and divine figures. The space between the main buildings and the outer enclosure wall was taken up by gardens and pavilions.

Hayes, W.C., *Journal of Near Eastern Studies* 10 (1951) 82ff; 156ff; 231ff

mamissi or birth house

A small chapel with plant-columns found in some Egyptian temple precincts. They represent the 'house' where the god (and by correlation the pharaoh) was born and reared. This clear reference to domestic architecture is emphasised by a comparatively light structure and easier access than in the large temples. Only late examples (from the Graeco-Roman period) built in stone have survived; they were probably built of more impermanent materials, like plant bundles and matting, or timber, in previous times.

The usual emplacement is at right angles to the main temple. Simple single-roomed chapels eventually developed into more elaborate structures with vestibules, store rooms and shrines. The mamissis at PHILAE and EDFU were surrounded by a colonnade, while those at KARNAK (temple of Mut), the older one at DENDERA, and the one at KOM OMBO had no external ambulatory. The roof of the colonnade can be higher than the one of the inner sanctuary, providing thus a secondary 'lid' of a box-like structure.

Badawy, A., 'The Architectural Symbolism of the Mamissi-Chapels in Egypt', *Chronique d'Egypte* 38 (Brussels 1933) 78-90
Borchardt, L., *Tempel mit Umgang* (Cairo 1938)
Daumas, F., *Les mamissis des temples égyptiens* (Paris 1958)

Mari (modern Tell Hariri)

Mesopotamia, see map p. xviii. This important site on the middle Euphrates has yielded not only a number of

Mamissi *at Dendera (Roman period)*

interesting architectural structures, such as temples and palaces dating from the 3rd and 2nd millennia BC, but also hundreds of statues and terracottas, wall paintings and some 23,000 cuneiform tablets.

The first important phase in Mari's history was the Early Dynastic (or Pre-Sargonic) Period (*c.* 2700-2400 BC). The Sumerian king-list records six kings of the Mari Dynasty. Several sanctuaries were found: the contiguous Ishtarat-Nini-zaza temples were laid-out regularly with symmetrical doorways and accessible through a courtyard *via* a BENT-AXIS APPROACH. The larger temple of Nini-zaza had a beautifully decorated square courtyard with manifold niches in the surrounding walls and an upright conical stela of stone. The Shamash and Ninhursag temples were only partially excavated. The so-called Massif rouge, a mass of mudbrick

core with baked-brick casing (40m × 25.9m high), surrounded by small shrines, was interpreted as an archaic ziggurat by the excavator.

Underneath the 2nd-millennium palace (see below) remains of Early Dynastic palaces were found (two levels). Their sacred precincts were well preserved with walls up to a height of 6.48m, complete with mud-plaster, recesses and niches. It has been suggested (Margueron, *Les palais mésopotamiens* p. 86) that the whole complex was a sanctuary rather than a royal residence. The bricks used in all Early Dynastic structures at Mari were flat and oblong and not the plano-convex ones usually associated with this period of Mesopotamian architecture. Mari was destroyed by Lugalzaggesi of URUK (*c.* 2400 BC) and only recovered some of its previous status during the Ur III period (*c.* 22nd-21st C BC). The old Ninhursag temple was enlarged by a porch with two columns.

The Lion or Dagan temple was a new foundation (*c.* 14m × 9m), probably featuring a BREITRAUM-CELLA with direct-axis approach and an entrance guarded by bronze lions. It was built against the SW facade of the Ziggurat (42m × 25m), erected over the levelled remains of the Early Dynastic Dagan temple and the Massif Rouge. It had a vast platform in front, and access to the top was by two parallel ramps perpendicular to the N face bordered by recessed and buttressed walls.

The fortunes of Mari prospered again during the Isin-Larsa period (*c.* 2017-1763 C BC), and Iahdunlim and his successor Zimrilim could afford to build a magnificent and admirably laid-out palace, which covered more than 2.5ha. It was burnt down by Hammurabi of Babylon (*c.* 1759 BC), never to be rebuilt. The result was that the ground plan could be re-covered by excavations and that some walls were preserved with plaster and occasionally murals, to a height of a few metres. A monumental entrance led to a sequence of two transverse courts and regulated the internal circulation of the vast complex, which was organised into several units distributed around open courts and linked by passages and corridors. The largest and most important courtyard (*Cour des palmiers*) (49m × 33m) was surrounded by the official reception rooms, sanctuaries and offices. It was paved with baked bricks except for a central depression which the excavator assumes to have been planted with trees. He also assigned precise functions to most of the rooms and chambers discovered which are questionable, as the existence of upper storeys over at least some parts of the palace meant that débris had fallen from above into the ground-floor rooms.

What can be ascertained is that the plan was extremely economical and that the circulation in all areas could be strictly controlled, avoiding congestion and disorder. An efficient system of drains underneath the foundations suggest careful overall planning before the palace was built. The various well-organised sectors were designed to meet the complex requirements of a building which combined facilities for secure storage of produced goods (cloth, wool, etc), their manufacture and distribution, a highly organised administration (with various offices and archives) as well as accommodation for the king and his entourage, reception rooms, sanctuaries and stables. The walls were well built throughout. The mudbricks were faced with plaster and sometimes painted with murals; there were bitumen lined bathrooms, but the luxuriously equipped living quarters doubtless occupied the upper storeys which have all but disappeared.

Margueron, J., *Recherches sur les palais mésopotamiens de l'âge du bronze* (Paris 1982) 86ff, 209ff

Parrot, A., *Le temple d'Ishtar* (Paris 1956)

Parrot, A., *Le Palais* I-III (Paris 1958-59)

Parrot, A., *Les temples d'Ishtarat et de Ninni-zaza* (Paris 1967)

Parrot, A., *Mari, capitale fabuleuse* (Paris 1974)

masonry

Building with regularly dressed stones, which could be fitted into compact and stable walls, was not possible before the suitable tools and techniques were available from the Bronze Age onwards. Large areas of the Near East do not have the right geological strata that could supply the necessary stones. Also, the quarrying, the transport and eventual assembly had to be coordinated and financed by a strong

Mari: palace of the Isin-Larsa period (after Parrot)

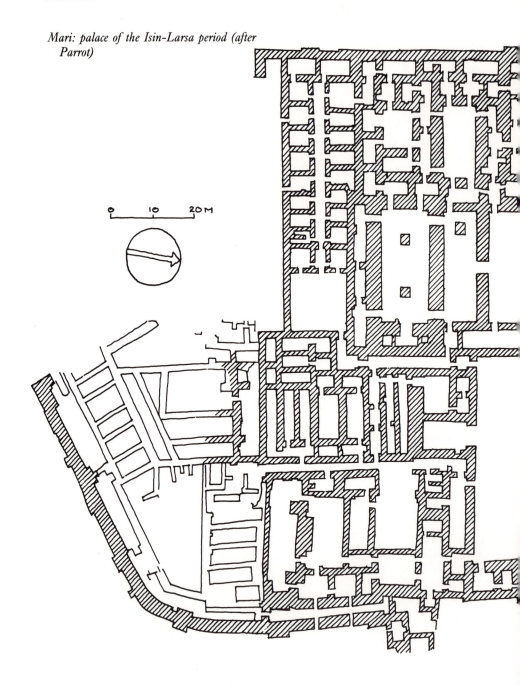

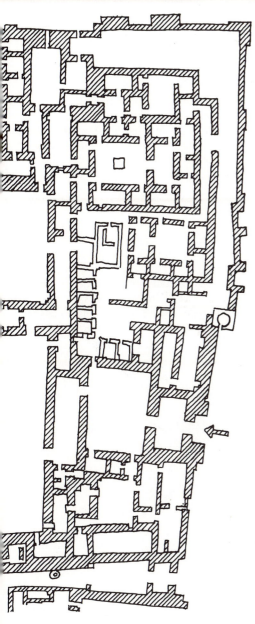

central government which was often lacking even in areas where good, hard rock was available. This is the reason why masonry-built architecture is an exception to the universal application of mudbrick. In Egypt, limestone of various qualities, sandstone and granite are piled up in horizontal layers along the Nile valley. Transport, even over long distances, was relatively easy by water. Limestone remained the principal building stone during the Old and Middle Kingdom, with granite being reserved for architraves, pillars and obelisks (eg GIZA: valley temple of Chephren). The hard sandstone from Silesia was more extensively used for the massive structures of the New Kingdom, and architraves of this material allowed the relatively wide spans of some hypostyle halls (eg KARNAK).

Stone architecture in Egypt was always a royal prerogative and only temples and tombs could be built 'to last forever'. During the III Dynasty, the first experiments in building in stone were initiated by Djoser in his funerary complex at SAQQARA (27th C BC). The blocks were small and the stones were laid like bricks with little pegs patching up broken edges. Such walls were not very strong, and when structures of the size of the great pyramids were being built in the IV Dynasty, the blocks became much larger. This in turn influenced the way they were dressed and laid. Blocks were dressed only on two surfaces before laying, those for the bedding and rising joint. They were then brought onto the course and laid close to the one laid last. Then the tops and front were dressed and the back if at all, only roughly. With megalithic masonry, where the blocks could be manoeuvred only on rollers or rockers, many were not truly rectangular and did not always have the same height. In a labour-saving technique, which still resulted in a perfect fit for the bedding joint, these blocks were cut obliquely and made to fit like a giant jigsaw puzzle.

Egyptian masonry: granite blocks from valley temple of Chephren, Giza (IV Dynasty)

Dovetail joints and peg-dowels, in wood or metal, were used for double architraves and occasionally in walls, to keep blocks in place during construction. The superior masonry techniques developed in the Old Kingdom deteriorated in the New Kingdom, where comparatively shoddy, badly bonded walls predominate, often re-using blocks from older structures (eg at Karnak). Rubble-filled double-walls were quicker and less expensive to construct and relied greatly on the consolidating pressure of the heavy architraves.

Clarke, S., Engelbach, R., *Ancient Egyptian Masonry* (London 1930)

In Middle Bronze Palestine (ET TELL, SHECHEM), fortifications could include massive battered walls of polygonal or cyclopean masonry, with a superstructure of mudbrick. Great boulders, some of them several metres across, with irregular outlines, were fitted together without

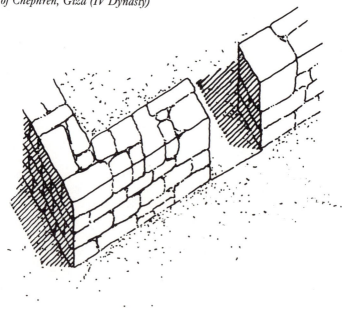

Iron Age wall, Palestine (after Albright)

mortar and the chinks between them were filled out with small stones. The outer face was then roughly hammer-dressed. The Hittites built similar walls for their fortresses (BOGHAZKÖY) and so did the Urartians (KARMIR-BLUR). The Phoenician-type masonry found in citadels and monumental buildings of the 2nd-millennium Levant was very regular ashlar masonry composed of well-hewn rectangular blocks laid alternately in groups of three or four headers and stretchers (RAS SHAMRA, SAMARIA, MEGIDDO, HAZOR). Bossed masonry blocks had slightly bulging outer faces with a regular trim around the edges (eg MEGIDDO, IV).

Lloyd, S., in Singer, C., *et al.*, *A History of Technology* I (Oxford 1954) 456-473

mastaba

The Arabic word denotes a bench on the outside of a peasant's house, but in Egyptian archaeology it is used for a type of tomb with a squat, rectangular superstructure and inclined walls in brick or stone, which somewhat resemble the mudbrick benches.

The mastabas seem to combine two traditional forms of burial, common in prehistoric times: the so-called Abydos tomb and the Nagada-type tomb. The former consisted of sand or stone heaped over the burial pit. Subsequently, these mounds were enforced by enclosure walls and marked by inscribed stelae (eg ABYDOS). The subterranean part was subject to architectural elaboration (by panelling of the lateral walls, internal division etc), considerably earlier than the superstructure. The Nagada-type tomb, on the other hand, is not primarily a pit-tomb, but provides a 'house' for the deceased; it had substantial superstructures with panelled walls and interior chambers. The monumental form of the mastaba was developed during the Early Dynastic period (first third of 3rd millennium BC), when it became a brick or stone structure enclosing a filling of rubble, with either plain (as in GIZA) or elaborately panelled and recessed outer walls. (The ritual requirements for the cult of the dead were first met by providing a simple niche in the facade, which then expanded into a chapel. By the middle of the Old Kingdom (*c.* 24th C BC), the body of the mastaba was utilised to accommodate cult rooms (at first on a cruciform plan) with a

Mastaba of King Aha, Saqqara (after Edwards)

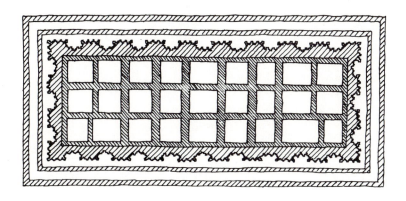

133

*Restored mastaba structure, tomb of Ankh-
  hor, Western Thebes*

stairway blockable by portcullises leading
to the underground burial chambers. The
ritual focus was the FALSE DOOR, often
containing a statue of the deceased.

The idea of providing the dead with a
house, as demonstrated by the Nagada
burials, led to very complex mastabas
imitating the layout of contemporary
houses with a succession of forecourt,
columned halls, living quarters and store
rooms, all decorated with painted reliefs
(ABUSIR, SAQQARA). While ROCK-CUT
TOMBS became popular wherever suitable
cliffs were at hand, mastabas continued to
be built in the flat areas (HAWARA,
ABYDOS, DENDERA). During the Middle
Kingdom they were predominantly made
of brick. The interior arrangements also
included various devices against tomb-
robbery such as false burial chambers,
dead ends, pits and portcullises.

Quibell, J.E., *Archaic Mastabas: Excavations
at Saqqara* VI (Cairo 1923)
Reisner, G.A., *The Development of the
Egyptian Tombs down to the Accession of
Cheops* (London 1936)
Scharff, A., 'Das Grab als Wohnhaus in
der Ägyptischen Frühzeit', *Sitzungsberichte
der Bayrischen Akademie der Wissenschaften,
philosophisch-historische Klasse* 6 1944/46
Simpson, W.K., *The Mastabas of Kawab,
Kafkufu I and II, Giza Mastabas* III
(Boston 1978)

Median architecture

The Medes were a people of Indo-
European stock who settled in the
northern and western parts of the Iranian

plateau around the beginning of the 1st millennium BC (first mentioned in Assyrian documents in 836 BC). The Assyrians had this area under control until their downfall in 612 BC, when the Median empire begun to dominate Northern Mesopotamia, most of Anatolia and Iran. The alliance with the Persians ended in a battle between Cyrus I and his Median father-in-law Astyages (*c.* 550 BC). The victorious Cyrus went on to establish the Achaemenian dynasty.

Comparatively little is known about Median architecture; most of the excavated Median sites are strongly fortified citadels or smaller 'manors', surrounded by thick walls with projecting TOWERS (eg GODIN-TEPE). They comprised several courtyards and oblong magazines. The square or rectangular columned halls may have been inspired by Urartian palace architecture, unless similar structures at the Iranian site of HASANLU, which seem to antedate the Urartian levels, point to a local tradition. The interior amenities included spiral staircases (Baba Jan), painted wall decorations and patterned glazed tiles which were much employed by the Elamites.

The religion of the Medes, at least of the ruling classes, was probably a form of monotheistic system associated with Zoroaster. The only extant sanctuary is a FIRE TEMPLE at NUSH-I-JAN. This was a free-standing tall structure of white plastered mudbrick, with a lozenge-shaped ground plan and a shaft-like room (11m × 7m; 8m high), containing the square fire altar.

Goff, C., 'Excavations at Baba Jan, 1968: Third Preliminary Report', *Iran* 8 (1970)
Stronach, D., 'Tepe Nush-i Jan, a Mound in Media', *The Bulletin of the Metropolitan Museum of Art* 27 (1968)
Cuyler Young Jr., T., and Levine, L.D., *Iran* 12 (1974)

Medinet-Habu: the High Gate (XIX Dynasty)

Medinet-Habu

Egypt (western Thebes), see map p. xvi. Site of the mortuary temple of Ramesses III (*c.* 1298-1167 BC) incorporating the XVIII Dynasty temple of Amun.

The whole complex (2230m × 320m) is surrounded by heavy mudbrick walls which were up to 10.5m thick and 18m high. The inner area was enclosed by another wall and contained the temple, store houses and magazines as well as residential quarters for the visiting king and his entourage. The entrance to the temple was heavily fortified by a massive gate, built in mudbrick with a limestone casing. Two tower-like structures on either side of the central opening were linked by a three-storeyed block containing small apartments, in one of which the king happened to have been assassinated. Another even stronger gate, which is now destroyed, was positioned in the W wall.

The pylon leading into the first court is the largest known pylon in Egypt (68m high). On the S side of this court behind a portico was the entrance to the royal residential quarters and the 'Window of Appearances', where the king could present himself to his subjects. The whole wing was built in mudbrick on a roughly square plan. When the original 'palace', which had barrel-vaulted ceilings, became too small, a second version was built instead. A central six-columned hall is surrounded by smaller rooms on three sides. The actual living quarters were probably located on an upper storey.

A second pylon, decorated with reliefs of the king's battles, leads to the second, larger court surrounded by a colonnade on the S and N and OSIRIDE PILLARS on the E and W side. A central ramp reaches the first hypostyle hall with small storage chambers on either side. The inner sanctuary consists of another, small hypostyle hall, a vestibule and the central shrine of Amun, surrounded by chapels dedicated to various gods and the cult of the dead king.

Between the great gate and the mortuary temple lie the XVIII Dynasty temple of Amun and four Late Period chapels for the funerary cult of princesses. One of them contains the earliest known example of a genuine stone vault (c. 720 BC).

Hoelscher, U., *The Excavation of Medinet-Habu* I-IV (Chicago 1934-54)

megaron

Term taken from classical architecture to describe oblong, narrow structures with extended lateral walls that form an open porch or a portico held up by columns. A pitched roof seems to have been another feature characteristic for timber-rich areas of Anatolia and North Syria where *megara* mainly occurred from the Early Bronze Age (TROY, BEYCESULTAN) to the 1st millennium (GORDIUM).

Hrouda, B., *Anatolia* XIV (1970) 1-4

Megiddo

Palestine, see map p. xix. Large mound with a long history of occupation beginning in the Early Bronze Age (3rd millennium BC) and ending just before the Hellenistic period.

Only a small portion of the TELL was cleared below level IV, revealing parts of the Early Bronze III town, which had an elaborate town plan laid out on several terraces with monumental buildings and private houses. The town wall itself was not recovered.

The best known architectural remains of Megiddo date from the Iron Age, from about the time of Solomo and the beginning of the Divided Monarchy (11th-9th C BC). The town then was surrounded by a circular casemate wall and entered by a fine three-chambered gateway. Two imposing buildings (palaces?) were found that have affinities with contemporary palaces in north Syria (CARCHEMISH, ZINJIRLI). Palace 1728 was set in a wide courtyard and entered by a gate built with bossed ashlar blocks. There was also a covered gallery, but little else of this building remains. The so-called 'Solomo's stables' were four sets of public buildings consisting of several units divided into three by rows of stone piers. The side aisles had cobbled floors, the central one was covered with lime-plaster. Between the piers were stone troughs. The interpretation as stables for the royal horses has not been universally accepted and the building may have had multiple functions.

Kenyon, K.M., *Levant* 1 (1969)
Lamon, R.S., Shipton, G.M., *Season of 1925-34, Strata I-V* (Chicago 1939)
Loud, G., *Seasons of 1935-9* (Chicago 1948)

Mesopotamian architecture

Mesopotamia, 'the land between two rivers', comprises an area defined by the waterways of the Tigris and the Euphrates that flow from the Anatolian mountains into the Persian Gulf. The land is a fairly flat alluvial plain in the south, but much hillier in the north (Assyria). Unlike the regular floods of the Nile, the yearly inundation of the twin rivers was more violent and the rivers were liable to change their courses. The agricultural potential of this fertile land could be exploited successfully only by communal efforts of canalisation, drainage and crop rotation. The reward was an economy able to produce a surplus of food; this could be

*Mesopotamian temple at Tell Harmal,
  beginning of 2nd millennium BC (restored)*

137

exchanged for goods such as timber and metals, that were lacking in this peculiar geological environment. The diversity of local conditions encouraged the rise of relatively small political units (city-states), responsible for the maintenance and administration of their immediate surroundings. Effective centralisation over the whole country, as in Egypt, was only established intermittently.

The architecture of Mesopotamia is essentially an earth architecture. The alluvial clay soil supplied the building material which, when shaped into mud-bricks, was used for all types of monumental architecture. Reeds and rushes were plentiful in the southern marshlands. Lightweight domed and arched shelters fashioned from bundles of reeds and covered with woven mats were most suitable for these particular conditions, a tradition kept up until recently by the modern Ma'dan living in the southern-most parts of Iraq.

The only kind of local timber was the date palm. Its trunk was used for beams, the branches for roof-coverings, screens etc. Other wood for building, as well as stone, had to be imported and was used sparingly.

The concentration on bricks as the main medium of construction distinguishes Mesopotamian architecture. It is also the reason that so few structures have survived above the foundations. The most important architectural element was the wall. Solid, vertical expanses of plastered mudbrick, with few but structurally emphasised openings, characterise the visual impact of Mesopotamian buildings. The walls not only protected the interior from heat, dust and physical attacks, they also had to bear the load of the flat or vaulted roofs. The exterior surfaces of these substantial walls could be articulated by buttresses, niches and recesses, in sometimes very complex and rhythmical patterns. (This exterior panelling was characteristic of public monuments, especially temples, from the prehistoric period (eg TEPE GAWRA VIII).)

The outer walls were conceived like a skin covering and concealed the interior structure. For instance, a round perimeter wall could surround an orthogonal house (eg Tepe Gawra XI A), and the height and panelling of the temple or palace wall obscured the disposition of the rooms behind it. This approach is made even more obvious by the methods of wall decoration. Apart from the predominantly vertical and geometric panelling, walls could be decorated with densely studded mosaics of stone or clay pegs in various colours, which covered the walls like tapestries or woven mats (eg URUK IV). Glazed bricks or tiles could be used in ornamental borders or, again, to cover the whole facade of a building (eg BABYLON: Ishtar Gate; Nebukadrezzar's Palace). The methods of building arches and vaults were known at any early date (at least from the Early Dynastic Period, eg UR: Royal Graves), but an arcuated architecture did not evolve before the Parthian period. Interior spaces therefore remained comparatively narrow, determined by the width of the roofing timbers or the span of the barrel-vaults (up to c. 12.5m). The column as an additional support was used only exceptionally.

The Mesopotamian house was built around a central courtyard, which was protected from the fierce heat by the high surrounding walls and offered shade and light for the daily activities (in the cooler north, the courtyards could be replaced by covered central halls lit from above by clerestories). The flat roofs could be used as terraces or for further storeys. The plans do not show any uniformity of orientation or distribution of space etc, as in Egypt for example. In the densely built-up urban conditions, house plots were constricted and many buildings grew gradually by agglutination not only outwards but upwards.

A disregard for symmetry and axiality is also characteristic of the monumental form of domestic architecture, the palace. The system of distributing architectural units around open spaces applied here too. Palaces had highly ingenious systems of internal circulation and the various functional sectors of the palaces were organised in such a way as to be independent and yet integrated in the overall design (eg MARI; KHORSABAD; BABYLON).

The majority of large temples in Mesopotamia were 'estates of the gods', not unlike the palaces, but with much more emphasis on the actual dwelling of the deity, within a large building suitable for ritual offerings and (at least in some periods) the congregation of worshippers and priests. The site of a temple was rarely changed; if a building fell into disrepair or was destroyed, the new building would still occupy the same place, very often on the same foundations. The accumulated debris elevated the temples high above the street-level, which kept them safe from floods as well. A further development of the temple above ground was the ZIGGURAT, a unique Mesopotamian invention consisting entirely of walls surrounding a dense and solid core of mudbricks. The ceremonial access to the top of these stepped pyramidical

Ishchali: temple of Ishtar-Kititum, reconstruction (early 2nd millennium BC) (after Hill)

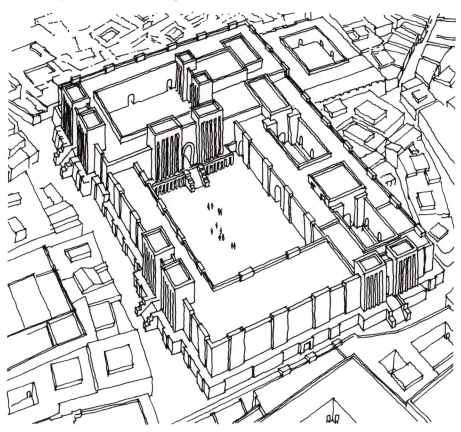

139

structures by various ramps and stairways was probably restricted to certain festivals. The ziggurats were the most conspicuous landmarks of Mesopotamian cities in the flat plains and virtually every town strove to build one.

The various periods of Mesopotamian architecture (see SUMERIAN, KASSITE, BABYLONIAN, ASSYRIAN ARCHITECTURE) have their characteristic style or at least a certain method of approach to a perennial theme, but they are all united in a continuous architectural tradition that was forged by a distinctive environment and a coherent civilisation.

Al-Khalesi, Y.M., *Mesopotamian Monumental Secular Architecture in the Second Millennium BC* (Ann Arbor 1975)
Andrae, W., *Das Gotteshaus und die Urformen des Bauens im Alten Orient* (Berlin 1930)
Badawy, A., *Architecture in Ancient Egypt and the Near East* (Cambridge, Massachusetts, London 1966) 75-120
Frankfort, H., *The Art and Architecture of the Ancient Orient* (4th ed., Harmondsworth 1970)

Margueron, J., 'Remarques sur l'organisation de l'espace architectural en Mésopotamie', *Colloques internationaux du CNRS* No 580 (Paris 1980) 157-169

Meydum

Egypt, see map p. xvi. Pyramid of IV Dynasty probably belonging to Sneferu (26th C BC). It underwent several stages of development, as it was built at a time before the techniques of building such structures were perfected. It might have originally been a MASTABA or a stepped pyramid as at SAQQARA. Eventually, however, the basic structure was extended upwards to form a steep inner core. Several thick shells of masonry enclosed this core, diminishing in height from the centre outwards until a seven-stepped pyramid resulted. This was enlarged further by adding more layers of casings. Finally, the steps were filled in with local stone and the whole building was overlaid with a smooth facing of Tura limestone and looked just like a geometrically true

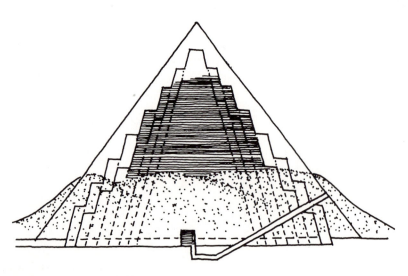

Meydum: section of pyramid (after Edwards)

pyramid. The entrance was at each stage of construction on the N face, where a steep corridor penetrated the core of the rock to reach a corbelled burial-chamber lined with limestone.

There was at least one subsidiary pyramid, and the remains of a mortuary temple with stelae, as well as a sloping open causeway leading to a valley temple, were discovered.

Petrie, W.M.F., Mackay, E., and Wright, G.A., *Meydum and Memphis* III (London 1910)
Rower, A., 'Excavations of the Eckley B. Coxe Jr. Expedition at Meydum, Egypt, 1929-30', *Museum Journal* (Pennsylvania 1931)

migdal/nigdol

A fortified, isolated tower built in stone and mudbrick. They were characteristic of the defences in Palestine during the time of the Divided Monarchy and later (first third of the 1st millennium BC) (BETH-SHAN, TELL EL-FUL). With their crenellated battlements they appear on Egyptian monuments which record campaigns in Palestine.

mortar

Used mainly for walls made of stone blocks or baked bricks. In Egypt, fine mud-mortar, or mortar composed of gypsum and sand, played an important role as a lubricant in the fitting of large masonry blocks. It was applied in a thin and watery consistency and brushed onto the vertical faces. Lime-mortar was used only during the Graeco-Roman period for baked-brick constructions.

In Mesopotamia and Iran, lime-mortar, as well as mud-cement and bitumen or a mixture of lime and ashes, was employed as an adhesive for baked bricks.

Generally, mudbricks were either laid in a sufficiently moist state to make them stick together, or on thin beds of mud-mortar, occasionally tempered with some straw.

mortuary temple

Mortuary temples in Egyptian architecture provided the setting for the rituals and offerings which assured the continuous well-being of the deceased pharaoh. Essentially they were monumental versions of the funerary chapel, focusing on a FALSE DOOR and attached to the pyramid. In the Old Kingdom, from the IV Dynasty onwards (DASHUR: Northern Pyramid), a tripartite arrangement evolved, consisting of a lower valley temple by the river, a causeway, and the funerary cult temple. The design of each of these units was determined by the rituals performed there, and also symbolised the various architectural traditions of Upper or Lower Egypt (GIZA: Chephren, Cheops). Due to the bad condition of most of these monuments, and lacking detailed descriptions, it is difficult to assign any specific function to the various architectural elements. Typical are the symmetrically laid-out pillared halls, a courtyard surrounded by porticoes and the niches for the royal statues with long, narrow chambers behind them (eg ABUSIR).

In the Middle Kingdom, the traditional pattern was still in use (LISHT), with the exception of the mortuary temple of Mentuhotep at DEIR-EL-BAHARI, where the court and the cult temple are superimposed on several terraces, a design which also influenced the adjacent XVIII Dynasty temple of Hatshepsut.

The mortuary temples of the New Kingdom were separate from the actual tombs and were positioned on the flat desert ground in western Thebes. The emphasis of the building's function also

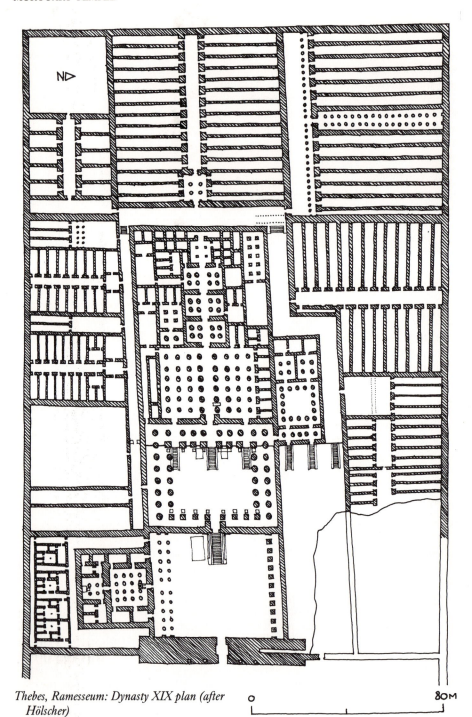

Thebes, Ramesseum: Dynasty XIX plan (after Hölscher)

shifted from a funerary cult to one of worship. The fact that the living king was already identified with Osiris meant that a cult of his image was perpetrated during his life-time, while after his death he merged with Amon and shared in the eternal divine kingship. The complex rituals and processions celebrating these various aspects were carried out in different sections of the mortuary temples, some of which are illustrated in the reliefs covering the walls of the shrines and chapels. The first completely excavated example was built by Ramesses III at MEDINET-HABU which follows closely the plan of the so-called Ramesseum, built by Ramesses II in western Thebes.

Hoelscher, U., *Die Wiederauffindung von Medinet Habu im westlichen Theben* (Tübingen 1958)

Ricke, H., *Bemerkungen zur ägyptischen Baukunst des Alten Reiches* II (Cairo 1950)

Schott, S., *Bemerkungen zum ägyptischen Pyramidenkult* (Cairo 1950)

mudbrick (in Arabic *libn*)

The most universally employed building material in the Ancient Near East. The necessary ingredients, river-mud or alluvial soil rich in clay sediments, plus a temper of sand or vegetal material such as chaff or straw, was readily available in most geographical areas. This material can be shaped or moulded on site, and the assembly into walls etc can be done fairly quickly by experienced workmen. The thermic qualities of thick brick walls make them particularly suited to the predominantly hot climate as they absorb and release heat very gradually. Coated with several layers of plaster they are draught- or wind-proof and not easily damaged by fire. The earliest bricks were shaped by hand into elongated ovals ('cigars') or bun-shaped lumps (eg JERICHO: Pre-Pottery Neolithic A).

Moulded bricks could be obtained either by passing a rectangular open mould or frame over pre-shaped clay

Making mudbricks in a wooden mould, Luxor, Egypt

143

lumps to get straight edges, or by filling the mould up with the unctuous, tempered clay and scraping off the surplus. The first method is quicker but the bricks have rounded, cushion-shaped tops (see PLANO-CONVEX BRICK). The second method was used with larger frames and resulted in flat bricks.

Sizes and formats of bricks vary considerably, but they could not be too large to lift (never more than 50cm long). In Egypt, bricks used for public buildings tended to be larger than those used for private buildings. The size and format of bricks has often been used as a dating device within a given area where no other chronological criteria have been available, but as there is much local variation this method is somewhat unreliable. The rectangular shape, as the most convenient for laying straight walls, was most universally employed but the square format was popular in Mesopotamia.

A special form of moulded bricks was used as architectural decoration by the Kassites and Babylonians to produce reliefs on facades in the shape of gods and goddesses (URUK: Karaindash temple) or mythological beasts (BABYLON: Processional way and Ishtar Gate).

Heinrich, E., *Schilf und Lehm* (Berlin 1934)

Salonen, A., *Die Ziegeleien im Alten Mesopotamien* (Helsinki 1972)

Spencer, A.J., *Brick Architecture in Ancient Egypt* (Warminster 1979)

mulqaf

A shaft with lateral openings protruding from the roof which serves to catch the breeze in order to provide ventilation to the interior of a building. Evidence for the use of this device, which is very common in traditional Islamic architecture, is limited to architectural representations in Egyptian reliefs (house of Neb-amun, papyrus of Nakht) and clay SOUL HOUSES; but one may assume that this useful and simple invention was widely known in the ancient world.

Davies, N. de G., *Metropolitan Museum Studies* I, part 2 (1929)

Fathy, H., *Natural Energies and Vernacular Architecture* (Chicago 1986) 56-61

naos

In the context of Ancient Near Eastern architecture, this Greek term signifies a container for the cult statue in an Egyptian temple. It probably derived from archaic tent or hut shelters. A naos could be made in wood like a box, or in stone, put together from different slabs. In the late Graeco-Roman period the whole naos was cut from a monolith of hard stone (eg EDFU). It had wooden doors which were kept closed, except for certain limited times when the High Priest opened them. The roof was either flat, sloping, domed, or surmounted by a pyramidion.

Nimrud (ancient Kalkhu or Kalakh)

Mesopotamia, see map p. xviii. Assyrian royal residence and administrative centre. It was founded by Shalmaneser I (*c.* 1274-1245 BC) but reached its greatest extension in the reign of Ashurnasirpal II (883-859 BC). When the Neo-Assyrian empire collapsed under the combined onslaught of Babylonians and Medes in 612 BC, Kalakh was destroyed. The town covered an area of some 350ha, but only a small part, the citadel, has been excavated. It was discovered in 1845 by Layard, who shipped quantities of carved slabs and several colossal winged bulls to London where they are still exhibited in the British Museum.

The North-West Palace was originally built by Ashurnasirpal II and extended by

Monolithic naos (Cairo Museum)

his successors. The whole complex measured 200m × 120m. Although the plan has only partially been recovered, it shows the division into various sectors characteristic of Assyrian palaces. The administrative quarter was situated to the north; the royal offices, reception halls and the treasury in the centre. The residential area was accommodated in the south. These units were arranged around two great courts. The throne room was reached directly from the *babanu*, the great

145

courtyard accessible to the public. The longitudinal room (47m × 10m), with the throne placed against the narrow wall on the east, was covered with carved slabs to a height of 3.6m. On the S side, a vestibule-hall led to the interior court (*bitanu*). The suite of oblong rooms to the east was also riveted with relief-slabs and may have been used for official banquets or religious ceremonies.

The Burnt Palace was built by Sargon II (*c.* 721-705 BC), adapting an existing older structure, which may explain certain irregularities in its layout (trapezoid courtyard and a throne room seemingly detached from the residential apartments). Ezida, the temple of Nabu (85m × 80m), commanded an elevated position on the SE end of the citadel. It was organised like a fortress, with a wall up to 8m thick that protected the exposed W side. There was only one entrance, through the heavily buttressed Fish Gate. This led into a transverse vestibule giving onto the great outer courtyard (27m × 21m) which was surrounded by various chambers. The actual temple area covered the southern half of the building and dates from the reign of Adad-nirari III (*c.* 798 BC). It was reached through a transverse vestibule leading into a rectangular courtyard surrounded on two sides by chambers like the first courtyard. In one of them quantities of cuneiform tablets have been found.

The double sanctuary of Nabu and his consort, Tashmetum, consists of two heavily buttressed gates which led to the parallel shrines each with a transverse ante-chamber and longitudinal cella. A southern extension by Sargon II was built behind the first courtyard and contained another double sanctuary believed to have been dedicated to Ea and Damkina. A richly decorated throne room contained various important historical documents, but its exact function in the context of a sanctuary is still doubtful. The Ekal-masharti, or arsenal, was built by Shalmaneser III (*c.* 853-824 BC). It was a vast complex (350m × 250m) surrounded by ramparts and bastions. Internally divided into five sectors, it contained a royal residence, apart from administrative quarters and military store rooms.

Mallowan, M.E.L., *Nimrud and its Remains* I-II (London 1966)

Nineveh (modern Kuyunjik)

Mesopotamia, see map p.xviii. This famous site is one of the oldest Assyrian towns, as its occupation goes back to the Chalcolithic Age (Hassuna period; 5th millennium BC). However, very few architectural remains antedating the Neo-Assyrian period (9th-7th C BC) have been found. The temple of Ishtar probably goes back to the Agade period (mid-3rd millennium BC), but its disposition is unclear.

Sennacherib (*c.* 705-681 BC) made Nineveh his capital city and built an extensive PALACE, which was discovered by Layard and subsequently rather ruthlessly excavated by Rassam. Many richly decorated relief-orthostats have reached the British Museum in London as a result of his efforts. The interior distribution is similar to that in the NW Palace in NIMRUD, with two courtyards, a longitudinal throne room with parallel halls, and various other chambers distributed around the private courtyard.

To the north of the mound, Ashurbanipal (*c.* 668-627 BC) built another larger palace with a seemingly more regular outline. Its interior arrangements, however, are completely obscure. It was here that the famous lion-hunt reliefs, some of the best examples of Assyrian art, were found.

The RAMPARTS of Nineveh with their regularly spaced towers, step-like crenellations and strongly fortified GATEWAYS have recently been reconstructed in parts.

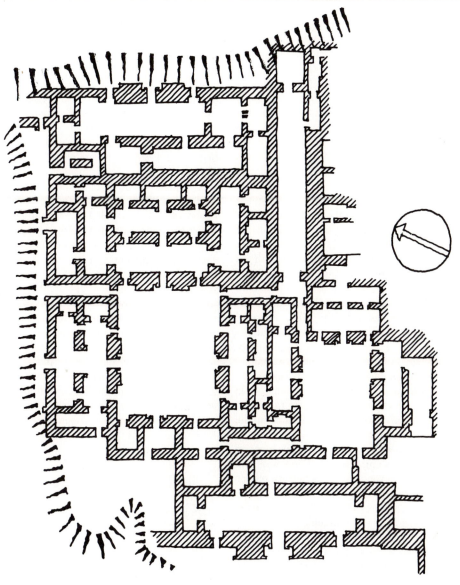

Nineveh: SW palace (after Paterson)

Campbell Thompson, R., and Mallowan, M.E.L., *Annals of Archaeology and Anthropology, University of Liverpool* 18 (1931) 79- 112; 19 (1932) 55-116; 20 (1933) 7ff
Layard, H., *Nineveh and its Remains* (London 1849)

Nippur (modern Niffer or Nuffar)

Mesopotamia, see map p. xviii. Nippur was one of Mesopotamia's most important religious centres, being the seat of Enlil, the supreme god of the Sumerian pantheon. It also had a distinguished scholastic tradition and many cuneiform records have been found in its 'scribal quarter' and the temple schools. The origins of the town go back to the end of the Uruk period (c. 3000 BC) and it was still occupied in the Parthian age (3rd C BC).

The temple of Inanna had at least ten different layers, from the Early Dynastic to the Parthian period (3rd millennium to 3rd C BC). The earliest structure (IX) consisted just of a simple cella with an antechamber. This was followed by a considerably more elaborate complex in the Early Dynastic (or Pre-Sargonic) II period (temples VIII and VII). An axial sequence of courtyards and various buildings was surrounded by walls with irregular outlines. The inner sanctuary consisted of two cellae side by side: one has the standard Sumerian oblong cella with a BENT-AXIS APPROACH, the other has a square cella with a podium in the middle. A central doorway led into an antechamber with two entrances, one on the main axis and one in the long wall next to the other sanctuary. Numerous statues were found in both shrines. Just before this DOUBLE SANCTUARY was a large courtyard with two columns, which probably formed a portico on either end. The rather haphazard layout of the Early Dynastic temple was replaced with a more regular structure by Shulgi, a king of the Third Dynasty of Ur (c. 2095-2048 BC). It was surrounded by a rectangular wall (50m × 100m) and the various buildings were distributed around several courtyards. The cella was not recovered due to the remodelling of the whole complex by the Parthians.

The temple of Enlil, 'Ekur', was built by Urnammu (c. 2113-2096 BC) over earlier but largely unexcavated structures. It remained fundamentally unchanged up to the 1st millennium BC. The large complex incorporated a ziggurat on a rectangular base (53 × 38m), with a T-shaped ramp abutting against the S face and a building resembling the priestesses' house at URUK. Both were set in a rectangular courtyard, enclosed by heavy walls which incorporated various rooms on the N and S side. A gateway led into another large square court to the S of the sanctuaries. Excavations carried out on the so-called Tablet Hill have revealed a great number of house plans from the Early Dynastic period onwards. They were predominantly simple arrangements of a few rooms disposed around a central courtyard. Standards were higher at later levels: brick-paved bathrooms with drains were found, the layout was more regular, and stairways leading to upper storeys were occasionally supported by true arches. Some rooms with bench- or pillar-like structures could have served for religious and/or social functions. The large number of cuneiform tablets recovered in these houses suggest that the scribes of Nippur lived there.

Crawford, V.E., *Archaeology* 12 (1959) 74-83

Hansen, D.P., Dales, G.F., *Archaeology* 15 (1962)

McCown, D.E., *Archaeology* 5 (1952) 70-75

McCown, D.E., Haines, R.C., *Nippur I: Temple of Enlil, Scribal Quarter and Soundings* (Oriental Institute Publications 78, Chicago 1967)

Nush-i-Jan

Iran, see map p. xvii. Median settlement (8th-6th C BC) including a fortress, a large

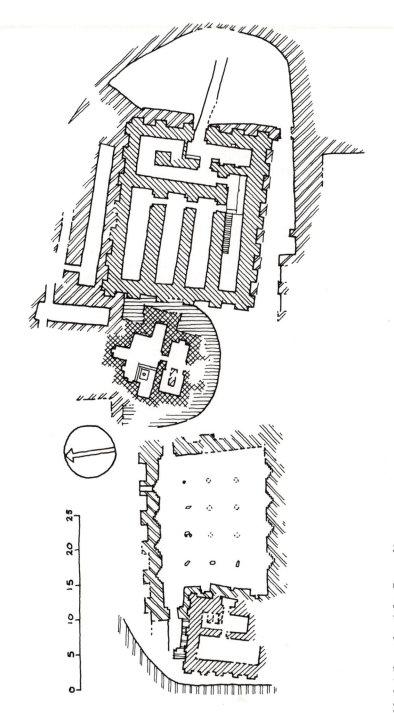

Nush-i-Jan: plan (after Stronach)

fire temple and the so-called 'Western Building' which was perhaps also a sanctuary.

The FIRE TEMPLE (or Central Temple, due to its position in the very centre of the mound) had a stepped, lozenge-shaped ground plan. A porch led to a low barrel-vaulted vestibule with a bench, basin and a deep niche. One door led to the base of a large spiral ramp with an anticlockwise revolution round a central pier which ran up to the roof. Another door of the vestibule with reveals on the inside gave onto the main room of the temple. It was one of triangular shape (11m × 7m and 8m high) and sheltered a large square fire altar behind a low screen wall. It consisted of a plain square shaft with four projecting rows of steps.

The fortress with its buttresses and arrow-slits still preserved, was really a defensible store house with residential quarters situated on the upper storey and four parallel magazines plus guardrooms on the ground floor.

The Western Building originally contained another fire altar but was converted into a columned hall (20m × 16m). The outer walls have an elaborate architectural pattern of stepped recesses and buttresses.

Stronach, D., *Bulletin of the Metropolitan Museum of Art* 27 (New York 1968)
Stronach, D., and Roaf, M., *Iran* 12 (1974); 13 (1975); 16 (1978)

Nuzi (modern Yorgan Tepe)

Mesopotamia, see map p. xviii. This site E of modern Kirkuk had been occupied since the 3rd millennium BC (Early Dynastic period) when it was called Gasur. Around the 18th C BC, the Hurrians, a group of non-Semitic immigrants from the Armenian region that had begun to settle in Northern Mesopotamia at the beginning of the 2nd millennium BC, took over the city and changed its name to Nuzi. Like TELL ATCHANA it became the residence of a provincial governor, probably one of the Indo-European aristocratic Mitanni. The TEMPLE, a double sanctuary, follows the layout of the Early Dynastic sanctuary (long cella with BENT-AXIS APPROACH). Throughout its long history the temple was restored and altered continuously, but kept to this basic ground plan, while the surrounding space, courtyards, subsidiary chambers and chapels, architectural decoration etc were changed several times. Wall paintings in private houses as well as in the palace were a standard form of interior decoration in the Hurrian stratum (II).

Starr, R.F.S., *Nuzi* (Cambridge, Massachusetts 1937, 1939)

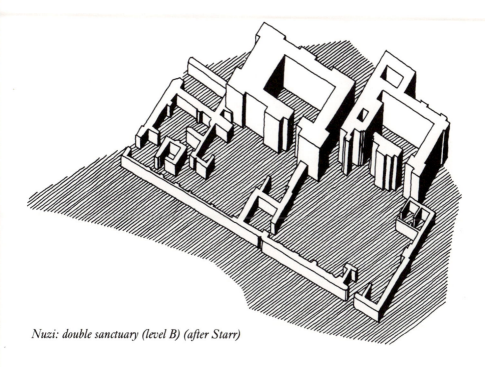

Nuzi: double sanctuary (level B) (after Starr)

O

obelisk

Freestanding monument in Egyptian sanctuaries, which represents a shaft of sunlight. The oldest excavated obelisk at ABU GHUROB (V Dynasty, 25th C BC) was a massive masonry structure with a pyramidical top, set upon a high plinth which was the focal point of the sun temple.

From the Middle Kingdom onwards, pairs of obelisks were erected in front of a temple on the occasion of a Royal Jubilee. These were much slimmer and taller than the Old Kingdom versions and were hewn from a single block of stone (mainly Aswan granite) (see KARNAK, LUXOR). Their sides were often inscribed, and the pyramidical top was cased in gold which dazzlingly reflected the light of the sun.

Engelbach, R., *The Problem of the Obelisks* (London 1923)

Obelisk of Hatshepsut, Karnak

*Orthostat, protecting lower courses of a wall,
  Ankara*

153

orthostat

Rectangular slab of stone, set on edge against the lower parts of a wall. In Anatolian buildings, the stone foundation could be extended upwards to render the lower courses of a mudbrick wall damp-proof and safe from erosion. Large rectangular blocks above ground fulfil the same function. In Anatolia and North Syria (ALAÇA HÜYÜK, Alalakh (TELL ATCHANA), CARCHEMISH), orthostats were decorated with reliefs of predominantly mythological subject matter. While these orthostats were primarily intended to protect and adorn the walls of a building's facade, those found in Assyrian palaces were employed exclusively in the interior courtyards, corridors and important official rooms. Assyrian orthostats had no structural function; they were made of large, thin slabs of gypsum (2-3m high), set on a bed of bitumen, and fastened to each other and probably to the mudbrick walls, by clamps and dowels of lead. The surface of this relatively soft stone was then carved in low relief, with various scenes depicting mainly the ritual and military activities of the Assyrian monarch. While the slabs decorating the courtyards could be inspected easily, it is difficult to imagine that the scenes carved on the grey background were visible in the dim light of corridors and rooms inside the palace, even if made more conspicuous by the application of paint.

Reade, J., *Assyrian Sculpture* (London 1983)

Osiride pillar

In New Kingdom MORTUARY TEMPLES, the PORTICOES of the inner courtyards were sometimes supported by pillars with monumental standing half-figures attached to the face of the pillar. Unlike caryatids or atlantes in a classical temple, they did not fulfil any structural function but represent the dead pharaoh in his 'Osiride' personification, dressed in long shroud, with arms crossed over the chest holding the ensigns of royalty, a reminder of the king's immortal power (eg DEIR-EL-BAHARI, KARNAK, MEDINET-HABU).

Osiride pillars, mortuary temple of Ramesses II, Ramesseum, Western Thebes (XIX Dynasty)

P

palace

Palaces are generally defined as royal residences. Building inscriptions sometimes provide names and chronological data of the kings who built, extended or refurbished them. In prehistoric levels, or in the absence of any written evidence, the designation of a building as a 'palace' is based mainly on architectural features, such as the size and number of rooms, the strength of its walls, the presence of defensive structures, the employment of expensive materials etc. Not every building with these or some of these characteristics need necessarily have been a 'royal residence'. Sanctuaries and palaces are not always easy to distinguish (eg MARI, Early dynastic 'palaces'). Industrial premises, barracks and armouries, or communal stores of goods are alternative purposes for large and well-protected buildings.

In order to analyse the organisation of a palace plan one has to understand the concept of kingship prevalent in the given time and place. At one end of the scale is the petty king who is little more than a chieftain, or a military leader in times of crises. If he is successful in establishing himself in peaceful times and comes to an arrangement with the local priesthood he might build himself a large and well-appointed house, where he would keep any accumulated wealth and his own person safe behind strong walls. His sons and successors would, if all went well, enlarge and strengthen the premises. Small kingdoms and city-states were very common throughout the Ancient Near East, especially in Mesopotamia, Syria and the Levant. Their political and economical prosperity was subject to sudden changes because of the continuous rivalries between them.

The classical example and probably the best preserved archaeological setting for such a 'petty kingdom' was Mari. This is also one of the rare cases where we have a very good idea of the sort of activities that went on in this vast building, due to the extensive cuneiform archives. Mari was a very important trading post and manufacturing centre that maintained a widespread net of diplomatic and economic connections. The plan of this palace reflects the efficient organisation and the strictly hierarchical structure of a successful 2nd-millennium small kingdom. It was planned carefully before construction began. (See also TELL MARDIKH, KISH, RAS SHAMRA, CARCHEMISH, TELL HALAF, ZINJIRLI.)

Then there was the concept of divinely decreed kingship. This could lead either to the deification of the living ruler (as in some Sumerian and Egyptian dynasties), or to his position as the representative of the community, who enjoyed the privilege of close contact with the gods (as in Assyria and Babylon, for instance). The emblematic and symbolic role of such a king transcended his functions as a political and military leader, important and crucial though they were. The palaces were built to meet the demands of royal rituals (almost exclusively so at PERSEPOLIS). There were temples within the palace complex allowing the king to

155

dwell in close proximity to the gods, and the vast dimensions of the official reception quarters and their carefully contrived schemes of decoration provided the appropriate setting for the king (eg NIMRUD, KHORSABAD, ASSUR, BABYLON, PASARGADAE, TELL EL-AMARNA).

The business of state was also conducted and controlled from the royal palaces as the numerous archives testify. Naturally, the royal residence was protected by fortifications which reflect the military standards of the time (see CITADEL). Such palaces are mainly known from MESOPOTAMIAN sites. They were very complex structures, functioning on several levels at the same time: as residence and sanctuary, foreign and home office, garrison and arsenal, treasury and law-court. Characteristic is a division into the public and the private sector with the reception suites between the large square forecourt and the smaller, private, inner courtyard. Archaeological research sometimes manages to identify specific localities by their layout (the throne rooms and temples most notably) or by material evidence (archives or store rooms). But generally, since only the ground plans remain in most cases, any attempt to explain the exact function of all units is highly speculative. It is probable that significant portions of the palace buildings had upper storeys to make best use of the available space, and that the residential quarters as well as most of the offices were situated upstairs. One can also assume that gardens and planted terraces as well as luxurious furnishing, wall paintings and glazed tiles, greatly enhanced the quality of living in the vast and seemingly stark surroundings of the mudbrick palaces.

Mari: palace of the Isin-Larsa period (after Parrot)

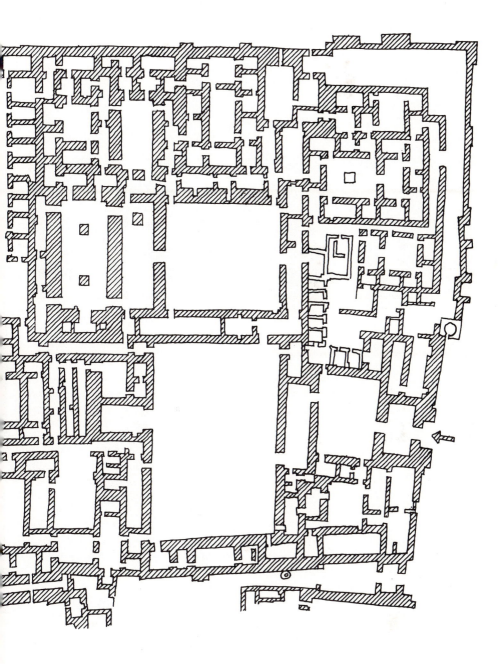

Palace of Nimrud: gate (restored)

Al-Khalesi, Y.M., *Mesopotamian Secular Architecture in the Second Millennium BC* (Ann Arbor 1975)

Loud, G., 'An Architectural Formula for Assyrian planning based on the results of excavations at Khorsabad', *Revue d'Assyriologie* 33 (1936) 153-160

Margueron, J., *Recherches sur les palais Mésopotamiens de l'âge du Bronze* (Paris 1982)

Moortgat, A., *The Art of Ancient Mesopotamia* (London, New York 1969) 20ff

Egyptian palaces are comparatively little known, especially before the New Kingdom. They were always built of bricks, and generally considered to be less important than the royal tomb projects. At MALKATTA in western Thebes, Amenophis III had four palaces built. They feature columned audience halls and an oblong room with two rooms of columns around which separate apartment-suites were arranged symmetrically for the use of the royal ladies. Such a suite comprised a columned vestibule, a central hall with a throne, and private rooms at the rear. The walls, ceilings and floors of this palace were lavishly decorated with paintings. At Tell el-Amarna, several palace complexes were excavated; two of them in the town centre on opposite sides of the Royal Road, connected by a bridge. They were built axially with a succession of vast courtyards lined by monumental statues, and large columned halls (one of them with 540 pillars). Some of the New Kingdom mortuary temples had a small palace suite to accommodate the king on his visits. They were also built in brick around central columned halls and connected with the courtyard of the temple by an ornamental Window of Appearances (eg MEDINET-HABU; also at ABYDOS: Temple of Seti I).

Badawy, A., *Architecture in Ancient Egypt and the Near East* (Cambridge, Massachusetts, London 1966) 28-33

Hittite, Urartian and Achaemenian palaces are characterised by columned halls and loosely grouped independent buildings within a fortified enclosure (see ALAÇA HÜYÜK, BOGHAZKÖY, ALTINTEPE, SUSA, PASARGADAE).

North Syrian palaces were also divided into several blocks (official, residential, private quarters). The rooms were comparatively small and the absence of large courtyards and pillared halls is conspicuous (see TELL MARDIKH, RAS SHAMRA, TELL ATCHANA). A particular structure, popular in the 8th C BC and later, was the BÎT-HILANI with its sculpturally decorated columned porch. The plan shows only accommodation of one transverse hall surrounded by smaller chambers. The thick walls and the staircases found in such buildings suggest elevations consisting of more than one storey. The Bît-Hilani was a free-standing, independent unit within the palace complex (see TELL HALAF, ZINJIRLI).

Naumann, R., *Architektur Kleinasiens* (Tübingen 1955) 364ff

parakku

Akkadian word, denoting the CELLA of a Babylonian temple.

Pasargadae

Iran, see map p. xvii. Achaemenian city founded by Cyrus the Great (559-530 BC). The site had previously been inhabited in prehistoric times (4th millennium BC) and in the 3rd millennium BC. It was destroyed by Seleucos I (3rd C BC).

The Achaemenian palaces (Palace 'S' or Audience Palace, and Palace 'P' or Residential Palace) were built on a rectangular plan and feature central columned halls surrounded by lower columned porticoes (on all four sides in the Audience Palace). They were built in mudbrick and black limestone (around the doors and windows); the columns were made of wood and covered with painted stucco. They have the typical impost-block capitals in the shape of two antithetically grouped crouching animals. Colossal winged bulls as in Assyrian palaces guarded the main doorways of the Gate-House. This was decorated with relief orthostats: the one representing a protective demon is the earliest extant Achaemenian relief.

The tomb of Cyrus is a large gabled structure set upon a stepped plinth (base: 13.5m × 12.2m; tomb: 5.2m × 5.3m; original height: *c.* 11m). It is built of megalithic masonry held together by swallow-tail clamps made of lead and iron. According to Greek writers, the tomb was richly furnished and the body of the king lay in a golden sarcophagus on a golden couch.

The Sacred Precinct was on a terrace surrounded by a dry-stone wall. There were two free-standing stone platforms which probably were surmounted by fire altars. There was also the (almost square) masonry tower (Zendan-i-Suleiman), set on a stepped plinth. A flight of 29 steps led to a chamber at the top of the monument. The purpose of this structure is still disputed.

Herzfeld, E., *Archäologische Mitteilungen aus dem Iran* 1 (1928)

Stronach, D., *Iran* 1 (1963); 2 (1964); 3 (1965)

Pasargadae: palace of Cyrus

Pasargadae: tomb of Cyrus

Persepolis (modern Takhti-i-Shamshid)

Iran, see map p. xvii. While PASARGADAE represents the still experimental phase of Achaemenian architecture, the magnificent palace complex of Persepolis is its ripest and most assured example. It was planned and built by Darius the Great (522-485 BC), extended by Xerxes and Artaxerxes I and finally destroyed by Alexander the Great in 330 BC. It is unique amongst Ancient Near Eastern palaces because it was only during the Persian New Year (*Nevruz*) Festival, that it was apparently ever used. On this occasion, representatives of all the nations united under the Persian rule were present to do homage to the Great King, as the famous reliefs on the Gateway of All Nations testify. The ceremonial function of the whole complex is underlined by the architectural design and decoration (and F. Krefter proposed to identify the various halls and courts according to the sequence of the festival as illustrated by the reliefs on the palace walls).

All buildings were set on a terrace built of well-fitted limestone blocks (450m × 300m and up to 20m high), surrounded by a mudbrick wall. The main entrance was by a monumental ramp-like stairway (suitable for horses), built of huge monoliths (up to 7m long). At the head of the stairway was the Gateway of All Nations, a square hall with four columns and three doors which were guarded by LAMASSU-bulls. Opposite the gate of Xerxes, across an oblong court, was the APADANA or Audience Hall. It was set on its own masonry-built terrace and approached by a double stairway in the N Wall. The central hall (60m × 60m) had 36 tapered and fluted columns with bull-impost capitals (*c.* 20m tall). It was surrounded on

Persepolis: view of the palace

Persepolis: Apadana

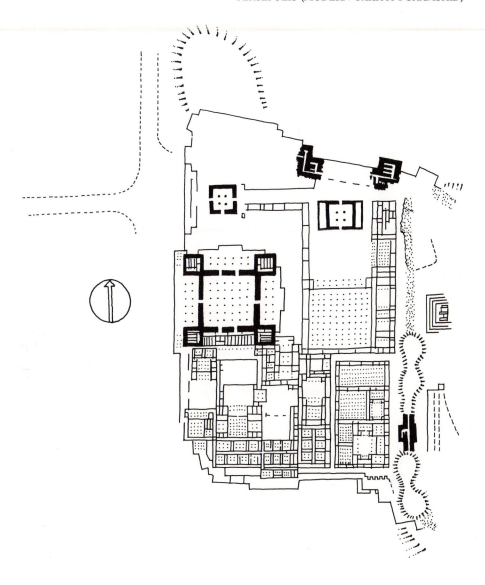

Persepolis: palace (after Hauser)

three sides by porticoes with two rows of columns. The symmetrically placed doors were made of wood covered in gold plate, while curtains of gold lace and glazed tiles adorned the walls. The ceiling was fashioned of cedar beams, ebony and teak, and was also plated with gold and inlaid with precious metals.

The largest building was the Hundred Column Hall (throne hall) (67m × 67m) with one portico and marble columns. Various other square and columned halls (residential palaces, banqueting halls, treasuries, *harem*) were grouped around several courtyards and connected by narrow corridors. The walls were built of mudbrick but the frames of doors and windows were made of stone and are occasionally still preserved (eg palace of Darius) with their Egyptian-inspired CAVETTO cornices.

Barnett, R.D., 'Persepolis', *Iraq* 19 (1957) 55ff

Krefter, F., *Persepolis Rekonstruktionen* (Berlin 1971)

Schmidt, E.F., *Persepolis* I-III (Chicago 1953-69)

Philae

Egypt, see map p. xvi. The temple complex of Isis, dating mainly from the Graeco-Roman period, was moved during the period 1972-80 from its original position on the island of Philae to the neighbouring Agilkia in order to save the monuments from submersion in the high waters of the Aswan dam.

The earliest preserved structure is a screen-walled kiosk or pavilion by Nectanebo I (4th C BC). From there, a processional way flanked by colonnades (only the western one was completed) with delicately carved composite floral capitals, led to the main sanctuary. The first pylon was built by Ptolemy XII (1st C BC). In the

Philae: temple of Isis, colonnade

forecourt of the temple stands the MAMISSI of Ptolemy VI (2nd C BC), with a portico and ambulatory supported by columns. The interior consists of two vestibules and the sanctuary along one axis. The second pylon (Ptolemy VIII), featuring the characteristic screen-walls of the period, opens to the transverse hypostyle hall with finely carved capitals. The inner sanctuary at the end of the three vestibules originally contained two shrines. On the roof were sunken chambers reserved for particular rites, as at DENDERA.

There are several other small temples and gateways built during the Roman imperial period.

Bénédicte, A., 'Le Temple de Philae', *Mémoires publiés par les membres de la mission archéologique française de Caire* 13 (1893)

pisé or tauf

These French and Arabic terms are used either as synonyms for tempered (alluvial) earth, clay or mud, or to describe a method of constructing earth walls. As with form concrete, this is done by ramming the prepared moist clay, mixed with straw or chaff, between two parallel temporary wooden walls (c. 0.5m high). When this has hardened another layer can be placed on top and so on until the required height is reached. The advantages of this technique are the prevention of vertical cracks, and the fact that fairly thick and high walls can be built quickly. It was used in Mesopotamia, Syro-Palestine and the Iranian plateau (JARMO, Mureybet) during the Neolithic period (c. 9th-7th millennium BC) as the predominant method of building with earth before brick-making was invented. In the Middle Bronze Age (2nd millennium BC), great pisé fortification walls of rectangular plan were much in use in Syria and Palestine (eg TEL EL-QADI, HAZOR, SHECHEM, Tell Beit Mirsim).

Aurenche, O., *La maison orientale* I (Paris 1981) 45ff

plano-convex brick

The characteristic building material in Southern Mesopotamia during the Early Dynastic period (c. 2700-2400 BC). Unlike the hand-made, bun or cigar-shaped bricks of the Neolithic period, which the excavators also sometimes describe as plano-convex, these bricks were made in a rectangular frame (at AL-UBAID for instance: 21cm × 16cm). The surplus clay was apparently not skimmed off, as the tops of these bricks are curved. They were either laid in flat courses with plenty of mortar to fill out the gaps or slanting sideways with the long sides outwards.

The latter method resulted in a herring-bone pattern when the direction of the inclination was changed after each course. The deep finger-impressions on the curved top surface were probably the marks of the brick-maker (especially if he was paid per brick). They also provided a better key for the mortar when the bricks were laid in stretchers.

The preference for this seemingly clumsy brick has been explained in various ways. Delougaz assumed that it imitated the techniques of dry-stone walling in a different medium. It has also been pointed out that such bricks could be laid quickly by comparatively unskilled workers. Parts of the wall (especially next to doorways) were built by specialists with straight courses and the spaces between could then be filled out with slanting courses (McGuire Gibson).

The curved outlines of many Early Dynastic structures (eg the Temple Oval at KHAFAJE) may have been the result of using plano-convex bricks. Rounded corners were obviously easier to build with these bricks than right angles.

Delougaz, P., *Planoconvex Bricks and their Methods of Employment* (Chicago 1933)
Gibson, M., Nissen, E., *et al.*, 'L'archéologie de l'Iraq du début de l'époque néolithique à 332 avant notre ère', *Colloques internationaux du Centre national de la recherche scientifique* 580 (Paris 1980)

plaster

Without a protective coat of plaster, mudbrick WALLS exposed to the weathering effects of sun, wind and rain, soon deteriorate. Applied on the inside, it helps to keep dust and insects away. The simplest type of plaster is made of clay (or alluvial mud), mixed with sand or a vegetal temper. It has to be renewed about once a year on the outside.

Plastered wall, Ur, Mesopotamia

Lime-plaster and gypsum (Arabic: *juss*), produced by burning chalky rocks on the fire or in kilns, were used in Palestine and Anatolia as early as the Neolithic period (late 9th-7th millennium BC). Mixed with clay and/or water it was applied to the outside walls, as well as the walls and floors of the interior. The floors could have several applications with a polished and painted top-layer (eg Beidha, JERICHO). Depending on the added quantity of clay, such lime-plastered walls are white or shades of white and grey. After repeated applications a thick skin covers the walls, softening the outlines and hiding the structural elements. Plaster mixed with earth-pigments can be used for murals or colour-washes.

Aurenche, O., *La maison orientale* I (Paris 1981) 23-30, 135-138
Petrie, W.M.F., *Egyptian Architecture* (London 1938) 67f

portico

An open gallery along a facade with columns or pillars supporting its roof. It is a monumental version of a porch which is usually placed just outside a doorway. Both provide shade and allow the air to circulate agreeably, marking a transitory space between the outside and inside of a building. Porticoes were especially popular in Egypt during the Middle Kingdom, as the SOUL HOUSES of that period testify. In monumental architecture, porticoes were found in palaces (KISH, NINEVEH), especially in Persia of the Achaemenians (PASARGADAE, PERSEPOLIS) and Egyptian and Urartian temples.

postern

A secondary gateway or corridor in a fortress which enabled people to emerge unseen to the outlying country. The posterns of RAS SHAMRA and BOGHAZKÖY ran several hundred metres underneath the ramparts and were roofed with corbelled stone vaults of triangular section.

processional street

Served to link a temple with another ritually important site in another part of the town or to provide a suitable access from a landing place to the temple. The cult statues throughout the Ancient Near East were taken on frequent journeys and some of these excursions had special significance when they were performed on high festival days. The divine statues were carried in procession along these routes. The most celebrated Mesopotamian processional street was found at BABYLON. It was used for the annual New Year festival (Akitu). It was raised above the level of the surrounding streets and had screen-walls of brick decorated with reliefs in glazed tiles. In Egypt, a sphinx-lined processional street linked the temple of Amon in KARNAK with that in LUXOR, while the one at PHILAE had a long and graceful colonnade on either side.

Andrae, W., *Alte Feststrassen im Alten Orient* (2nd ed., Berlin 1964)

proportions, harmonic

While it is generally accepted that the architects of classical Greece and Rome made use of an integrated system of proportions, based on modules such as the square and the isosceles triangle, the application of harmonic design in the Ancient Near East has often been questioned. But if one takes into consideration the high standards of Egyptian and Mesopotamian mathematics, as well as their

Postern entrance, Ras Shamra

view of the world as a mirror of celestial harmony, it would be surprising if their monumental architecture disregarded harmonic principles. Modern units of measurement naturally differ from those employed by the ancient builders, which tends to obscure the internal relationships between building units in the modern publications. In some cases, however, we know the dimensions of the old measurement; for instance in Egypt, where a number of cubit rods have been found. The researches by A. Badawy suggest that the Egyptians combined in some buildings (especially at TELL EL-AMARNA) the module of the square and the proportion of 8:5 derived from the isosceles triangle, with the consecutive summation known as the Fibonacci Series. These were also used by Alberti and Palladio during the Renaissance.

Badawy, A., *Ancient Egyptian Architectural Design: A Study of the Harmonic System* (Berkeley 1965)

pylon (Greek: 'portal')

The double-towered monumental entrance of Egyptian temples from the New Kingdom onwards. The walls have a trapezoid section and feature the characteristic cornice at the top and torus along the sides. The facade was flat, except for some small window-slits and the recesses for the FLAGSTAFFS. This flat surface provided the background for large-scale, deeply incised reliefs which covered the whole facade with scenes of enthroned gods and the pharaoh triumphant over his enemies. These reliefs were originally painted in vivid colours on the white plastered facade of the pylon. The central doorway was closed with heavy wooden gates. Colossal statues of the king on either side of the entrance were popular during the Ramesside period.

First pylon, temple of Amun, Karnak (XXII Dynasty)

Pylons were usually built of rubble-filled double masonry walls. The earth ramp which used to bring the building materials to the upper courses is still preserved at the first pylon at KARNAK. The symbolism of the pylon combines the ideas of the 'Sun Rising between the Mountains' and the 'Heavenly Boundary'.

Dombardt, T., 'Der zweitürige Tempel-pylon altägyptischer Baukunst und seine religiöse Symbolik', *Egyptian Religion* I (New York 1933) 87-98

pyramid

The pyramids of Egypt were built to provide suitable tombs for the pharaoh, to secure the undisturbed rest of his mortal body and to assist in the resurrection of his divine soul. The theological concepts

*Lower courses of Chephren's pyramid, Giza
(IV Dynasty)*

of the Old Kingdom, which merged different existing beliefs about the underworld with a cult of the Sun, are still relatively obscure, but their architectural expression was the pyramid complex.

Experiments with the pyramidical form began in the III Dynasty. The pyramid at Zawiyet al-Arian was built in layers of small limestone blocks set at an angle of 68°. The larger Step-pyramid of Djoser at SAQQARA was originally a MASTABA with a subterranean burial chamber. It was extended by adding further superimposed platforms up to a height of 60m, but the rectangular plan was maintained. A similar stepped structure at MEYDUM was filled in with a casing of limestone, resulting in the first 'true' pyramid – with a square base and four inclined faces meeting at an apex.

Builders became more experienced in handling masonry and the IV Dynasty can be regarded as the classic age of the pyramid, beginning with Sneferu's structures at DASHUR and culminating in the Great Pyramids of GIZA. The scale of these monuments (the pyramid of Cheops had a base of 230m × 230m and was originally 46m high) and the precision of workmanship was never surpassed. The funerary cult complexes of the great pyramids, comprising mortuary temples, causeways and valley temples, were built in the same uncompromising monumentality that characterises the pyramids. They catered for the various rituals and devotional services associated with the royal funerary cults of the Old Kingdom (see Giza: Chephren's mortuary temple).

The pyramids of the V and VI Dynasties are markedly smaller and have less-well-built superstructures. The burial apartments on the other hand became more elaborate and were inscribed with the so-called 'pyramid-texts', which have shed much light on the funerary beliefs and practices of the time (see Saqqara, ABUSIR). The pyramids of the Middle Kingdom were built in brick faced with limestone, while the subterranean burial chambers were surrounded with extensive, labyrinthine arrangements designed to confuse the potential tomb-robbers (LISHT, HAWARA). During the New Kingdom, the pyramids were replaced by concealed rock-cut tombs (Valley of the Kings in Thebes) and separate mortuary temples.

The XXV Dynasty Nubian kings built steeply inclined pyramids with a flat top of stone or plaster-faced brick, with an adjoining offering-chapel at Meroë.

The construction of the IV Dynasty pyramids is still a subject of speculation. None of the various attempts to use echo-technology and X-rays has succeeded in gaining definitive information about the internal structure of the great stone pyramids. Were they built round a natural outcrop of rock and if so to what extent? Are there any other yet unknown internal chambers? The problems of how the work was organised and how the upper faces and the monolithic top were put in place, are also still unexplained. The inner blocks of local limestone were dressed *in situ* and fitted together without levelling their height to a uniform measure. The material for the outer casing was transported by ships and the individual blocks were fitted to measure on site. Traces of numerous transport-ramps have been found but exactly how they were utilised is unknown. In any case, the organisation of such an undertaking, which must have needed a considerable workforce, in such a relatively short time (*c.* twenty years for the pyramid of Cheops) was a miracle of effective management. It may have relied on the voluntary cooperation of the people, which weaker or less popular dynasties apparently failed to achieve.

Arnold, A., 'Überlegungen zum Problem des Pyramidenbaues', *Mitteilungen des Deutschen Archäologischen Instituts Abteilung Kairo* 37 (1981) 15-28

Borchardt, L., *Die Pyramiden, ihre Entstehung und Entwicklung* (Berlin 1911)

Borchardt, L., *Die Entstehung der Pyramide an der Baugeschichte von Meydum nachgewiesen* (Berlin 1928)

Brinks, J., *Die Entstehung der königlichen Grabanlagen des Alten Reiches* (Hildesheim 1979)

Edwards, I.E., *The Pyramids of Egypt* (2nd ed., Harmondsworth 1961)

Grinsell, L., *Egyptian Pyramids* (Gloucester 1947)

Mendelsohn, K., *The Riddle of the Pyramids* (London 1974)

Petrie, W.M.F., 'The Building of a Pyramid', *Ancient Egypt* II (London 1930) 33-39

pyramidion

Small pyramidical structure in Egyptian architecture which could either be a decorative element, as on a naos for instance, or the superstructure of certain private New Kingdom tombs (eg DEIR-EL-MEDINEH). The apex of the pyramids of Giza consisted of a monolithic pyramidion which was said to have been gilded.

Rammant-Peeters, A., *Les pyramidions égyptiens du Nouvel-Empire* (Leiden 1983)

Pyramidion superstructure on a tomb at Deir-el-Medineh, Western Thebes (New Kingdom)

Q

Qubbet-el-Hawwa

Egypt (Aswan), see map p. xvi. ROCK-CUT TOMBS of the governors of Aswan, dating from the Old and Middle Kingdom (mainly the VI and XII Dynasties). The tombs were cut into the sheer face of the cliffs, which overlook the western bank of the Nile. Steep causeways, with steps and a central rail for the transport of the sarcophagus, led straight from the river to the entrances of the tombs. The older tombs (eg that of Sebni and Mekhu; Harkuf) had broad, transverse chambers cut out of the rock, with squared pillars and offering tables. The exterior was plain except for stelae at the entrance. The Middle Kingdom tombs (eg Sarenput I and II) were more elaborate on the outside; there was a columned rock-cut forecourt (11m × 15.25m, Sarenput I) with six pillars and a central gate, and the BATTERED facade was decorated with reliefs. The interior was aligned on a straight axis, an oblong 'reception room' with four pillars narrowed to a niched corridor which ended in the pillared cult chamber with the FALSE DOOR. The sarcophagus was placed in a subsidiary pit reached by a low corridor.

Müller, H.W., 'Die Felsgräber der Fürsten von Elephantine aus der Zeit des Mittleren Reiches', *Ägyptologische Forschungen* 9 (1940)

quoin

In masonry, the prominent and sometimes enlarged cornerstones usually laid in alternative headers and stretchers. Quoins were characteristic for Israelite buildings in Palestine (eg MEGIDDO, or the Solomonic wall in JERUSALEM).

Qubbet-el-Hawwa: tombs of Sabni and Mekhu, offering table and false door (VI Dynasty)

R

rampart

Generally, ramparts are fortified walls surrounding a citadel or a settlement. More specifically, the term is used like the German *Wall, Erdwall* for banks of earth, sometimes faced with plaster or stones (eg JERICHO MB II), which could constitute either a primitive defensive wall (as in Neolithic GEZER for instance), or a secondary line of fortification, outside the city walls. Ramparts are sometimes found in connection with dry ditches as the by-product of their excavation (BOGHAZKÖY, TELL HALAF: Iron Age, BUHEN).

Ras Shamra (ancient Ugarit)

Syro-Palestine/Levant, see map p. xix. The site was already inhabited during the Pre-Pottery Neolithic period (7th millennium BC) and from then almost continuously until the 12th C BC. There are some eighteen layers of occupation. Excavations of architectural structures concentrated on those of the Phoenician city (Ugarit) of the Late Bronze period (14th-12th C BC), but only a small part of the city, which covered some 22ha, has been investigated. The palace and other official buildings were situated in the NW of the town. The acropolis in the centre contained two temples and the priests' quarters. The residential area of the upper classes was near the palaces, while the craftsmen and traders occupied the southern part of the city. The palace quarter was crossed by a transverse road.

The fortress on the W flank of the mound had a stone glacis with an inclination of 45°. A corbel-vaulted postern with a right-hand turn led directly to a staircase which gave access to the interior.

The Royal Palace is one of the largest and most luxuriously appointed palaces discovered in the Ancient Near East. It was built in at least four stages from the 18th to the 13th C BC. The area covered was 6500m². There were five large and four smaller courtyards, some seventy rooms and halls, gardens and a tower. The existence of a substantial upper storey is made highly probable by remains of twelve staircases. The palace was built in stone (except for the upper storeys) and the main walls, some of which are preserved up to a height of up to 4m, were made of beautifully dressed ashlar masonry. The N facade, which overlooked the main road, was further distinguished by buttresses and bossed masonry. On the main facade and on the great courtyards, there were porticoes with wooden columns on stone bases. Corbel-vaulted subterranean tombs built of large stone blocks were found under the second court and even larger ones in the so-called Palais Sud. These funerary apartments consisted of three rooms, entered by a double-columned portico. The palace covered an area of 1600m², roughly the same size as the Northern Palace, the construction of which dates back to the 17th C BC. It ceased to be used in the 15th C and served as a quarry for stones. The careful and compact layout of this palace contrasts

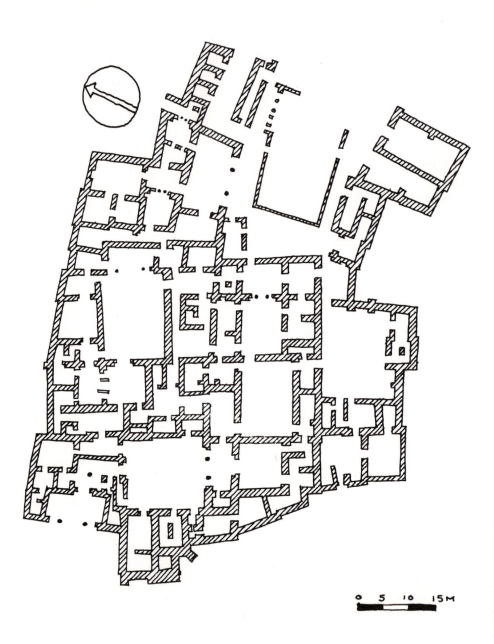

Ras Shamra: Royal Palace (after Hanna)

with the rather haphazard and irregular Royal Palace. The outside walls and those of the courtyards were lined with orthostats in the Hittite manner. The floors were covered with a gravel-mixed lime-plaster which produced a cement-like hard surface.

The largest HOUSE in the upper residential area belonged to a certain Rap'anu and contained thirty-six rooms on the ground floor. It had a curiously uneven plan and irregularly shaped rooms. The sanitary arrangements comprised bath-rooms and latrines, connected with a cesspool. Most houses, including those in the Artisans' Quarter and the Lower Town, were built around an interior courtyard. They seem to have had upper storeys and funerary vaults and were built of local sandstone and cement. Some walls had timber reinforcements as a provision against earthquakes.

The temples of Baal and Dagan(?) (probably built during the Middle Bronze period) were situated on the acropolis and had almost identical dispositions. They were surrounded by thick enclosure walls (up to 4m) and entered through monumental stairways leading to a courtyard with a podium or altar (2m × 2.2m) and special installations for libation offerings. Behind was a vestibule and a broad cella. The continuing excavations at Ras Shamra have also brought to light various other religious installations of more modest architectural pretensions but with adequate cult furniture and objects (eg 'Sanctuaire aux rhytons').

Saadé, G., Ugarit, métropole Canaanéenne (Beirut 1979)
Schaeffer, C.F.A., Ugartica II-VI (Paris 1949, 1952, 1956, 1968, 1969)
Virrolleaud, C., Nougayrol, J., Le Palais Royale d'Ugarit II-VI (Paris 1955, 1956, 1957, 1965, 1970)
Yon, M., 'Sanctuaires d'Ougarit', Temples et Sanctuaires: Séminaire de recherche 1981-1983 (Lyon 1984)

recess

A part of the wall which is set back from the main surface. (A niche is technically speaking a recess.) In the context of Mesopotamian architectural decoration, recesses were vertical grooves with a curved or rectangular profile. They alternated with buttresses (projecting from the wall-surface) to produce the rhythmically articulated panelling characteristic of Mesopotamian monumental architecture from the Protoliterate period. Multiple recesses produced step-like serrated patterns (see URUK IV, TELL AL-RIMAH, TEPE GAWRA VIII). The technique required considerable skills in brick-laying and the model bricks discovered at Tepe Gawra, which comprised various half- and quarter-bricks, may have been used experimentally. (For the use of recesses in Egyptian architecture see SEREKH.)

reed

Reeds were an important building material in Egypt and Mesopotamia, where they grew abundantly in the river marshes. Lightweight vaulted structures were made of long, tightly wrapped bundles of reeds that were bent into arches and covered with woven reed-mats. They were ideally suited to the unstable ground of the marshes. On the dry mainland, reed-huts provided the cheapest if temporary accommodation, and most Egyptian and Southern Mesopotamian cities built along the rivers had 'shanty towns' consisting of such shelters.

In brick-built architecture, especially in massive structures such as town walls or ziggurats, layers of reeds or reed-mats were used between courses to distribute the weight evenly and to prevent vertical cracks from developing.

In Egypt, drawings and models of boats show cabins (either with vaulted roofs or

*Domed reed-structure, Sumerian vase-
fragment*

flat slanting ones) made of papyrus or
other reeds, which probably imitated the
type of shelters built around the banks of
the Nile. Certain decorative elements in
Egyptian monumental buildings derive
from reed structures, such as the DJED-
ORNAMENT, KHEKHER-ORNAMENT, the
TORUS and the CORNICE. In Mesopotamian architecture, the engaged semi-
columns of certain archaic temples
(URUK IV), the practice of covering mudbrick walls with a mosaic of cones that
imitate woven mats, and possibly the
panelling of the facade with vertical
recesses, are reminiscent of reed buildings.

Andrae, W., *Das Gotteshaus und die
Urformen des Bauens im Alten Orient* (Berlin
1930)
Badawy, A., *Le dessin architectural chez les
anciens Egyptiens* (Cairo 1948) 4-8

Heinrich, E., *Schilf und Lehm* (Berlin
1934)
Heinrich, E., *Bauwerke in der altsumerischen
Bildkunst* (Wiesbaden 1957)

Riemchen

Mudbricks of small dimension with a
square section (*c.* 6cm × 6cm × 16cm)
used together with large irregular bricks
(*Patzen*) in URUK IV.

rock-cut tomb

In most parts of Upper and Middle Egypt,
sheer cliff-faces and rocky hills, in parallel
formation to the river, overlook the Nile
valley. The mainly horizontal lime and
sandstone strata were easily quarried with

'Saff' *tombs, Western Thebes, Egypt*

bronze tools and, towards the end of the Old Kingdom, tombs were cut into the rock-faces (GIZA). The custom was established by the nobles and officials during the First Intermediate period (*c.* 2160-2140) who had their tombs carved in the cliffs overlooking their cities (at Asyut, Meir, Bersha, BENI-HASAN). During the XI Dynasty, the first pharaohs of the Middle Kingdom, who refrained from building pyramids, had rock-cut tombs prepared at western Thebes. These were large tombs with wide porticoes in front and deep shafts descending far into the mountain. The courtyards of such tombs were flanked by rows of subsidiary rock-tombs of courtiers, the so-called 'saff' tombs (*saff*: Arabic for 'row'), which also featured pillared or columned porticoes. The pharaohs of the XII Dynasty felt sufficiently established to revert to build-

ing pyramids again (eg LISHT, HAWARA). However, the tradition of the rock-tomb was kept up by the provincial nomarchs for the next millennium, until the kings themselves decided to be buried in secret rock-tombs during the New Kingdom because they considered them to be safer from the ever-active tomb-robbers than mastabas or even pyramids.

The basic layout of a rock-tomb from the Middle Kingdom onwards consisted of four main parts: a forecourt, a portico (or transverse front hall), a long hall oriented towards a niche with a FALSE DOOR (or a shrine), and the burial chamber (sometimes several for the various members of the family). The main rectangular hall was cut deep into the mountain and the whole tomb was laid out symmetrically along a longitudinal axis defined by the entrance and at right angles to the facade. In

177

Rock-cut tomb, Qubbet-el-Hawwa, Egypt (Middle Kingdom, XII Dynasty)

Middle Egypt and Thebes, the architectural emphasis was on the porticoed facade, which could be structured by niches containing statues. The vaulted porticoes at BENI-HASAN were supported by gracefully tapered and fluted polygonal pillars. The tombs were decorated with painted reliefs or wall paintings depicting scenes from the daily life of the tomb owners and the funerary rituals. The terraced tombs at Qaw el-Kebir (Wahka I and II) had a temple-like sequence of buildings leading up to the cliffs, comprising a covered causeway leading to a pylon with a columned court behind. The tomb-chapel was reached through a succession of transverse and oblong 'hypostyle halls' and was cut out of the rock.

The royal rock-cut tombs of the New Kingdom (Valley of the Kings in western Thebes) were excavated and furnished under strict security and the entrances were carefully concealed. The tombs consist of a long corridor, intercepted by various shafts, chambers and staircases, and the sarcophagus chamber. This could be a pillared hall, preceded by an antechamber. In some tombs the whole sequence is along one straight axis (eg Horemheb, Seti I, Merneptah); in others there is an abrupt change of direction (eg Tuthmosis III, Amenhotep II, Tutankhamun) at an angle to the entrance and turning right or left in an attempt to confuse the potential robbers. The mural decoration of the royal tombs consists of brightly painted scenes from the main religious texts concerning the Underworld.

Some of the private rock-tombs at TELL EL-AMARNA have cruciform plans consisting of a long corridor (sometimes penetrated by an almost square hall) ending in a transverse broad room (eg Huya, Ahmose, Merye, Pentu) and a niche for statues cut into the rear wall. The relief decorations of the Amarna tombs are mainly concerned with the person of Akhenaten.

Brunner, H., 'Die Anlagen der ägyptischen Felsgräber', *Ägyptologische Forschungen* 5 (Glückstadt 1937)
Garis Davies, N. de, *The Rock-tombs of Amarna* (London 1905)
Giedion, S., *The Eternal Present: The Beginnings of Architecture* II (London 1963) 403ff
Müller, H.W., *Die Felsgräber der Fürsten von Elephantine aus der Zeit des Mittleren Reiches* (Glückstadt, Hamburg, New York 1940)
Steckeweh, H., *Die Fürstengräber von Qaw* (Leipzig 1936)
Steindorff, G., and Wolf, W., 'Die Thebanische Gräberwelt', *Leipziger Ägyptologische Studien* 4 (1936)

In Palestine, the practice of formal burials

in excavated rock-shafts complete with funerary offerings goes back to the beginning of the 'Proto-Urban Period' (last third of the 4th millennium BC; Kenyon). At JERICHO, for instance, tombs were cut into the limestone hills surrounding the settlement. Only the bases and walls of the large chambers have survived, but in analogy to later tombs, they were probably entered by a circular, vertical entrance shaft which led into the tomb chambers. Large numbers of bones were found in these tombs and they may have been ossuaries or secondary collective burial places.

During the Iron Age, rock-cut underground tombs existed side by side with stone-lined earth graves. They comprised one, and in post-exilic times, several tomb chambers with benches along the walls.

Barrois, A.G., *Manuel d'archéologie biblique* II (Paris 1939) 295ff
Kenyon, K.M., *Archaeology in the Holy Land* (4th ed., London 1985) 67ff

In Iran, the Achaemenian kings from Darius I (521-485 BC) had their tombs cut into the sheer cliffs at Naqsh-i-Rustam and PERSEPOLIS. The overall shape is that of a Greek cross, but they represent the facade of a palace: pairs of semi-engaged columns with bull-protome capitals flanking the entrance. The high-relief carvings above depict the king in the act of worship before a fire altar. The interior of Darius's tomb contains several chambers each with space for three sarcophagi. Many more rock-cut tombs with stepped facades, sometimes representing fire altars, were found in the western Zagros mountains.

Herzfeld, E., *Iranische Felsreliefs* (Berlin 1910)
Matheson, A.S., *Persia: An Archaeological Guide* (London 1972)

For rock-cut tombs in Anatolia see URARTIAN ARCHITECTURE and TOMB.

roof

The flat roof is characteristic for most Ancient Near Eastern architecture. It was the most convenient type of covering for most buildings since it was easily constructed and the flat terraces afforded additional space for open-air quarters or further vertical extensions. As the walls and roofs did not form a structural unit, the timber could be used again for another house (Sumerian contracts specify whether a house was to be sold with or without a roof). The method of construction was to rest parallel beams or simply tree-trunks across the upper ends of the outside walls. Across them were laid thinner planks, branches or saplings and then came a thick layer of mud-plaster. This surface had to be well maintained by rolling it with large cylindrical stone rollers, especially after the rainy season. For a greater span, wooden posts or columns in the middle of the room provided additional support.

In Egyptian stone architecture, the principles of the flat roof were maintained. The beams were replaced by longitudinal slabs of limestone or sandstone (the latter afforded a greater span) which rested on walls and architraves. The protruding ends could be hollowed underneath to form a cornice.

The drainage of rainwater could either be effected by a tilt of the roof surface outwards from the centre, or by semi-circular channels conducting the water to a spout (eg lion-shaped spouts at DENDERA: Temple of Hathor).

Vaulted and domed roofs were probably more common for smaller rural houses, huts, stables and stores. Built primarily of impermanent materials, there is little archaeological evidence for such structures, but architectural representations from Egypt and Mesopotamia occasionally depict cabins, huts and barns with spherical roofs (see REED). Interior vaulted

*Roof drainage by lion-shaped spout,
Dendera, Egypt (Graeco-Roman period)*

Pitched and gabled roofs were reconstructed for the prehistoric houses and *megara* of certain Anatolian sites (Hassuna, BEYCESULTAN, TROY). The mountainous areas, rich in timber, doubtlessly produced their own wood architecture alongside the prevalent mudbrick techniques. Traces of such a tradition can still be found in the Phrygian rock-monuments which seem to imitate wooden houses with gabled roofs (GORDIUM). The Urartian temple of Musasir is depicted in an Assyrian relief as having a pitched roof.

rubble

Rough unhewn stones used either for dry-walling or as an infill between parallel brick walls. Used in Egyptian temple walls and pylons, and in Anatolia for fortifications.

rustication

A type of bossed masonry where the surface of each block projects from the wall level indicated by the joints. It was used mainly in the monumental architecture of Iron Age Palestine, the Levant and in Achaemenian palaces.

ceilings (see VAULT) were flat on the roof-side, particularly when they were built by corbelling, because the vault needed to be weighed down with a covering of flat stones, bricks, or a thick layer of plaster from above.

saff-tomb *see* ROCK-CUT TOMB

Sam'al *see* ZINJIRLI

Samaria

Palestine, see map p. xix. Israelite city founded by Omri (885-874 BC), who had moved the capital of the northern kingdom here from Tirzah Far'ah. It was further enlarged by the dynasty of Jehu and destroyed by the Assyrians in 705 BC. The town continued to be inhabited until the Byzantine era, but the royal quarters on the summit of the mound were left in ruins, and their stones re-used for other buildings to such an extent as to make an exact reconstruction of the ground plan impossible. The layout of the royal quarter was regular, and the buildings were aligned with the rectangular enclosure wall. There was a large courtyard, plastered with hard lime-mortar. Some pilaster capitals of the Proto-Aeolian type, which may have been part of a doorway originally, have been found re-used in later structures. Numerous fragments of ivory inlays among the débris of mud-

Proto-Aeolian capitals from Samaria (restored) (after Albright)

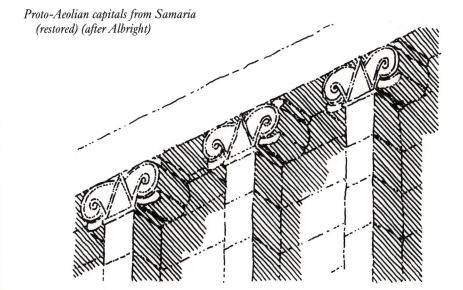

bricks fallen from the superstructure give some indication of the luxurious furnishings of this palace. The quality of the masonry is excellent throughout; flat-dressed ashlar blocks were fitted with great exactitude. The fortifications could be traded all round the summit plateau. Well-built casemate walls (up to 10m thick) have survived in parts. On the N side, the casemates had their axes perpendicular to the wall; on the S and W the compartments were smaller and in line with the wall. The flat-dressed blocks and the irregularly bossed foundation courses testify to the skill of the (Phoenician?) masons.

Crawfoot, J.W., Kenyon, K.M., Sukenik, E.L., *Samaria-Sebaste I: The Buildings* (London 1942)

Saqqara

Egypt, see map p. xvi. Extensive necropolis outside Memphis, in use throughout the pharaonic period from the I Dynasty until the Roman era. The tombs of Saqqara therefore reflect almost all the major developments of Egyptian funerary architecture.

The I Dynasty royal mastabas (around 3000 BC) were built in mudbrick and with elaborate panelling. The substructure was originally a simple pit subdivided by walls. Further magazines were accommodated in the superstructure and were raised by fillings of sand and rubble. Gradually, the burial pits were sunk deeper and contained the burial chamber, store rooms etc, until they imitated the houses of the period, while the superstructure became solid. The excavators Lauer and Emery support the theory that these mastabas were the real tombs of the I Dynasty kings and that those at ABYDOS were cenotaphs (against that, Reisner, *Tomb Development*; see TOMB).

The underground arrangements and the subsidiary structures surrounding the mastabas became increasingly elaborate and advanced towards the general concept of the later pyramid complexes (eg tombs 3505, 3504 with painted stucco decorations, a low bench with bulls' heads surrounding the outer walls, magazines and a funerary chapel, all enclosed by a plain wall). Twin mastabas were common during the II and III Dynasties (first half of 3rd millennium BC), when larger structures combined model or dummy buildings to serve as 'eternal estates' for the deceased. The most extensive and best preserved structure of this kind is the funerary complex of Djoser (*c.* 2667-2648 BC). It is also the first Egyptian architectural monument to be built entirely in stone (the experimental handling of this material is made obvious by the small size of the individual building blocks or the tongue walls between columns of the entrance hall). The architect credited with the design was IMHOTEP. He also transformed the conventional mastaba into a six-stepped pyramid above a substructure (7m square, 28m deep) which contained the burial chambers. They were lined with blue faience tiles imitating woven mats.

A rectangular enclosure wall (544m long, 277m wide, 10m high) surrounded the complex. It has recesses and niches like those of the brick walls of ABYDOS or Nagada and several dummy gates, irregularly spaced, which seem to imitate the famous 'White Walls of Memphis'. The single entrance flanked by buttresses led to a narrow passage with forty fluted columns engaged to low tongue-walls forming niches, which probably contained statues of the king. The passage was roofed with stone slabs carved on the underside to resemble logs. At the end of the passage was a rectangular hall with eight columns that led to the large courtyard S of the pyramid. It was surrounded by panelled walls on three

*Step-pyramid and Jubilee Court in Djoser's
funerary complex, Saqqara (III Dynasty)*

sides and the 'Southern Tomb' took up one side. To the E of this large court lay the so-called 'Heb-sed' Court with its 'chapels'. These consisted of carefully dressed facades and rubble-filled interiors. The chapels on the E have narrow elevations and curved roofs typical of the shrines of Lower Egypt, while those on the W side, with their simulated doorways and model fences, recall Upper Egyptian shrines. Some of these also had stairways leading to a statue-niche.

North of this court, next to the pyramid, were two structures set in separate courtyards distinguished by their columns. The 'southern' facade had fluted columns with 'lily' capitals, the 'northern' had open-papyrus ones. Inside these buildings were cruciform cult rooms with niches. The mortuary temple of the king was on the N side of the pyramid, next to the SERDAB, which contained the seated statue of Djoser. The temple comprised two interior courts, and the entrance to the pyramid.

The complex of Djoser is remarkable for recording in stone, architectural structures normally executed in more ephemeral materials, such as wood and reed. It is also unique in providing for a variety of cults (associated with kingship and the afterlife) in one single complex by arranging symbolic and 'real' buildings in a monumental and legible manner.

The royal pyramids of the V and VI Dynasty are smaller and less well built than those of GIZA. The pyramid of Unas is known best. Here, the causeway was decorated with finely carved reliefs on the inner corridors while the mortuary temple resembled Sahura's at ABUSIR. The internal passages and chambers of the pyramid were inscribed with magic spells, the so-called Pyramid texts. The extensive cemetery contains a large number of private tombs. Some of the best preserved

Saqqara: engaged columns in Djoser's complex (III Dynasty)

date from the V and VI Dynasties. Their ground plans vary considerably, some containing columned halls, courts and a great many chambers as in the houses of that period. These tombs are beautifully decorated with painted reliefs. The actual burial chambers behind the FALSE DOORS were frequently lined with limestone and roofed with stone slabs over relieving vaults in mudbrick.

The XVIII Dynasty Serapeum is a series of subterranean corridors with large chambers on either side which contained the huge granite or limestone sarcophagi of the sacred bulls.

Drioton, E., Lauer, J.P., *Sakkarah: The Monuments of Zoser* (Cairo 1939)
Emergy, W.B., *Great Tombs of the First Dynasty* I-III (Cairo 1949, 1954, 1958)
Lauer, J.P., *Saqqara, the Royal Cemetery of Memphis* (London 1976)

school-room

When A. Parrot discovered a bench-lined room in the palace of MARI, where so many written documents had been found, he provisionally assigned to it the function of a school-room, which has since been quoted in most popular textbooks. Parrot's erstwhile collaborator J. Margueron has criticised this identification as a case for 'cultural projection' in archaeology. He pointed out that most of the tablets in Mari seem to have fallen from above and that it was reasonable to assume that the archives and offices were accommodated on the upper storeys, where the lighting conditions must have been much better than on the heavily built-up ground floor. There is certainly no specific room in the whole of the Near East which could be described as a 'school-room', although we know of the existence of schools at certain periods. Benches are hardly characteristic, but the presence of 'school texts' (bilingual lists, exercises etc), vessels containing clay for the tablets, and kilns for their baking, are obvious clues for scribal activities which might have entailed some training. A good example for the Old Babylonian period (2nd millennium BC) comes from Isin. (See also RAS SHAMRA, TELL MARDIKH, NIPPUR.)

Ayoub, S., et al., 'Isin-Ishan Bahriyat I (Die Ergebnisse der Ausgrabungen 1973-1974)', *Abhandlungen der Bayrischen Akademie der Wissenschaften, philosophisch-historische Klasse, Neue Folge* 79 (Munich 1977) 22f
Margueron, J., *Recherches sur les palais Mésopotamiens de l'âge du Bronze* (Paris 1982) 345f

Senmut

Egyptian ARCHITECT of the XVIII Dynasty; 'Overseer of the Works' and close adviser of Queen Hatshepsut (c. 1503-1482 BC). He is credited with the planning and supervision of the queen's mortuary temple at DEIR-EL-BAHARI, and the transport and erection of her obelisks at KARNAK.

Meyer, C., 'Senmut, eine prosographische Untersuchung', *Hamburger Ägypto-logische Studien* 2 (1982)

serdab

Arabic word for subterranean chamber or corridor which can be used as living room in the heat of the hot summer. In Egyptian archaeology a *serdab* is a closed room in a tomb where the statues of the deceased were kept. It had no openings except for a small slit at eye-level of the statue (eg at Djoser's step-pyramid in SAQQARA, or the pyramid of Unas, also in Saqqara).

serekh or palace-facade ornament

The Egyptian hieroglyphic sign seems to represent the ceremonial double gateway of a palace, flanked by lateral buttresses and surmounted either by a cornice or a frieze, with diamond-shaped ornaments. Later versions are often quite elaborate and even imitate the weaving pattern of textile wall-hangings. As an architectural ornament it is often found on sarcophagi, on the exterior walls of funerary structures or inside a tomb (see also FALSE DOOR). The question as to what kind of building provided the prototype for the sign is not conclusively settled. Vertical panelling is not necessarily a sign for a brick building. Timber or reed structures, or those built in mixed techniques (brick and wood for instance), can also show such articulation.

Shechem (modern Balata)

Palestine, see map p. xix. A site with a long history of occupation, from the Pre-Pottery Neolithic to the 1st century BC. The excavated architectural remains date from the Middle Bronze Period (2nd millennium BC). The battered walls of the fortifications are partly preserved to a height of 10m. They were built in cyclopean masonry and the inside face of the wall is straight, while the outer one has a pronounced slope and bulges slightly. A mudbrick superstructure was erected on top. A triple-buttressed gateway belonged to these walls. Near this gate was a large building, probably a temple, as similar structures are known from RAS SHAMRA or MEGIDDO. It measured some 25m × 21m; its entrance was flanked by towers and there were two rows of three columns in the interior. The very thick exterior walls (5m) probably supported one or several upper storeys, similar to the model-shrines found at BETH-SHAN. During the Iron Age, Israelite Shechem was surrounded by casemate walls (11th C BC) of a type similar to the one at TELL EL-FUL.

Wright, G.E., *Shechem: The Biography of a Biblical City* (New York 1964)

soul house

Between the VI and XI Dynasties in Egypt, little terracotta or clay models of houses were deposited in tombs of poorer people in order to provide the soul of the owner with a suitable home. The models represent simple peasant dwellings, from one-room houses within rectangular enclosures to more elaborate types with porticoes and upper storeys.

Badawy, A., *A History of Egyptian Architecture* I (Giza 1954) 55ff
Petrie, W.M.F., *Gizeh and Rifeh* (London 1907) 14-20

speos

A building entirely cut out of a rock-face. In Egypt mainly tombs, but also some temples (ABU SIMBEL). The mason began by cutting the upper part of the projected rooms first and then working downwards on either side of the access.

sphinx

The best-known example of this creature, with a recumbent lion's body and the head of a human being, belongs to Chephren's mortuary temple at GIZA. The monumental version with the facial characteristics of his king was shaped from a rocky outcrop and guards the royal necropolis. Sphinxes were very popular during the Middle Kingdom and many beautifully sculpted examples are known, though none of them in their original architectural context. During the New Kingdom, the crio-sphinx (with a ram's head) became associated with the god Amon. At KARNAK there were long avenues lined with such sphinxes, which are partly preserved. The sphinx was also a popular image outside Egypt, even reaching Anatolia via Syria-Palestine, and the frontal part of a sphinx with shoulder-length 'Hathor-locks' appears on Hittite sculpted gate-jambs (eg ALAÇA HÜYÜK).

stairs and stairway

Wooden ladders were the simplest and most common type of access to the flat roof or upper storeys. The ladders were leant against the outside wall of the house and people could move them or pull them up at will. At ÇATAL HÜYÜK, they were the only means of entering the houses in the absence of doorways. In larger private houses (eg the TELL EL-AMARNA villas, the houses at RAS SHAMRA, UR, ASSUR etc), internal stair-wells could be fitted with wooden or brick stairs. Stairways in Egyptian monumental architecture were not a prominent feature (an exception is the large, ramped stairway at DEIR-EL-BAHARI: Hatshepsut's mortuary temple). The stone steps were usually cut to the block or consisted of single separate blocks, resting on solid masonry or a system of brick vaults. Sloping treads were very common. The stairways in temples and tombs had flat plain borders to facilitate the transport of ritual equipment. The short flight of steps leading to the Jubilee pavilions had straight low parapets.

In Anatolia and North Syria, monumental stairways were an important element in temples or palaces. They were very wide (in ZINJIRLI 20m, YAZILIKAYA 12m) and could be flanked by high parapets lined with orthostats (eg TELL ATCHANA, BOGHAZKÖY: temple V). The oldest stone staircase was found inside the tower of Pre-Pottery Neolithic A JERICHO

(8th millennium BC); it was a steep flight of twenty-two steps reaching the top of the tower.

In Mesopotamia, stairways made of bricks led to the temples on their high platforms, ending in a monumental gateway, flanked by towers or buttresses. The ziggurats had great ramps and stairs leading to the various stages, but none has survived. The ritual processions moving along these ramps and steps must have presented an astonishing spectacle.

In Persia, the great stairway of PERSEPOLIS is one of the most impressive remains of Achaemenian architecture. Several steps were cut out of colossal monoliths, and the carved reliefs on the walls behind have immortalised the emissaries and kings of the many nations who came to pay tribute to the Persian king in the very act of mounting these stairs.

Stairway in the temple of Seti I, Abydos, Egypt (XIX Dynasty)

Monumental stairway, Persepolis

'Clay cone temple', Uruk (Uruk IV)

Stiftmosaik

German expression sometimes used to describe a type of wall decoration used in some Mesopotamian temples of the Uruk period (last quarter of the 4th millennium BC). Cones made of clay or stone were either laid in courses between layers of gypsum mortar, or pressed into the still-soft brick walls. As the rounded heads of the cones were dipped in different colours (red, white or black) before laying, various geometrical patterns (zigzag bands, triangles etc) were produced, which probably imitated woven reed or textile hangings. This technique, though very laborious, also provided a weather-proof skin for the mudbrick walls which made them almost indestructible.

stone

Although the use of stone in Ancient Near Eastern architecture was of secondary importance compared to mudbrick, it was already utilised in the earliest permanent settlements. It was used for walls (particularly of fortifications in Syro-Palestine), foundations (also in the relatively stoneless regions of Mesopotamia; see URUK: Limestone temple; TELL CHUERA; TEPE GAWRA), and most commonly, for doorsockets, sills and column-bases. Stones could be used in their natural state as boulders, blocks and pebbles or dressed (see MASONRY). An architecture of stone was only developed in Egypt where it was an exclusive royal privilege to build 'eternal' structures for the gods and the dead. The original architecture of the Ancient Near East was based on the use of earth and clay.

Sumerian architecture

The southern regions of Mesopotamia were called Shumer (Sumer) after an

Stone orthostats, palace of Nimrud, Mesopotamia

important group of its inhabitants who emerged as the first historical people at the beginning of the 3rd millennium BC. The earliest intelligible cuneiform documents were written in their language and although the country was also inhabited by several other ethnic communities, especially Semites, the Sumerians seem to have been culturally dominant.

The first stage of Sumerian civilisation is associated with the URUK IV period, before writing was commonly used (last third of the 4th millennium BC). It was a time of great artistic activity when some of the best works of Mesopotamian art and architecture were produced. The great temples of Uruk (Eanna) were like cathedrals, with huge and spacious halls and often cruciform plans. The temples were freely accessible through multiple door-

ways on their elevated brick terraces and the design is clear, harmonious and symmetrical. It was still an age of structural experiments and a variety of building materials were used simultaneously: limestone (Kalksteintempel), stone cones imbedded in gypsum-concrete (Steinstift-tempel) and mudbrick covered with a 'skin' of multi-coloured clay pegs inserted into the walls (see STIFTMOSAIK). Semi-engaged large cylindrical pillars, as well as vertical recesses and buttresses, could articulate the walls in an effort to develop an aesthetic suitable to the medium of mudbrick. The individual bricks employed were mainly long and narrow. Despite this diversity, the standard of workmanship was excellent and the boldness of design was unrivalled by later developments.

There was a marked stylistic break at the end of Uruk IV. The sanctuary of Anu comprised a vast artificial 'mountain' or ZIGGURAT with a small sanctuary on top. In *Eanna*, the buildings of the preceding period were levelled and the new structures, built predominantly with 'Patzen-bricks' (see RIEMCHEN), had thick walls and dark interiors, as openings were kept to a minimum. The reasons for these changes are unknown; they might have had something to do with an upheaval of religious beliefs and practices.

In the ensuing Early Dynastic period (*c.* 2700-2400 BC), the population was concentrated mainly in numerous city-states, engaged in cultivating the irrigated land around the cities and in profitable trade with far-flung regions. The economy of these communities was regulated by the temples, with the city gods officially owning the means of production. The Sumerian temple buildings became large precincts, complete with magazines and workshops, offices and archives. The actual sanctuaries were situated far from the commercial quarters and relatively remote from public access which was probably restricted to the large temple

189

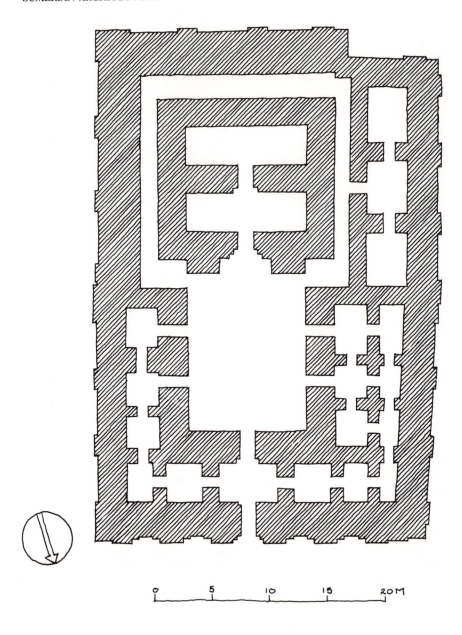

Ur: Enki temple (Ur III period) (after Woolley)

courtyards. PLANO-CONVEX bricks were used for most buildings, which often had curved rather than orthogonal outlines (see KHAFAJE).

The gradual emergence of a secular leadership, especially in the more northern parts of Sumer, led to a new type of building, the palace. It was defensible by high and strong walls, with fortified entrances, and the interior rooms and halls were distributed around several courtyards (see KISH, TELL ASMAR, MARI).

The country was united for the first time by Sargon (c. 2334-2279 BC), who established himself in the still unlocated city of Agade. The architecture of this era does not show any marked differences from the traditions of the preceding periods. The reign of the Akkadian dynasty ended in confusion and an invasion from the East. Eventually, the kings of the third dynasty of UR presided over the so-called 'Sumerian revival' (c. 2113-2004 BC), the final phase of Sumerian culture. Intensive building programmes went on in all major Sumerian cities and two types of buildings evolved which were to become typical of the Mesopotamian architectural repertoire. One was the ZIGGURAT, the other the broad-cella temple (see BREITRAUM). Ziggurats were not invented in the Neo-Sumerian period, but the methods of construction and the overall design were perfected and formalised. The best-known example comes from Ur and was built by Urnammu. It had a rectangular plan, battered facades of baked bricks surrounding a mudbrick core, and a treble ramp which led to the first stage. The ziggurats stood in their own precincts and like the archaic ziggurat at Uruk they probably had a sanctuary on the platform on top, although no such structure from the 2nd millennium BC has yet been found. The temples of this period have a strictly axial layout: entrance, courtyard

and cella were aligned in succession so that there was direct access from the outside to the inner sanctum. The facades of these temples were dominated by monumental gate-towers and elaborate vertical panelling (see UR: Enki-temple; TELL ASMAR: Shu-Sin temple).

Standards of domestic architecture were high; the houses in Ur had well-built rooms surrounding a central courtyard, often upper storeys, chapels, and bathrooms with drains.

The technical expertise of the Sumerian builders can be seen in the subterranean tombs of the Early Dynastic and Neo-Sumerian period. True and corbelled vaults, arches and domes were found in the royal cemeteries of Ur.

Crawford, H.E.W., *The Architecture of Iraq in the Third Millennium BC* (London 1977)
Frankfort, H., *The Art and Architecture of the Ancient Orient* (4th ed., Harmondsworth 1970)
Moortgat, A., *The Art of Ancient Mesopotamia* (London 1969)

sun temple

Intended for the worship of the solar deities in Egypt (Re-harakhte and Aten). As there was no cult statue to be accommodated, all the rituals and sacrifices were performed in the open air. The oldest sun temple was at Heliopolis, but little is known of this structure except that it contained the famous *benben* stone. The sanctuary at ABU GHUROB, built by the V-Dynasty pharaoh Niuserre (c. 2456-2425 BC), comprised a valley portal at the canal-side, a causeway, the temple proper and a brick sun boat. Within the enclosure wall of the temple was a large courtyard with an alabaster altar oriented to the points of the compass, and store rooms and slaughter houses along the walls. The whole complex was dominated by a massive squat obelisk set on a platform.

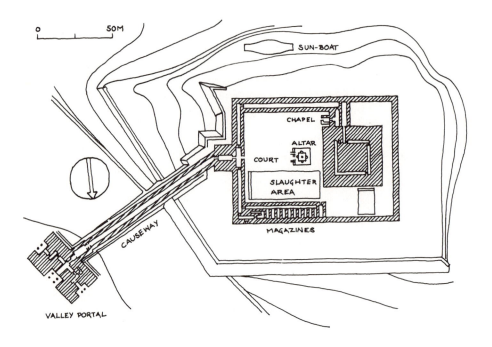

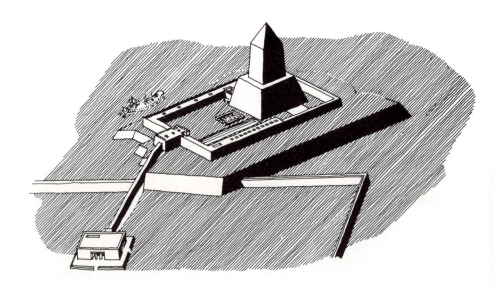

Abu Ghurob: sun temple (V Dynasty) (after Badawy)

192

When Amenophis IV (*c.* 1379-1362 BC) changed his name to Akhenaten and instigated a religious reform centred around the *Aten*, the creative principle revealed in the Sun, he had several new temples built at his new capital TELL EL-AMARNA, at KARNAK, and elsewhere. These temples are oriented towards the setting sun and consist of vast courtyards separated by screen walls pierced by gate-pylons. There were small cell-like rooms along the enclosure walls, but the courts were filled with rows of small offering tables of brick. The largest temple, *Gem-Aten*, was preceded by three courts with a total number of 365 altars. It was entered by a columned pavilion with an open central passage.

Barguet, P., 'Note sur le grand temple d'Aton à el-Amarna', *Revue d'Egyptologie* 28 (1976) 148-151

Pendlebury, J.D.S., *The City of Akhenaten* III (1951)

Uphill, E.P., 'The Per-Aten at Amarna', *Journal of Near Eastern Studies* 29 (1970) 151-166

Winter, E., 'Zur Deutung der Sonnen-heiligtümer der 5 Dynastie', *Wiener Zeitschrift für die Kunde des Morgenlandes* 54 (1957) 222-233

Susa (modern Shush)

Iran, see map p. xvii. Susa was almost continuously occupied from the 5th millennium BC to the 15th C AD, and traces of the many levels have been found on the so-called Acropolis.

One of the oldest architectural structures from the first period of occupation (Susa I, 5th millennium BC) is a large platform (80m × 80m × 10?m) which seems to have been associated with the so-called '*massif funéraire*' in which over 2,000 bodies were interred.

Susa: Elamite town

The town grew in the Elamite period (2nd millennium BC). Large, well-built private houses within rectangular enclosures were arranged in an ordered urban pattern dominated by two main streets intersecting at right angles. While the general layout of the mudbrick houses resembles those of Mesopotamia, there was one feature that was different. This was a large rectangular and probably vaulted reception room with four pilasters on the short wall, which was entered from the courtyard. Little monumental architecture of that period is known, due to the later encroachments, but part of a temple facade has been reconstructed which featured moulded bricks similar to those of the Kassite temple at URUK.

The 1st-millennium Neo-Elamite town was destroyed by Ashurbanipal in the

193

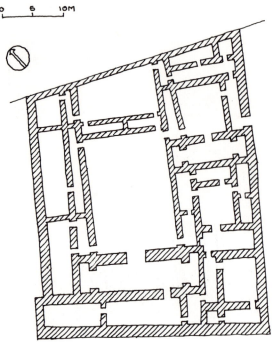

0   5   10M

Susa: house of Attura-Uktuh (Elamite period)
(after Gascha)

7th C, and little is known of its architectural wealth except a small one-room shrine which was decorated with glazed bricks and probably guarded by large pottery lions. The Achaemenians built a citadel and large palace at Susa (from the time of Darius I, 6th C BC, to Artaxerxes II, 5th C BC). It was built shortly before the great palace of PERSEPOLIS but there are significant differences, except for the APADANA which was even larger than at Persepolis and had seventy-two fluted columns with bull protome capitals. The general layout, however, resembles the great palaces of BABYLON. There was the same axially arranged series of courtyards giving access to main halls, rather than the loosely grouped blocks linked by corridors, as in Persepolis or PASARGADAE. The decoration consists predominantly of coloured glazed-brick reliefs as in Babylonian palaces, although with a different iconography.

Ghirshman, R., *Arts Asiatiques* 11 (1965) 3-21; 13 (1966) 3-22; 15 (1967) 3-27; 17 (1968) 3-44
Le Brun, R., *Cahiers de le Délégation archéologique française en Iran* 1 (1971) 163-216; 9 (1978) 57-154
Mecquenem, R. de, *Mémoires de la Délégation en Perse* 25 (1934)

Susi temple

Urartian sanctuary built around a square, tower-like structure, accommodating a single cella. The thick mudbrick walls (4.35m at ALTINTEPE) could be enforced with corner towers and probably termin-

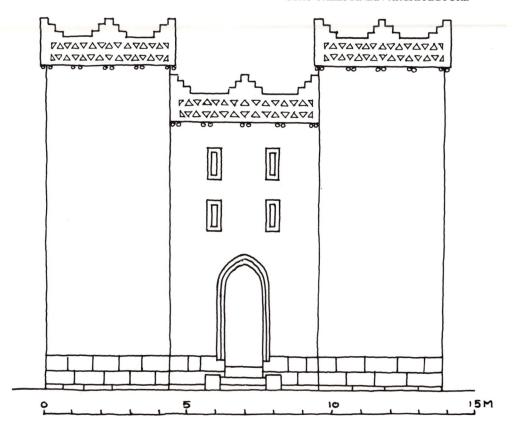

Urartian 'Susi' temple (reconstruction after Naumann)

ated in crenellations. These free-standing tall buildings were surrounded partially or on all sides by porticoes with wooden columns (see Altintepe, KARMIR-BLUR).

Naumann, R., 'Bemerkungen zu Urartäischen Tempeln', *Istanbuler Mitteilungen* 18 (1968) 45-57
Salvini, R., 'Das Susi-Heiligtum von Karmir-Blur und der Urartäische Turmtempel', *Archäologische Mitteilungen aus dem Iran* 12 (1979) 249ff

Syro-Palestinian architecture

The area along and beyond the eastern coast of the Mediterranean lies in the middle of the Fertile Crescent, bordered by Egypt in the S, Mesopotamia in the E, and Anatolia in the N. The cultural and political influence of these civilisations has always been very strong. The geographical conditions are extremely diverse: deeply eroded mountain ranges and arid valleys contrast with fertile lowlands and wooded hill-sides, deserts with pastures and olive groves. The coast is long and has numerous good harbours. It was not a land that was easily united and for most of its long and varied history it was inhabited by nomadic groups, some of which eventually settled in small city-states that were almost continually at risk from rapacious tribes or

195

the interventions of the great political powers of Egypt, Mesopotamia and Asia Minor.

However, trade between Egypt and Anatolia, as well as Mesopotamia, flourished. The densely wooded mountains of the Lebanon and Anti-Lebanon provided timber, probably the most coveted export article of the area. The Phoenicians built various large cities close to the sea and established an extensive network of trading posts throughout the Mediterranean.

There is no Syro-Palestinian monumental 'style' of architecture. The extensive palaces typical of the Syro-Hittite period (beginning of the 1st millennium BC; see TELL HALAF, ZINJIRLI, CARCHEMISH) were strongly influenced by Anatolian methods of construction (eg the extensive use of timber within the brick walls; sculpted orthostats) and Mesopotamian architectural traditions (ground plans). The elaborate architectural treatment of the palace facades, with their pillared porches or porticoes ornamented with sculpted reliefs, is one of the few constant features of Syrian architecture (see TELL MARDIKH, TELL ATCHANA, TELL HALAF, CARCHEMISH, ZINJIRLI, RAS SHAMRA). The wealthy Phoenician towns (eg Ras Shamra, BYBLOS) combine stylistic elements borrowed from Egypt, Greece and Asia Minor in a tastefully eclectic manner, admirably executed in finely dressed stone. The cities of Palestine which prospered briefly during the United Monarchy employed craftsmen and builders from Phoenicia to build monumental defences and spacious palaces. But the lack of political stability prevented any stylistic continuity. The violent destructions suffered by this area during the 2nd and 1st millennia BC severely disrupted or annihilated local traditions.

Phoenician masonry, Ras Shamra

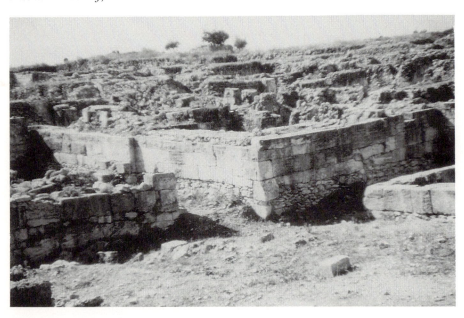

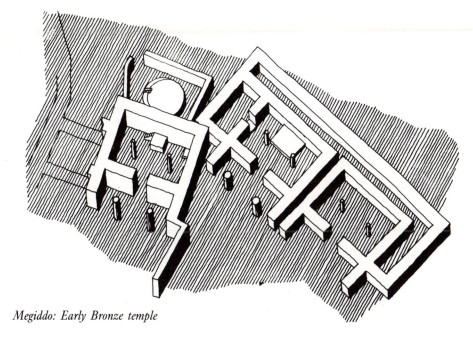

Megiddo: Early Bronze temple

Syro-Palestine is nevertheless of great interest to architectural historians, for it was here that architecture began. The Neolithic agricultural communities began to build permanent settlements sometime in the 9th millennium BC. All available building materials were utilised in an experimental way and there was a great diversity of techniques (stone walls using mortar at Abu Salem; PISÉ on a sub-structure of stones at Mureybet, etc). Pre-shaped elements, such as cut limestone, hand-shaped mudbricks, and timber fashioned into planks, began to be used in the 8th millennium BC, when rectilinear ground plans replaced the predominantly round or oval plans of the first phase. More people lived together in larger communities and engaged in collective building activities such as constructing fortifications (see JERICHO pre-Pottery Neolithic A). By the 7th millennium BC, more complex architectural structures were built in mudbrick. Moulded bricks were introduced during the second half of the millennium (eg Beidha).

During the Bronze Age, the architectural development of Syro-Palestine fell behind those of the great Near Eastern civilisations. But relatively small and prosperous manufacturing and trading communities such as Tell Mardikh, level IIB (middle of 3rd millennium BC), show surprisingly high standards of civic architecture including large palaces with pillared porticoes and effective fortifications.

The art of MASONRY was highly developed in the Syro-Palestinian area from the 3rd millennium BC. Very large smoothed blocks were used in the Middle Euphrates region (eg Mumbaqat; 3rd millennium BC). The Phoenician masonry was composed of smaller, more regular and well-dressed blocks of limestone (see Ras Shamra, Byblos). During the time of the United Monarchy in Palestine, ashlar walls in the Phoenician style were common for civic monuments (see MEGIDDO, HAZOR).

Little is known about Syrian and Canaanite religion. Open-air cults of fertility- and weather-gods have left few archaeological traces. The temples of the 3rd and 2nd millennia BC are mainly of a bipartite plan, comprising a vestibule and cella (or tripartite if one counts the niche at the end of the cella as an independent unit with its own ritual significance). The cult room was either oblong or a BREITRAUM (eg: Tell Mardikh levels B, C, N; Megiddo Early Bronze III; Hazor Middle Bronze-Late Bronze; Tell Atchana MB II, etc). Some temples with oblong cellae had projecting walls, forming a porch *in antis*, reminiscent of the *megaron*-type plan of western Anatolia (eg TELL CHUERA, and Tell Meskene-Emar, a 14th C town: see Margueron, J., 'Quatre Campagnes de Fouilles à Emar (1972-74). Un Bilan Provisoire', *Syria* 52 (1975) 53-85).

Another type of temple appeared during the Middle Bronze period often in connection with the impressive fortifications of this time. It had an oblong cella, preceded by a vestibule and the entrance was apparently flanked by gate-towers on either side (eg SHECHEM).

The palaces of the 2nd millennium seem to have more affinity with Aegean architecture than Mesopotamian (eg Tell Atchana, Tell Tayanat).

Avi-Yonah, M. (ed.), *Encyclopedia of Archaeological Excavations in the Holy Land*, English edition I-III (London, Jerusalem 1975, 1976, 1977)

Cauvin, J., *Les premiers villages de Syrie-Palestine du IXième au VIIième millénaire avant JC* (Lyon 1978)

Kenyon, K.M., *Archaeology in the Holy Land* (4th ed., London 1985)

Margueron, J.C. (ed.), 'Le Moyen Euphrate', *Actes du Colloque de Strasbourg* 5 (Strasbourg 1977)

Moorey, R., and Parr, P. (eds), *Archaeology in the Levant: Essays for Kathleen Kenyon* (Warminster 1978)

Paul, S.M., Dever, W.G. (eds), *Biblical Archaeology* (Jerusalem 1973)

T

tell

Arabic word describing the mound formed by accumulated débris of successive mud-brick settlements. When a mudbrick structure falls into disrepair, the fabric of the walls soon disintegrates and the bricks are not worth salvaging. Instead, the walls are levelled and a new building erected on top. This slow process of decay and reconstruction builds up multiple layers of habitation which are detectable by arch-aeological soundings. Wholesale destruction in raids or wars afflicts large sectors of a settlement and thereby gives the excavators a change to investigate buildings that are contemporary. A mature *tell* is composed of many occupational layers of various thicknesses and the lowest is usually the earliest stratum. But when the surface of a mound's summit became too small, the foot of the mound might have been inhabited as well, perhaps building up a new *tell* alongside the older one. At any rate, evidence of pottery and written texts, if available, is needed to establish a valid stratigraphic sequence of habitation.

Tell Abada

Mesopotamia, see map xviii. Chalco-lithic settlement of the Ubaid period (5th millennium BC). The houses of the earlier level III had several rooms surrounding rectangular courtyards. At level II, T-shaped (cruciform) courtyards (or halls) became characteristic, and there is evidence for industrial installations (domed kilns for firing pottery). One large building (temple?) had three T-shaped courts/halls and buttresses on the outside, another with a similar internal organisation – entrance to a small square room leading to courtyard/hall and other rooms – lacked buttresses. These buildings remained fundamentally unchanged to level I. The tripartite plan and the T-shaped spaces are the earliest examples of an architectural tradition which culminated in buildings of the *Eanna* precinct at URUK.

Jasim, S.A., *Iraq* 45 II (1983) 165-186

Tell Agrab

Mesopotamia, see map p. xviii. The best-known building on this site is a large sanctuary, the Shara temple, dating from the Early Dynastic (or Pre-Sargonic) period (*c.* 2700-2400 BC). It was surrounded by an almost square, several-metre-thick enclosure wall with external buttresses. The entrance was a monumental gateway flanked by projecting towers. The interior space was divided into a number of clearly defined units grouped around a courtyard, comprising two major and some minor shrines, residences for the priesthood, store rooms and magazines etc. The central shrine (19m × 5.5m) was on a BENT-AXIS between an ante-chamber and a side room, with two doorways at the far end of the long walls, on opposite sides. A double row of altars(?) was set across the centre of the room, with a screen wall behind. The

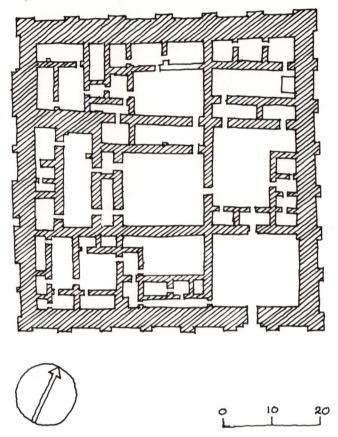

Tell Agrab: Shara temple (after Delougaz, Lloyd)

other shrine had two cellae, also with a bent-axis approach from the inner court-yard.

Delougaz, P., Lloyd, S., 'Presargonic Temples in the Diyala Region', *Oriental Institute Publications* 58 (Chicago 1942) 218-288

Tell al-Rimah (ancient Karuna)

Mesopotamia, see map p. xviii. The most extensive and interesting architectural

remains date from the 19th C BC. The Temple of Ishtar is better preserved than any other early 2nd-millennium sanctuary. Though within the Mesopotamian tradition, it has individual characteristics. The temple has a square ground plan (46m × 46m), a central courtyard and a symmetrically disposed double range of rooms. The ante-cella and the smaller BREITRAUM-CELLA behind it, abutted against the ziggurat set against the W side of the temple. The exterior walls and those of the courtyard were articulated with an intricate system of slender half-columns, reveals and pilasters, which were

200

*Tell al-Rimah: temple and ziggurat (after
  Oates)*

201

carefully adjusted to the viewpoint of the observer. They also reflect the disposition of rooms in the interior. The main entrance was emphasised by projecting towers. A staircase next to the entrance led *via* a right turning to the roof terrace. It was supported by a series of brick vaults constructed with great ingenuity. When the temple was restored during the 15th C BC its main dispositions remained unchanged.

The Palace is contemporary with Yasmah-Adad's of MARI, although much smaller. It is divided into two rectangular blocks with an inner courtyard each and surrounded by a massive (2.5m thick) wall. The western block was for representative functions and had higher walls, whereas the eastern unit was the residential area. Noteworthy is the extensive use of vaulting. The Late Assyrian temple (9th C BC) conformed to the standard type of the Assyrian long-room sanctuary, with a small cella partitioned off from the single shrine-room by tongue walls. The walls were faced with orthostats representing lions.

Oates, D., *Iraq* 27 (1965) 62-80; 28 (1966) 122-139; 29 (1967) 70-96; 30 (1968) 115-138; 34 (1972) 77-86

Tell Arpachiya

Mesopotamia, see map p. xviii. Chalcolithic settlement (Halaf period: late 6th, early 5th millennium BC) of peasants and potters, who lived in large houses with long rectangular rooms without interior courtyards. The walls and floors were made of PISÉ. Of special interest are the sixteen *tholoi*. They were circular buildings built of pisé, on stone foundations with a low dome (not higher than 1.5m). These domes seem to have been 'real' domes, constructed with radiating courses.

Some had a rectangular ante-chamber with a gabled roof. It is not clear whether these buildings had any specific ritual function.

Mallowan, M.E.L., Cruikshank, Rose J., 'Excavations at Tall Arpachiya, 1933', *Iraq* 2 (1934) 1-78

Tell Asmar (ancient Eshnunna)

Mesopotamia, see map p. xviii. Important site with a wealth of architectural remains dating from the beginning of the 3rd millennium to the 18th C BC.

The earliest excavated buildings were found in the N of the mound. Most notable is the Abu temple, which was begun at the end of the Djemdet-Nasr period (beginning of the 3rd millennium BC) as a very irregularly shaped cluster of rooms built of hand-shaped mudbricks. This was transformed in the Early Dynastic I (or Pre-Sargonic I) period into a more formal arrangement consisting of a vestibule, courtyards and an oblong cella (9m × 3.5m), which contained an altar/podium set against the short side, a circular hearth, and a lateral doorway at the far end. The temple was again completely rebuilt in level II (Pre-Sargonic/Early Dynastic II; *c.* 2700-2400 BC). It was even oriented towards N rather than W, like the previous archaic sanctuary. The ground plan is almost square and three oblong cellae were grouped around a central square space, which may or may not have been open to the sky. The building material was PLANO-CONVEX BRICKS. When this temple fell into disrepair it was levelled and the new building, the so-called 'Single shrine temple' (Early Dynastic III), was erected in its place. It was essentially just one large oblong with an annex to the northern side, entered through a gateway with triple-stepped

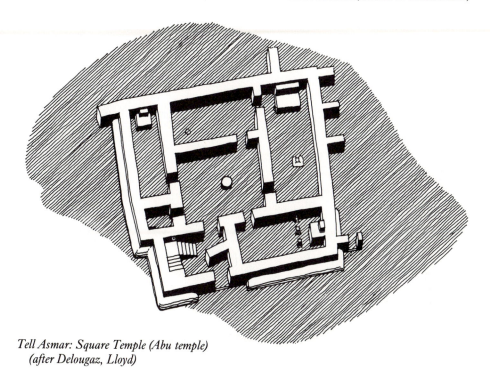

Tell Asmar: Square Temple (Abu temple)
(after Delougaz, Lloyd)

flanking buttresses. The walls were twice as thick as in the preceding structures and have simple flat buttresses on all four exterior sides. The excavators assumed that the temple was roofed with a huge barrel vault and lit by small windows high up in the walls.

The Northern Palace, previously called 'Akkadian Palace', is now thought to date from the late Early Dynastic period (*c.* 2700-2400 BC). The exact purpose of this vast and only partially excavated complex is still disputed. The large court-yard and its adjoining long-room seem to have remained a constant feature through-out the successive stages of adaptation, which might point to a representative function, probably combined with extensive storage facilities and possibly workshops in other parts of the building.

The central area of the site is occupied by the buildings dating from the III Dynasty of Ur (2113-2004 BC). The Palace of Shu-Sin contained a square sanctuary dedicated to the worship of the deified king. Its walls are much thicker than those of the adjoining palace build-ing. The plan conforms to the standard Mesopotamian pattern of the period, with a central courtyard, a BREITRAUM-cella and ante-cella, and various subsidiary rooms. An almost identically laid-out if smaller version, constitutes the palace chapel. The palace itself, which abuts against the E temple with an acute angle, seems to have been accessible through a single gate at the SW. A succession of narrow corridors led to a vestibule, which gave access to the central square court-yard. A path paved with baked bricks led

203

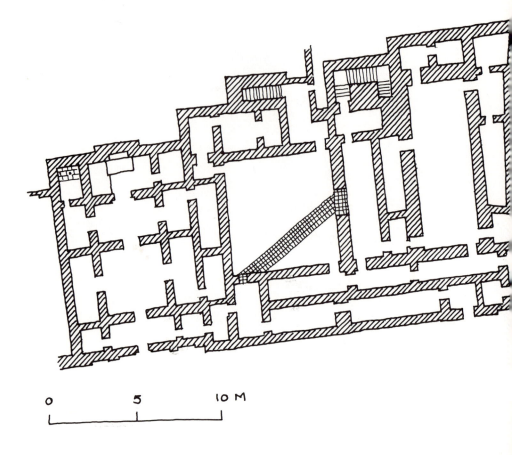

Tell Asmar: temple and palace (Ur III period)
(after Frankfort, Lloyd, Jacobsen)

to an oblong room with a central doorway (the throne room?). Behind it lay a rectangular hall flanked by corridors (administrative quarters?). The varying thickness of the walls and the many narrow corridors suggest an upper storey over at least some parts of the palace.

Delougaz, P., Lloyd, S., 'Presargonic Temples in the Diyala Region', *Oriental Institute Publications* 58 (Chicago 1942)
Frankfort, H., Jacobsen, Th., Preusser, C., 'Tell Asmar and Khafaje: The First Seasons at work in Eshnunna 1930/31', *Oriental Institute Communications* 13 (Chicago 1932)
Frankfort, H., 'Tell Asmar, Khafaje and Khorsabad: Second preliminary report of the Irak Expedition', *Oriental Institute Communications* 16 (Chicago 1933)
Frankfort, H., Jacobsen, Th., 'The Gimilsin Temple and the Palace of the Rulers of Tell Asmar', *Oriental Institute Publications* 43 (Chicago 1940)

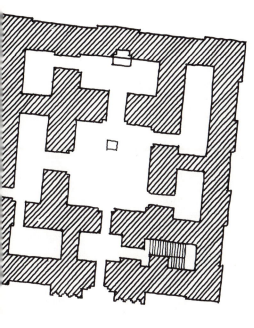

S was the temple or chapel. The official apartments had orthostats of basalt lining the lower parts of the walls. Wood was used extensively, incorporated in the mud-brick walls, as well as for columns ('Audience hall'). Staircases and substantial amounts of painted plaster, column-bases and furniture inlays, obviously fallen from above, point to the existence of upper storeys. Purely utilitarian rooms were added onto the southern residential area accommodating a mason's workshop and a pottery. The temple (16m × 13m) consisted of a long and narrow vestibule and a rectangular cella both with central doorways. It is thought that there was at least one upper storey, since a well, designed to catch libations poured from above, was found behind the altar wall.

The Palace of Niqmepa (level IV, 15th C BC) has a much more compact layout than the older structure of Yarimlim. The ground plan is rectangular (33m × 30m) and the various sectors were distributed around a series of inner court-yards, retaining the functional division. An irregular forecourt was reached by stairs and a columned portico. As in the earlier palace, quantities of luxurious furnishings in an Egyptian style had fallen from the private apartments on the upper storey.

The building techniques at Tell Atchana reflect a local tradition and easy access to timber. The foundations were of stone and the walls consisted of a timber grid filled out with mudbrick, lined with basalt orthostats inside and coursed rubble outside. All was covered with plaster.

The architecture was influenced by western traditions rather than Meso-potamian ones: the temples resemble those at MEGIDDO and the palace of Niqmepa follows the design of the ones at RAS SHAMRA rather than at MARI.

Tell Atchana (ancient Alalakh)

Syria, see map p. xix. The site was occupied from the end of the 3rd millen-nium BC until the 12th C BC. The best-documented architectural remains belong to level VII (18th C BC) and level IV (15th C BC).

The Palace of Yarimlim (18th C BC; destroyed by the Hittites c. 1595 BC) was built against the fortified walls on three successively raised platforms. To the N were the official state apartments, with a large courtyard between the representative quarters and the domestic and private sector. Abutting against the palace to the

Woolley, L., *Alalakh: An Account of the Excavations at Tell Atchana in the Hatay, 1937-49* (Oxford 1955)

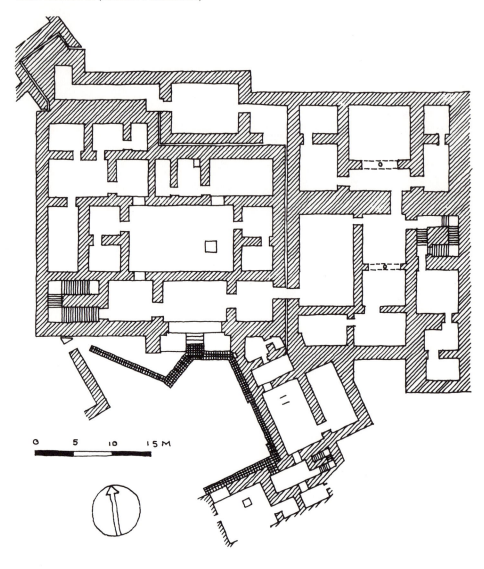

Tell Atchana: palace of Niqmepa (after Woolley)

Tell Brak

Mesopotamia, see map p. xviii. A large mound with occupational levels from the Chalcolithic to the 14th C BC.

The most prominent early building (Uruk period, last third of the 4th millennium BC) is the 'Eye temple' named after the numerous eye-shaped objects found there. The largest and most interesting temple dates from the Djemdet-Nasr period (beginning of 3rd millennium BC). It was built directly on a platform, covering 6m of rubble from previous temples (Red Eye temple: Uruk period; Grey temple; White temple). Their sequence bears considerable similarity to contemporary structures at KHAFAJE (Sin temple) and URUK. The brickwork of superior quality consists of rectangular bricks laid in alternate courses of headers and stretchers. The exterior walls were built on slightly projecting stone plinths (80cm high) and had simple, evenly spaced flat buttresses. The walls were plastered and whitewashed and decorated with strips of 'pencil cones' on the outside niches. The cruciform oblong cella was lavishly decorated with stone rosettes, coloured limestone inlays and copper panelling impressed with the eye motif. The podium set against the short end of the room was also adorned with a panelled frieze. The dimensions (18m × 6m) of the cella are identical with those of the White Temple at Uruk and the proportion of the room's length to its width is 3:1. The considerable thickness of the walls between the cella and the subsidiary rooms might indicate that the walls were carried up to a greater height in the centre, possibly providing clerestory lighting.

Another large building, its southern facade decorated with deep niches, as well as the so-called Palace of Naramsin, both date from the Agade period (c. 23rd C BC). The latter is an almost square complex (111m × 93m), with 10m-thick exterior walls. One large and three successive smaller spaces, each surrounded by double rows of narrow corridors, might have served as light-wells if one assumes that the very thick walls supported more than one floor. The building was destroyed at the end of the Agade period and seems to have been rebuilt on the identical ground plan by the Urnammu of the III Dynasty of Ur (22nd C BC).

Mallowan, M.E.L., 'Excavations at Brak and Chagar Bazar', *Iraq* 9 (1947) 48ff

Tell Chuera

North Syria, see map p. xix. Early Dynastic (2nd millennium) site with several *megaron*-type buildings (two in stone and one in mudbrick); simple rectangular rooms with projecting lateral walls formed a kind of porch. Statues of 'worshippers' found in one building suggest that they might have been sanctuaries.

Mallowan, M.E.L., 'Tell Chuera in Nordostsyrien', *Iraq* 28 (1966) 89ff
Moortgat, A., *Tell Chuera in Nordostsyrien* (Cologne, Opladen 1960, 1963, 1967)

Tell Duweir *see* LACHISH

Tell el-Amarna (ancient Akhetaten)

Egypt, see map p. xvi. Site of the new capital of the XVIII Dynasty during the reign of Amenophis IV/Akhenaten (c. 1379-1362 BC). Previously uninhabited, it was only occupied for a few years before it was destroyed and abandoned for good.

The various parts of the town, which extended about twenty miles, were linked by a main road running parallel to the

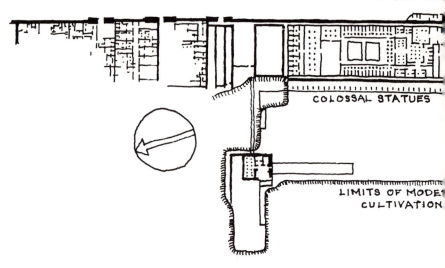

ROYAL ROA

COLOSSAL STATUES

LIMITS OF MODE
CULTIVATION

*Tell el-Amarna: palace in the central quarter
(XVIII Dynasty) (after Pendlebury)*

river. Transverse natural ravines divided the built-up areas into several zones, with the royal palaces, temples and official buildings occupying the central quarter. There was a palace and a stable(?) enclosure at the N end of the town and a religious complex or royal domain at the S end. The residential areas were in between and an enclosed workmen's village was situated out of town, near the cliff-side where the tombs were prepared.

A great variety of HOUSES have been excavated. The private villas of the nobles were set like country estates in comparatively spacious grounds with gardens and various outbuildings. The plan of the main house conformed to the usual tripartite arrangement (vestibules, reception halls, private quarters). The central hall could be supported by wooden columns and rose above the surrounding rooms that were probably lighted by a clerestory. The private quarters had bathrooms and latrines.

The royal palaces in the town centre were on either side of the main road and linked by a bridge with a 'Window of Appearance', from which the pharaoh would distribute gifts to his subjects. The palace on the western side had large open

O   120M

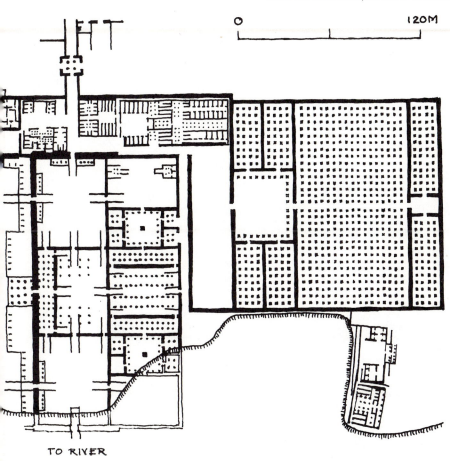

TO RIVER

spaces bordered with monumental statues of the king and the queen in front of great hypostyle halls (the great Pillared Hall had 540 pillars in rows). The second palace across the road, the 'King's house', was smaller and more intimate. It was decorated with painted murals representing unusually informal family scenes. Both palaces had gardens and made extensive use of limestone in the lining of walls. Maru-Aten, in the S of the city, seems to have served as a royal retreat. It contained an enclosed park or pleasure garden with various pavilions and little shrines. The architectural representations in the carved rock-tombs of Tell el-Amarna show that the columns had brightly painted palm or other floral capitals.

The temples were specially built for the new cult of Aten and consist mainly of huge open-air offering spaces with a large number of altars, linked by pylons and surrounded by rectangular walls (see SUN TEMPLE).

Assmann, J., 'Palast oder Tempel? Überlegungen zur Architektur und Topographie von Amarna', *Journal of Near Eastern Studies* 31 (1972) 143-155

Borchardt, L., Ricke, H., *Die Wohnhäuser in Amarna* (Berlin 1984)

Frankfort, H., Pendlebury, J.D.S., *The City of Akhenaten* II (London 1933)
Peet, T.E., Woolley, L., Gunn, B., *The City of Akhenaten* I (London 1923)
Pendlebury, J.D.S., *The City of Akhenaten* III (London 1951)

Tell el-Ful (ancient Gibeah)

Palestine, see map p. xix. Iron Age fortified settlement with four building levels. At the beginning of the 1st millennium (period of Saul) it was a 15m-square, tower-like structure surrounded by a village. In the 12th C BC it was completely destroyed and rebuilt at the end of the 10th C to serve as an outpost for the defences of Jerusalem. It was then an isolated fortified tower or *migdal*. The plan was still square, with a casemate wall consisting of two shells (the outer was 1.5m thick, the inner *c.* 1.20m), each built of dressed stone blocks laid in rough courses. Between these walls was a narrow space divided by transverse partitions into long chambers. Some of these were filled with rubble, others were used for storage and had access to the interior of the fortress. There was also a stone glacis, bringing the total width of the defences to some 9m. The internal space (13m^2) had a series of massive piers.

Albright, W.F., *Annual of the American Schools of Oriental Research* 4 (New Haven 1923)

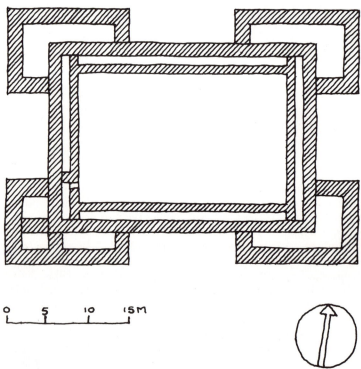

Tell el-Ful: citadel (c. 1000 BC) (restored) (after Albright)

Tell el-Qadi (ancient Laish and later Dan)

Palestein, see map p. xix. The Middle Bronze (2nd millennium BC) Canaanite town was called Laish and parts of its fortifications were excavated. They included a plastered glacis, built with rammed earth against an inner core of stone, sloping both ways. Around the 12th C BC, the Israelite tribe of Dan captured the town and renamed it. The well-built fortifications, including a double gate with an inner courtyard, were executed in stone with a type of masonry known from SAMARIA: finely dressed ashlar in alternate courses of headers and stretchers. A paved road led to the summit where a sanctuary stood. It was a BAMAH, consisting of an 18m² platform, approached by a flight of steps.

Biran, A., 'Tel Dan', *The Biblical Archaeologist* 37.2

Tell Halaf (ancient Guzana)

North Syria, see map p. xix. This large mound overlooking the river Khabur gave its name to a prehistoric culture (late 6th and early 5th millennia BC) because of the considerable amounts of distinctive, polychrome pottery which were found there underneath the ruins of much later buildings (see below). Architectural evidence of this period comes from other sites (see TELL ARPACHIYA, TEPE GAWRA); the farming population lived in villages with simple houses built of hand-shaped mudbricks, often with domed roofs. During the 9th C BC, Tell Halaf was a prosperous town known as Guzana, and paid tribute to the Assyrian king Adadnirari II. The local dynasty of Kapara built a strong citadel on a steep hill by the river, with a well-built ceremonial palace. It was approached by the 'Scorpion-gate' (so called because of the sculpted figures of scorpion-men on the orthostats of the gateway), that gave access to a public square. A monumental stairway led to the BÎT-HILANI that stood on a high terrace. This was a shallow building with three parallel broad and narrow halls which may have been vaulted. Strong bastions and buttresses at the back gave it a fortified aspect. Although details of the ground plan are lost because of denudation, the rich sculptural ornamentation of the portico was relatively well preserved. The outside walls of the terrace itself were decorated with relief orthostats, as was the facade of the palace. Sphinx-like creatures and griffins on the jambs protected the doorways. The three columns of the portico were technically caryatids, human figures in the round, supporting the architrave on their heads. There were two male figures and one female, and all stood on animal-shaped bases (a bull flanked by two lions).

Oppenheim, M. Freiherr von, *Tell Halaf: II, Die Bauwerke* (Berlin 1950)

Tell Harmal (ancient Shaduppum)

Mesopotamia, see map p. xviii. Small fortified administrative centre dating from the beginning of the 2nd millennium BC and a good example of Mesopotamian town planning. It was surrounded by a trapezoid strong wall (147m × 133.5m × 146.5m × 97m) with shallow buttresses (6.36m wide). A single gateway flanked by grooved buttresses opened onto the main road which crossed the town from E to W. Transverse side streets separated densely built-up housing blocks. The main temple dedicated to Nisaba and her consort Khani (28m × 18m) was approached by a flight of steps flanked by life-size terracotta lions. The facade was articulated by buttresses and stepped niches. The layout of the temple consisted of a transverse

vestibule, a large rectangular courtyard, a BREITRAUM ante-cella and CELLA. At right angles to the main cult rooms were the smaller shrine and ante-cella of the divine consort. Another religious building of interest was a double sanctuary with two parallel, axially laid-out Breitraum-cellae of equal dimensions. Nearby was a large private house (25m × 23m) built around a central courtyard. A stairway was accessible from the courtyard. One of the rooms contained a mudbrick pedestal (or altar) in the shape of a miniature temple, complete with the characteristic corru-

Tell Harmal: Nisaba temple (after Lloyd)

gated façade, doorways and windows.

Baqir, T., Lloyd, S., *Sumer* 2 (1946) 23-24; (1948) 137ff

Tell Mardikh (ancient Ebla)

North Syria, see map p. xix. Large site with a long and varied history of occupation from the middle of the 3rd to the end of the 2nd millennium BC. The first urban settlement of importance (Mardikh II B1, *c.* 2400-2250 BC) was protected by a stone wall with salient towers, and divided into a lower town and an acropolis on the natural limestone plateau. The so-called 'Court of Audience' (52m × 32m) formed the monumentally conceived threshold between the two areas. It was surrounded on at least two sides by porticoes (*c.* 5m deep) held up by wooden columns (70cm thick). The thick mudbrick walls (2.80m) of the facades rested on low ashlar foundations. Under the N portico was a platform of mudbrick (4.5cm × 3m, 55cm high), which probably served as a dais for the royal throne when the king gave public audiences. Nearby was a high narrow door which opened to the 'Ceremonial Stairway' inside a square tower. The stairway connected the inner apartments of the palace with the court. The palace was destroyed by the Akkadian king Naramsin (23rd C BC).

The second major phase is Mardikh III AB (*c.* 2000-1600 BC). The town was surrounded by powerful ramparts of PISÉ (20m high), covered at the base with large stone boulders, while the upper part was faced with a plaster of mud and gypsum. There were four gates, the most important being the one on the SW. This was a triple gateway, consisting of an outer gate flanked by buttresses, a trapezoid courtyard and an inner gate between three pairs of buttresses flanking two successive entrances. The gateway was lined with thick orthostats of basalt or limestone supported by ashlar.

The private HOUSES had stone foundations (40-90cm high) and a mudbrick superstructure. The basic tripartite plan comprised a vestibule, a wide rectangular

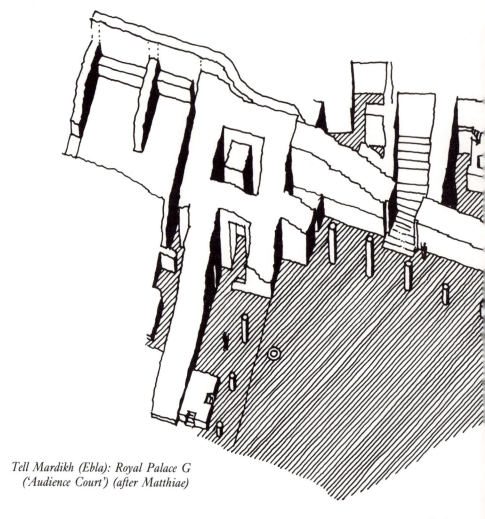

*Tell Mardikh (Ebla): Royal Palace G
('Audience Court') (after Matthiae)*

courtyard and two rooms opposite the vestibule (or on all sides of the courtyard).

The temples, B, C and N, were one-room structures with a rectangular or square CELLA and strong walls (3-4m thick), which probably rose to consider-able heights. Temple B2 was a more complex building with a large cella and forecourt surrounded by small square cellae, resembling the Double Temple at HAZOR. Matthiae suggested that it may have been used for particular rites and sacrifices, probably in connection with the nearby rock-tombs. Temple D was the largest sanctuary at Ebla (overall length 30m). The foundations are almost 5m thick, the walls above 2m. It was a tripartite axial arrangement of a centrally placed doorway, a transverse vestibule, a narrow ante-cella and an oblong cella (12.40m × 7.20m). Benches and square niches, as well as carved basins, were found in several Ebla temples.

Matthiae, P., *Missione archeologia italiana*

l'époque amorrhéenne', *Akkadica* 28 (1982) 41-87

Tell Uqair

Mesopotamia, see map p. xviii. The site was inhabited from the Obeid period (5th millennium BC). From this time, houses first built in PISÉ and then in mudbrick were discovered. An important architectural monument of the Uruk period (last quarter of the 4th millennium BC) is the so-called Painted Temple (level VII A). It was set on a two-stage platform in the shape of a flat curve with a straight front (5m high and *c.* 54m long), and decorated with pilasters and STIFTMOSAIK around the border. Two stairways on either end of it led onto the first terrace on which the second platform was erected (1.60m high, rectangular and *c.* 34m long). The temple resembles the contemporary White Temple at URUK and has similar dimensions (18.50m × 22.50m). The outside walls were articulated by pilasters and niches and covered with white gypsum plaster. The interior walls had painted designs and figurative scenes, as did the podium (altar?) set against the far wall which featured a large design of a spotted leopard painted in earth pigments.

Lloyd, S., Safar, F., 'Tell Uqair. Excavations by the Iraq Government Directorate of Antiquities 1940 and 1941', *Journal of Near Eastern Studies* 2 (1943) 132-158

in Siria: Rapporto preliminare della campagna 1964, 1965, 1966 Tell Mardikh (Rome 1965, 1966, 1967)
Matthiae, P., 'Ebla in the Early Syrian Period: The Royal Palace and the State Archives', *Biblical Archaeologist* 39, no. 2 (1976) 44-55
Matthiae, P., 'Tell Mardikh: Ancient Ebla', *American Journal of Archaeology* 8 (1978) 540ff
Matthiae, P., 'Fouilles à Tell Mardikh-Ebla 1980: Le palais occidental de

temple

Our knowledge about the religious beliefs and ritual practices of the Ancient Near East is still very scanty. We know a little about some of the official cults of the Egyptians, Babylonians and Hebrews, because they were described in contemporary texts, but such evidence is

215

extremely rare. We know next to nothing about the content and form of worship during the prehistoric and the archaic periods. The architectural evaluation of religious buildings of the time without a knowledge of their actual usage is therefore a somewhat spurious endeavour.

The Latin word *templum* described not only the actual building dedicated to a god, but any location or area deemed sacred by tradition and association. This extended usage also applies to the sanctuaries of the Ancient Near East. Anthropological research has shown that the sacred locality does not require any architectural distinctions. A grove, hillside, spring, cave, or any parts of the landscape that have acquired some special significance, can be used for seasonal assemblies and festivals, as well as for regular rituals and sacrifices. The Old Testament refers frequently to the local Canaanite cult of the 'Groves and High Places', and in Anatolia and Iran open-air sanctuaries predominated.

It is not clear why and when solid buildings destined for religious worship were first constructed. The designation of prehistoric structures as temples rests only on secondary evidence. Certain objects may be found within the confines of a building which are found in none of the others and suggest a religious connotation (for instance, the various 'fertility-idols'). Sometimes a building is distinguished by its careful construction, the size of rooms, unusual wall decorations (see eg ÇATAL HÜYÜK), or the presence of certain interior features, such as pedestals or niches. The expectations of the excavator, who is not always free from certain cultural stereotypes, may influence his identification. Unless the evidence is substantiated by other factors, such as a long tradition of sacred buildings on the same spot, continuing into the historic period, as for instance in ABU SHAHREIN, the designation 'temple' ought to be hypothetical.

With the emergence of the literate urban civilisations of Egypt and Mesopotamia (*c.* end of the 4th millennium BC), concrete information in the form of building inscriptions or inscribed votive offerings becomes available, which not only confirms an architectural complex as a temple, but also specifies to whom it was dedicated and who built it.

Many ancient myths describe how a new and interdependent relationship between gods and humans came to be established. In exchange for regular offerings, the gods promised to look after the people, to 'hear their prayers and grant them a long life'. The gods were given a permanent and suitably prominent residence, where the ritual duties could be performed by the deputy of the community, either the king or the high priest.

Apart from the large and well-endowed temples of city or national gods, there must also have been a fair number of small and less distinguished chapels and shrines, dedicated to purely local deities, which remain often undetected by archaeological excavations.

As so little is known about the priestly rituals, the participation of a worshipping community and the number and duties of the temple personnel, it is almost impossible to assign a specific function to the various architectural units of an excavated temple. There are some Egyptian and late Babylonian texts that describe the daily attendance to the divine statue which needed to be provided with clothes, food and drink and other diverse offerings, but that concerns only a fraction of the cultic offices that must have been performed. The analogy with domestic architecture is suggested by the ancient words for temple, such as 'house of the God', 'Great House' etc, but this does not explain everything. The question of access to the Holy of Holies, or of orientation, was obviously of some consequence but it is not clear in what way it was determined by the ritual.

Furthermore, the space surrounding the inner sanctuary, as well as the various chambers and corridors, the roofs and the courtyards were doubtlessly important too. But again it is often impossible to designate any specific function to these seemingly subsidiary architectural spaces. The archaeological description of an ancient temple therefore remains vague or primarily concerned with formal considerations. Since there is a tendency towards conservatism in ancient temple-building parallel with a diversity of local solutions it is difficult to establish a typology of temple buildings based entirely on architectural analysis (such as attempted by the German school in respect of Mesopotamian sanctuaries).

Only a very small fraction of Egyptian temples have survived and those were built relatively late in Egypt's long history. Countless deities were worshipped in shrines, chapels and small temples that were built of more transient materials than stone, such as wood, wicker or mudbrick. They have completely vanished and only some hieroglyphic signs and certain elements in the late stone temples hint at the appearance of these sanctuaries. The variety of religious dogma in Egypt partly explains the many different types of temples (see SUN TEMPLE, MORTUARY TEMPLE, CULT TEMPLE) since it demanded different rituals. Such plurality was balanced by a tendency towards a canonisation of forms, which resulted in an almost homogeneous style of Egyptian sacred architecture during the New Kingdom and later periods. The temples stood within a *temenos* or precinct, surrounded by high brick walls. The various spatial units (portals or pylons, courtyards and colonnades, hypostyle halls and vestibules, and finally the inner sanctum) were arranged in an axial sequence, one behind the other, as if to emphasise the idea of a passage. All architectural elements had specific or even multiple symbolic connotations, quite apart from the superficial relief decorations, which could be read and understood by the initiated – in this respect the Egyptian temple is very much like the medieval cathedral with its architectural semiotics. The painted reliefs, preserved on the interior walls of still existing temples, were put there in an attempt to perpetuate the rites performed in them by magical means and are now some of the few extant sources about the Egyptian rituals.

Ruszczyc, B., 'The Egyptian Sacred Architecture of the Late Period: A Study against the Background of the Epoch', *Archaeologia* 24 (Warsaw 1973) 12-49

Sauneron, S., Stierlin, H., *Die letzten Tempel Ägyptens* (Freiburg 1978)

Spencer, P., *The Egyptian Temple, a Lexicographical Study* (London 1983)

Varille, A., 'Quelques caractéristiques du temple pharaonique', *Le Musée Vivant* 2 (Paris 1954)

Mesopotamian temples were built in mudbrick. Their structures are only exceptionally preserved above the lowest courses and not one has been found with its roof and interior intact. There are very few texts, primarily from the Neo-Babylonian period, that relate to ritual practices performed within the temples. Because of this lack of information, a typology of Mesopotamian sacred architecture tends to be based on spatial organisation of the buildings rather than a functional analysis. This approach, which ignores the anthropological dimension (eg the relationship between temple and community, the daily routine of the personal etc) remains necessarily one-dimensional.

During the 4th millennium BC, a great number of monumental buildings were designed which the excavators have generally interpreted as temples (see URUK, TEPE GAWRA). They were vast and spacious buildings, often strictly symmetrical, and the main hall, that could be surrounded by subsidiary rooms, was accessible by more than a single entrance. The walls were rhythmically articulated by multiple recesses, buttresses and vertical grooves. These buildings seem to have opened onto an open (public?) space in the middle of the settlement.

In the course of the 3rd millennium, temple estates (mostly identified by inscriptions) developed, which were separated from the surrounding town by their elevated position on high platforms or terraces and by high perimeter walls. Various buildings were accommodated around courtyards within this enclosure and the sanctuary commanded its own internal precinct. It was comparatively remote from public access and the numerous inscribed statues, their hands folded in the attitude of prayer, which were found in and around the sanctuary, presumably acted as magical substitutes for the worshipping individual.

ZIGGURATS had already been built towards the beginning of the 3rd millennium BC, but they became a characteristic landmark of a Mesopotamian town during the 2nd millennium BC. The denuded state of these monuments and the lack of pertinent texts have led to much speculation concerning their function. It is not clear whether all ziggurats had a 'high temple' at the top level, as at URUK, and the relationship between a ziggurat and the religious structures on the ground is also unclear. There seems to have been a tendency towards more axially arranged hall buildings with central doorways. A vestibule or ante-chamber generally preceded the cella which was transverse in Babylonia and oblong in Assyria. (See SUMERIAN, KASSITE, BABYLONIAN and ASSYRIAN ARCHITECTURE.)

Lenzen, H.J., 'Mesopotamische Tempelanlagen von der Frühzeit bis zum zweiten Jahrtausend', *Zeitschrift für Assyriologie, Neue Folge* 16 (1955) 1-36

Le temple et le culte, XXième Rencontre Assyriologique Internationale (1972)
Heinrich, E., *Die Tempel und Heiligtümer im Alten Mesopotamien* I-II (Berlin 1982)
Temples et sanctuaires: Seminaire de recherche 1981-1983 (Lyon 1984)

In the area of Syria-Palestine, open-air sanctuaries and formal temples seem to have existed side by side from the Early Bronze Age. A combination of both elements in one architecturally defined space or building seems to be characteristic for this area (see BAMAH). Altars and cult-stelae set up in courtyards, on platforms or terraces, indicate that rituals were carried out under the sky (see MEGIDDO). The architecturally void spaces were probably of equal importance to the cult as the actual buildings, but their precise purpose is difficult to assess in the absence of any textual evidence concerning the religious practices of the area. Most temples destined to accommodate a divine emblem or statue were organised along the lines of a private residence, with a vestibule and a main hall behind. This bipartite arrangement predominates. The *cella* or *adyton* could be divided off the main hall by wooden partitions, or provided by a deep niche at the back of the main room. Benches along the walls of the sanctuary are another typical feature of Syro-Palestinian temples. The strong cultural influence of Egypt left a mark on the temple design of the Middle and Late Bronze Age (eg BETH-SHAN, BYBLOS).

Ottoson, M., *Temples and Cult Places in Palestine* (Stockholm 1982)
Le temple et le culte, XXième Rencontre Assyriologique Internationale (1972)
Temples et sanctuaires: Seminaire de recherche 1981-1983 (Lyon 1984)

For Anatolian temples see BOGHAZKÖY.
For temples in Iran see ELAMITE ARCHITECTURE and FIRE TEMPLE.

Tepe Gawra

Mesopotamia, see map p. xviii. A very important site with a long and continuous sequence of habitation (twenty archaeological strata), beginning in the Halaf period (late 6th and early 5th millennia BC) and ending in the 3rd millennium BC.

An astonishing architectural development, hand in hand with the process of urbanisation, began at level XIX. The 'temple' (extant measurements: 10.50m × 7m) was centred on an oblong chamber flanked by smaller rooms. A podium at the rear of the central chamber, built of PISÉ, suggests a religious purpose. On the N facade three simple piers or buttresses were found, which appear to have had some structural purpose, probably supporting roofing beams.

At level XVIII, circular *tholoi* (4.25m in diameter) appear, some with interior buttresses and very narrow openings. They were probably roofed with a dome or a conical structure and are associated with the Halaf culture (see TELL ARPACHIYA). The first great period of monumental architecture occurred at the end of the Obeid period (*c.* 4400-4300 BC), documented by level XIII. Three large 'temples' built of mudbrick were arranged around an open square. All three had their corners oriented towards the cardinal points. Only the plan of the Northern Temple is completely preserved. It was the smallest (12.65m × 8.65m) of the three and consisted of a single long hall. Each long side had a deep niche in the centre which divided the building into three zones: two transverse spaces balanced by a narrow oblong in the middle. Recessed niches inside and outside were found on the exterior walls. The entrance in one of the long walls afforded indirect access to the interior. Otherwise, the design is symmetrical and carefully balanced. The Central Temple had a front facade dominated by a central niche, with quarter-pilasters at the corners. It was also built along a long axis, with indirect access.

The building material was mudbrick of high quality and almost uniform size. In the Eastern Temple, model bricks of well-baked terracotta were discovered (full brick 43cm × 23cm × 7cm; also square, half and quarter bricks), which may have been used for experiments in brick-laying, especially useful for the complicated, multiple recessed pilasters.

After a period of transition (XII A), Tepe Gawra was a densely populated town at level XII. No obviously religious structures were found; the 'White Room' (plastered white) was the only outstanding building, formally planned with a central long room and flanking chambers at both long sides. At level XI, the settlement was fortified and organised around a circular tower or small fortress (the 'Round House') in the middle of the town. This was a large structure (outside diameter 18-19m), forming a perfect circle with a single entrance on the W. The exterior walls were 1m thick. The interior was divided into seventeen rooms, six rectangular ones in the middle and a central oblong room (preceded by an antechamber) which determined the axis to which all other rooms were subordinated. Levels XI, X, IX constitute a unit; at the time the settlement had a peaceful and predominantly religious character. The temples had long axes, a central sanctuary with a podium flanked by smaller rooms, decorative piers, and were entered by a central doorway. The private houses were closely packed together and had almost uniform ground plans composed of long and short rooms flanking a central chamber. Beehive ovens were ubiquitous in level X.

Level VIII C, B, A (around 3000 BC, contemporary with the end of the Uruk period/Jemdet-Nasr period in the south) apparently saw a shift from a predomin-

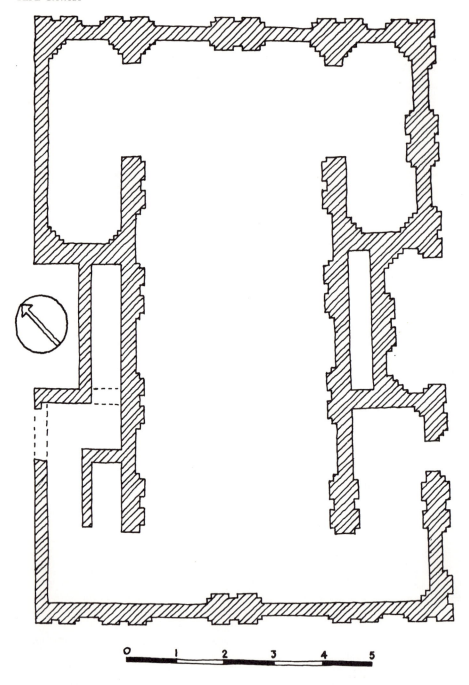

Tepe Gawra: northern temple of stratum XIII
  (after Tobler)

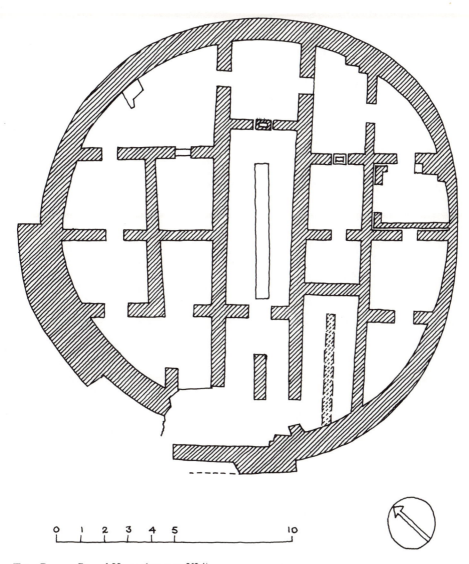

Tepe Gawra: Round House (stratum XIA)
  (after Tobler)

antly religious community to one with a more pronounced residential and commercial character, since the temples were gradually outnumbered by secular installations and houses (if the previous structures had indeed been temples). Building 940 (VIIIA) had a vaulted hall. It was constructed with a true arch, in mudbrick (average span 3.25m, length 8.5m), with proper wedge-shaped voussoirs, which became wider with the increasing height of the room to fill the gaps formed by the curving of the vault. The temples were mainly of the traditional Long-room type with an entrance porch flanked by triple recesses on both sides. The niches on the outside contained windows; one was found in a good state of preservation. During the 3rd millennium BC, the site gradually became less important and few architectural remains of interest have been found. For a short while, at level IV, stone replaced mudbrick as the predominant building material in the sacred precinct.

Speiser, E.A., *Excavations at Tepe Gawra* I (Philadelphia 1935)
Tobler, A.J., *Excavations at Tepe Gawra* II (Philadelphia 1950)

terre pisé *see* PISÉ

tomb

All groups of human beings have their specific funerary customs and methods of dealing with the mortal remains of the dead. The basically conservative nature of such practices is of great importance for prehistoric archaeology, as graves and their contents often furnish the only available evidence for cultural change and continuity within a given area.

The Egyptians developed various theories about the afterlife, which made it imperative that the mortal remains of the deceased should be kept from decay and corruption. Hand in hand with techniques of mummification, architectural structures were developed which guaranteed a permanent and safe repository for the body. Equally important were the funerary gifts and the rituals performed by the surviving members of the family. The tomb became the 'house of eternity' or the 'castle of the *ka*' for the deceased, and a place of offerings and rites for the surviving relations. The majority of the population, however, at any time during Egypt's history, did not have the necessary means to have a tomb built and maintained and had to be content with simple earth-burials accompanied by magical amulets. Architecturally, there is a correlation with the house and the shrine or chapel and both features were combined in the mature Egyptian tomb.

The MASTABA originated from an artificial memorial mound above the simple pit-grave of the prehistoric period, but developed into a complex structure with subterranean burial chambers and cult rooms, especially for offerings, in the superstructure. During the early dynasties, only kings were buried in mastabas, but when pyramids became the royal tombs in the III Dynasty, private people of rank were buried in such structures around the pyramids. The great pyramids of the IV Dynasty, the largest and most convincingly monumental tombs ever built, were surrounded by large numbers of mastabas, carefully aligned on orthogonal streets, running from N to S (see GIZA).

ROCK-CUT TOMBS were comparatively safe from the constant threat of the grave-robbers, and the limestone cliffs bordering the Nile were convenient locations for the rock cemeteries of provincial nomarchs. The Middle Kingdom rock tombs often have elaborate porticoed forecourts and pillared, vaulted interior apartments decorated with painted reliefs (see BENI-

Intra-mural tomb at Kültepe (Anatolia)

HASAN, QUBBET-EL-HAWWA). During the New Kingdom, in an attempt to reduce the danger of pillage by grave-robbers, the pharaohs had their tombs sunk into secret mountain-sides while their funerary rites were performed in special MORTUARY TEMPLES elsewhere. The private tombs now sometimes had pyramidical super-structures above subterranean burial chambers (DEIR-EL-MEDINEH).

Badawy, A., *A History of Egyptian Architecture* I-III (Giza 1954, Berkeley 1966, 1968)
Brinks, J., 'Die Entwicklung der königlichen Grabanlagen des alten Reiches', *Hildesheimer ägyptologische Beiträge* 10 (1979)
Reisner, G.A., *The Development of the Egyptian Tomb down to the Accession of Cheops* (London 1936)
Scharff, A., 'Das Grab als Wohnhaus in der ägyptischen Frühzeit', *Sitzungsberichte der Bayrischen Akademie der Wissenschaften, philosophisch-historische Klasse* 1944/46, Heft 6
Steindorff, G. and Wolf, W., 'Die Thebanische Gräberwelt', *Leipziger ägypt-ologische Studien* 4 (1936)

In Mesopotamia people were more afraid of the restless and tormenting spirits of the dead who, deprived of their proper burial places, haunted the living, than preoccupied with the celestial destiny of the soul as in Egypt. The spirits of dead relatives were kept at bay by allowing the bodies to remain at home; the burial *intra muros*, usually underneath the house, was very common in Mesopotamia, espec-ially in the South, from prehistoric times onwards. Extramural burials, in cemeteries outside the city walls, were sometimes an alternative within the same culture, probably for those wealthy enough to afford the erection and maintenance of a specifically built tomb.

In the North, separate tombs or tomb chapels were more frequent. At TEPE GAWRA X, for instance, tombs were rectangular chambers built mostly of brick and roofed over with stone. The most famous tombs of the Early Dynastic period were those discovered by L. Woolley at UR, which date from the I Dynasty of that city (middle of the 3rd millennium BC). The rich funerary offerings and the mysterious circumstances of a collective burial somewhat eclipse the architectural merits of these structures. The royal tombs (eg PG 1236) resembled houses whose entrance was a *dromos* leading down from the ground level. Walls and roofs were of heavy limestone rubble, plastered on the inside with fine white cement. The mudbrick floors sloped sideways and had terracotta drains to draw away the fluids. All contemporary methods of roofing were employed: chambers were corbel-vaulted, domed or flat, and there were radial as well as corbel arches above the internal doorways. Royal intramural burials within the palace grounds were found at KISH ('Chariot Burial' *c.* 2600 BC), MARI (large stone-vaulted tombs beneath the Early Dynastic Ishtar temple and the Amorite family vaults), and at UR. The kings of the III Dynasty of Ur, some of whom were deified during their lifetime, built impressive monumental structures commonly referred to as the Royal Tombs. They had elaborately niched walls, built of baked bricks set in bitumen, vaulted burial chambers accessible through internal stairways and a final superstructure (replacing a temporary structure built to receive funerary offerings), in the form of a well-appointed private house with platforms for statues and altars. It has been suggested

(Moorey), on the basis of textual evidence, that these monuments were cenotaphs and that the actual burial places of the kings were within the palace grounds.

The Assyrian kings, from Ashurnasirpal II (*c.* 883-859 BC) onwards, were buried in the Old Palace at ASSUR, in basalt sarcophagi deposited within large vaulted brick tombs (6-8m, 3m high).

Al-Khalesi, Y., 'The Bît-Kispim in Mesopotamian architecture', *Mesopotamia* 12 (1977) 53ff

Andrae, W., *Das wiedererstandene Assur* (2nd ed., Berlin 1977)

Moorey, P.R.S., 'Where did they bury the Kings of the Third Dynasty of Ur?', *Iraq* 46 (1984) 1-18

Strommenger, E., in *Reallexikon der Assyriologie* III, 581ff

Woolley, L., 'Excavations at Ur 1928-29', *Antiquaries Journal* 9 (1929) 306ff

There are few Anatolian tombs of architectural interest. Intramural burials were common in the South; the Hittites cremated their dead and buried the ashes in earthenware urns, and caves and crevices in rocky mountains provided suitable locations for simple burials. The tombs of ALAÇA HÜYÜK are famous for the lavish funerary equipment; the graves were rectangular pits, lined with stones and roofed over with wooden beams. At TELL HALAF, spacious tombs with vaulted burial chambers and funerary chapels were found. The Urartians provided similar structures for their kings, possibly also under Assyrian influence. They consisted of underground burial rooms of stone masonry and mudbrick superstructures containing cult rooms (see ALTINTEPE). Characteristic for the Phrygian period (*c.* 8th-7th C BC) are the tumuli burials. The tomb chamber was inside a shaft, with wooden walls and wooden roofs. Heaps of stones were carefully piled up high above the grave and its centre could be marked with intersecting lines of stones. For the so-called Tomb of Midas and other rock monuments see GORDIUM and ANATOLIAN ARCHITECTURE.

Naumann, K., *Die Architektur Kleinasiens* (2nd ed., Tübingen 1971)
Lloyd, S., *Early Anatolia* (Harmondsworth 1956)

In Syria-Palestine, prehistoric burials in communal pits or individual graves received no architectural elaboration. In the Proto-Urban period (around 3000 BC), large numbers of bones and detached skulls were put into rock-cut chambers (4.30m × 3m) with a circular entrance shaft; some were discovered near JERICHO.

The practice of multiple interments was carried on throughout the Early Bronze Age (Jericho). In the Intermediate Early Bronze-Middle Bronze (Kenyon) (*c.* 2300-1900 BC), however, people were buried individually, and much more attention than hitherto was paid to providing suitable 'houses for the dead'. Five different types of tombs can be distinguished by their funerary equipment as well as their architectural characteristics. This variety may have been due to divergent traditions of the various nomadic tribes moving into Palestine at that time. Some tombs were small, carefully excavated shafts ('Dagger tombs'); some were very large and roughly cut ('Outsize type'; up to 3.43m in diameter and 2.44m high); some had predominantly square burial chambers; and others were of a mixed type. The rock-cut tombs at MEGIDDO were in use for a long time. They had a vertical square shaft, about 2m deep, that led into a central chamber surrounded by three others at a slightly higher level.

In Phoenicia, burials in stone-covered shafts were accompanied by rich funerary gifts, often imported Egyptian articles. The architecturally most elaborate tombs were found at RAS SHAMRA. A stairway or *dromos* led down to a rectangular chamber of dressed masonry, roofed with a pointed corbel vault, adjacent to an ossuary.

Kenyon, K.M., *Archaeology in the Holy Land* (4th ed., London 1985)
Schaeffer, C., *Ugaritica* I (Paris 1949) 68ff

Intramural burials for private people were the norm in Iran from prehistoric times. Royal tombs from the Elamite period (middle of the 2nd millennium BC) feature monumental underground vaults built in mudbrick (see CHOGA ZANBIL, HAFT TEPE, SUSA). The Achaemenians first buried their kings in monumental, free-standing stone structures resembling houses (eg the tomb of Cyrus at PASARGADAE). Darius I had his tomb cut out of the rock-face near Naqsh-i-Rustam, which featured a cruciform facade imitating the porticoed front of an Achaemenian palace, and the rock-cut tombs remained the favourite type of royal (and private) tomb in the Persian, Sassanian and Parthian periods (see ROCK-CUT TOMB).

Ghirshman, R., *Iran in the Ancient East* (Oxford 1941)

torus

A moulding with semi-circular section underneath a cornice or at the top and along the edges of Egyptian buildings. Executed in stone, it probably derives from bundled reeds used in the primitive vegetal shelters. The diagonal bindings are carved or painted onto the stone torus.

tower

Only a few structures which can be

Torus moulding, Great Hypostyle Hall, Karnak (XIX Dynasty)

feature a variety of tower-like buildings. Egyptian hieroglyphic signs show two types of towers; one round structure with a diagonal exterior stairway, windows at the top and a KHEKHER topping; the other has battered sides, crenellated battlements and what could be interpreted as a rope ladder hanging from the top.

Structurally, three types of tower can be distinguished: (1) prismatic towers in pairs, one on each side of an entrance (gate-towers); (2) round or prismatic towers projecting from the walls of fortifications, usually at the angles (defence towers); (3) free-standing towers. The first type was very common throughout the Ancient Near East, as the practice of strengthening the walls on either side of a monumental entrance was generally observed. In Mesopotamia, the thick-walled temple enclosures had elaborately stepped entrance funnels flanked by high buttress-like towers (eg TELL AGRAB: Shara temple; KHAFAJE: Sin temple VIII; KISH etc). The gates of cities were almost

recognised as towers by their height, have survived. The best-known and the earliest example is probably the round stone tower from 8th-millennium JERICHO. It is preserved to a height of 9.14m and its diameter is 8.5m. A passage from the eastern side led to a steep stairway with twenty-two steps climbing to the top of the tower, which formed part of the defence system of the town.

Substantially projecting parts of a facade or a perimeter wall are often interpreted as towers, even when only the foundations or the lowest courses of the building remain. It is not always clear whether these structures were accessible, if the space at ground level is filled in. Architectural representations, primarily from Egyptian and Assyrian sources,

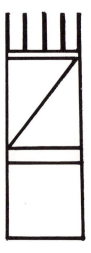

Egyptian hieroglyph: 'palace', 'tower'

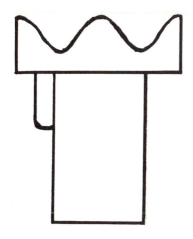

Egyptian hieroglyph: 'tower'

universally protected by towers; certainly in Syria-Palestine (Beth Shemesh, Tell el-Nasbeh: 10m wide, 2m projection, GEZER, RAS SHAMRA, Hama etc), in Assyria (eg ASSUR, *gurigurri* gate: 8-10m wide, 4m projection, 15m high), and Anatolia (especially in Hittite fortresses).

Towers in fortifications cannot always be distinguished from BASTIONS; they seem to have been characteristic of Hittite, Assyrian, Palestinian and Elamite fortresses. Egyptian and Assyrian reliefs show such crenellated structures defended by guards fighting on the battlements (eg Qadesh, LACHISH, Elam).

For free-standing watchtowers see MIGDAL. Certain high tower-like structures in Urartian and Persian architecture had religious purposes (see SUSI TEMPLE and FIRE TEMPLE).

trabeated architecture

Making use of vertical supports and flat ceilings or architraves, in contrast to an arcuated style, characterised by the employment of arches and vaults. Egyptian and Achaemenian architecture were trabeated.

Trabeated structure, 'post and lintel', from mortuary temple of Hatshepsut, Deir-el-Bahari

Troy (modern Hissarlik)

Anatolia, see map p. xv. Citadel with nine successive layers of occupation, which gradually extended southwards. Troy I (30th-26th C BC) was a small fortified enclosure (*c.* 50m across), surrounded by a mudbrick wall on stone foundations, with irregular outlines and projecting towers. The private houses have also stone foundations and are of the MEGARON type. In the fortress of Troy II (*c.* 26th C BC) the walls formed an irregular polygon. There were square towers (*c.* 18m²) flanking the colossal gate-ways with a tunnel-like passageway. The strong mudbrick walls (2.8-4m thick) rested on a stone substructure and were enforced with horizontally embedded wooden beams. The interior stone walls had upright

227

wooden posts spaced at intervals of 2m, probably supporting the roof beams. The *megara* buildings of the citadel have a square porch and an oblong room with a central hearth. In the bigger building (33m × 11m), the internal space was subdivided into two units. During the Hittite period (Troy VI; 18th-13th C BC), Troy was surrounded by a stone enclosure (*c.* 200m across) of irregular outlines and a projecting tower at each of the entrances with a bent-axis approach. The *megara* were replaced by large rectangular houses.

Blegen, C.W., *et al.*, *Troy* I-III (Princeton 1950-53)

Ugarit *see* RAS SHAMRA

upper storey

With the exception of some Egyptian stone monuments which are exceptionally well preserved, most Ancient Near Eastern buildings were discovered through archaeological investigations. Stone structures survived better than those built with mudbrick. The tracing of mudbrick walls, often subjected to successive rebuilding, is a difficult and meticulous task. Many of the older publications dealt with architectural remains rather summarily, concentrating on the ground plans. As the archaeological techniques become more advanced, much more detailed information about the structures of excavated buildings is made available. A statistical and chemical analysis of débris inside a ruined building, for instance, contributes valuable information regarding the displaced superstructure.

The existence of upper storeys in Ancient Near Eastern architecture has always been surmised as possible but not very common and the flat-roof skyline was generally postulated. Comparisons with contemporary vernacular building traditions and the functional analysis of excavated ancient buildings have shown that these flat roof terraces lend themselves readily for vertical extensions, especially if lightweight materials are used. Architectural representations or model houses also depict buildings with several storeys. The construction methods are identical to those for the ground floor and access by ladders or stairs is easily provided. In very closely built-up domestic conglomerations, the lighting and ventilation are better on the upper floor, which makes it likely that the bedrooms and family apartments were installed there. In palaces especially, upper storeys would make optimal use of the existing space; in fact many structures do not make any sense unless one postulates that the ground-floor accommodation was primarily utilitarian. Supporting circumstantial evidence, such as furnishings and plaster fallen from above, the emplacements of stairs and the thickness of walls is not always clearly recorded in the excavation reports. Although the exact nature and extent of upper storeys in an individual building is naturally impossible to establish, one has to admit the general principle of vertical extensions throughout Ancient Near Eastern architecture.

Ur (modern Muqqayir)

Mesopotamia, see map p. xviii. Important Mesopotamian site, seat of the moon-god Nannar and dynastic city with a variety of interesting architectural remains, some of which have been partially restored and reconstructed.

Ur was first inhabited during the Obeid period (beginning of the 4th millennium BC) and the earliest settlements of mud and reeds provided a firm substratum for later and more solid constructions. The buildings of the Early Dynastic period (*c.* 2700-2400 BC) are largely superseded by the grandiose structures of the 20th C BC (see below). The most celebrated complexes of the mid-3rd millennium BC are the Royal Graves, communal subterranean chambers, some with corbelled dome roofs, reached by descending ramps. Royal personages together with their personnel, chariots and draught animals were buried there, accompanied by lavish funerary equipment (see TOMB).

During the III Dynasty (*c.* 2113–2004 BC), Ur was a very prosperous trading community and enjoyed political and economic supremacy through Mesopotamia. Numerous buildings from this period have been excavated. Most prominent was the newly reconstructed ZIGGURAT. It was built by Urnammu (*c.* 2113-2096 BC) over an existing structure going back to the Early Dynastic period, and eventually restored by the Neo-Babylonian king Nabonidus (556-539 BC). It is one of the best preserved ziggurats in Mesopotamia and has been partially reconstructed. It stood within a rectangular court and was oriented to the points of the compass; the measurements at the base are 62.5m × 43m. The outer faces of baked brick, which encase the well-drained solid core of mudbricks, are inclined to a pronounced batter and have regularly spaced, flat buttresses. Access to the 11m-high first stage was achieved by building a projecting bastion against one face which supported a vertical ramp in the middle and two lateral ramps parallel with the body of the ziggurat. These ramps converged at another structure doubling as a gatehouse, from where a central stairway continued to the second stage. As the upper parts of the original ziggurat are denuded, it is uncertain in which manner the stairs proceeded to the top of a third stage (if there was one) and whether there was a High Temple on the ultimate platform.

The NW side of the ziggurat's *temenos* was traditionally sacred to the moon-god Nannar, the SE to his spouse Ningal. The NW side comprised the Court of Nannar, enclosed by a double wall with casemate(?) chambers with an elaborately buttressed facade and one massive gate-tower. Next to it was a large square building, the *Enunmah*, which probably served for storage purposes. At the SE corner of the ziggurat enclosure is the *Edublalmah*, a monumental gateway which was substantially transformed by the Kassite ruler Kurigalzu (*c.* 1345-1324 BC) into a vaulted sanctuary, the archway of which has been restored. The SE quarter, dedicated to Ningal, is known as the *Giparu*. Enclosed by the same kind of regularly buttressed walls characteristic for all other buildings in the *temenos*, this complex was internally divided in half by a corridor separating the quarters of the priestesses and the rooms reserved for the rituals associated with the Sacred Marriage ceremonies, from the temple and the surrounding 'kitchens'.

An isolated square building S of the *Giparu* is thought to have been the Palace of the kings of Ur. It is built around a large courtyard but not much of the internal arrangement could be ascertained. Much better preserved is the so-called Mausoleum of Shulgi, which is planned like a large private house but was in fact a shrine dedicated to the memory of the kings who may have been buried in great vaulted tombs beneath the floor. The quality of its brickwork, and the slightly convex curve of its walls, are similar to those of the ziggurat.

The whole *temenos* was built on an artificial platform retained by a heavy brick wall (up to 22m thick and 8m high), with a strongly battered outer face (45°) strongly resembling an earth ramp. The flat buttresses echoed the rhythmical articulation of the ziggurat, which underlined the conceptual unity of the Ur precinct. The wall was later rebuilt and strengthened several times.

Sir Leonard Woolley also excavated

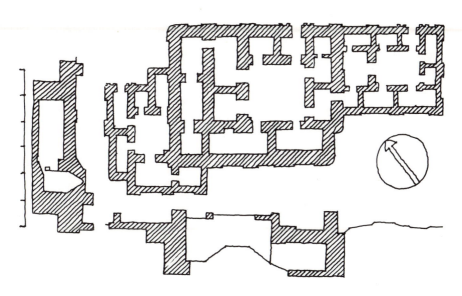

Ur: royal graves (plan and cross-section)
(Ur III period) (after Woolley)

part of the old town outside the religious enclosure; with its winding streets and crowded quarter it is a good example of a naturally grown Mesopotamian town. The houses of the richer people had paved courtyards, bathrooms and latrines (emptying into the streets), kitchens with bread ovens, reception rooms with benches and upper storeys. The Neo-Babylonian town erased the old layout of the 2nd millennium as it was built on an entirely new plan with broad avenues intersected by narrower streets at right angles. The houses were larger and built entirely in mudbrick (the old town had houses with baked-brick foundations). Their facades show the serrated, flat projections typical for the Neo-Babylonian town-houses.

There was also a Neo-Babylonian palace built for Nabonidus's daughter in the manner of other contemporary palaces, with a very large court and adjacent shallow reception room, audience chamber and utilitarian rooms.

Gadd, C.J., *History and Monuments of Ur* (London 1929)

Hall, H.R., Woolley, C.L., *Ur Excavations* I, II, V (London 1927-39)

Oates, J., 'Ur, Eridu: The Prehistory', *Iraq* 22 (1960) 32-50

Weadcock, P.N., 'The *Giparu* at Ur', *Iraq* 37 (1975) 101ff

Woolley, C.L., *Antiquary's Journal* 5 (1925); 9 (1929); 10 (1930); 11 (1931); 12 (1932); 13 (1933); 14 (1934)

Urartian architecture

Urartu was the name the Assyrians gave to a kingdom situated in the far eastern parts of Asia Minor (later Armenia), which repeatedly and successfully challenged the Assyrian claims of sovereignty during the 9th and 8th C BC, until it was in turn defeated by the Scythians and Medes in the middle of the 6th C BC.

Urartian fortification walls, Arinberd

The Urartians built strongly fortified towns of rocky promontories and developed a ruggedly monumental style of architecture. They were famous for their metalwork and small sculpture, which was distributed as far as the Mediterranean area; but they were also skilful hydraulic engineers, and various AQUEDUCTS and canals built by Urartian kings still function today (eg the 'Shamiran-su' which brought drinking water to the eastern shore of lake Van from a distance of some 75km). Urartian citadels, sited on impregnable mountain spurs, were surrounded by a glacis and strong walls. These were built with semi-cyclopean masonry, using large blocks of the local black basalt, 3-4m thick, and laid in stepped courses. The mudbrick superstructure was strengthened by regularly spaced buttresses and projecting parapets (as shown on a bronze model found at Toprakkale). The various buildings were distributed on the uneven levels of the site (see KARMIR-BLUR) and linked by rock-cut steps and stairways. Palaces and temples were decorated with wall paintings in vivid colours. The column played an important part in Urartian architecture. They supported the ceilings of spacious columned halls in private houses and palaces or provided graceful porticoes. Urartian temples were either tall, tower-like structures with projecting corner-bastions (see SUSI TEMPLE), or oblong, rectangular in plan and preceded by a portico. An Assyrian relief representing the temple of Musasir shows a facade hung with great round shields and a sloping roof, which may have been gabled. There were also open-air sanctuaries with rock-cut rectangular niches. (See ALTINTEPE, BASTAM.)

Akurgal, E., *Urartäische und altiranische Kultzentren* (Ankara 1968)

Forbes, T.B., *Urartian Architecture* (Oxford 1983)

Van Loon, M.N., *Urartian Art* (Istanbul 1966)

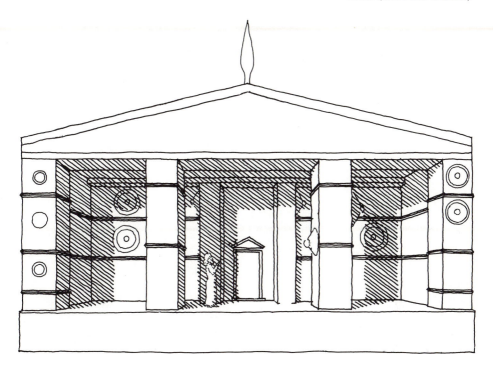

Urartian temple at Musasir (reconstruction after an Assyrian relief by Naumann)

Uruk (modern Warka)

Mesopotamia, see map p. xviii. A site with an unparalleled wealth of architectural monuments from the archaic to the Seleucid period. The results of the excavations carried out by the Deutsche Orientgesellschaft (since 1928) have been made available in publications of exemplary thoroughness.

There are two principal sites. One was dedicated to the goddess Inanna and is called *Eanna*; the other belonged to the sky-god Anu and encompasses the ziggurat. These deities were worshipped throughout Mesopotamian history and the numerous levels (nineteen at *Eanna*) testify to the continuous building activity spanning some 3,000 years.

The beginnings of monumental architecture fall into the 'Uruk period' (last third of the 4th millennium BC), following a long experimental phase (twelve levels since the Obeid period; first half of the 4th millennium BC). The oldest temple is the 'Steinstift-tempel' (Uruk VI-IVa), whose building methods are characteristically experimental. It was built on a platform of rammed earth (or *pisé*) and made water-proof with a layer of bitumen. The foundations for the temple were limestone blocks set in lime-mortar, and the actual walls consisted of a kind of cast concrete made of white gypsum and pulverised baked bricks. The inside of the temple was decorated with a cone mosaic, made with white alabaster and limestone, black limestone and red sandstone. It produced geometric patterns resembling those of woven reed-mats or textiles. The temple measured 28m × 19m and was set in a separate court surrounded by a limestone wall, with shallow niches outside and deep niches inside. On the SE of the temple was an L-shaped room (4m × 2.40m), surrounded by a parapet. The floor consisted of limestone blocks set in bitumen, which prompted the excavators tentatively to designate it as a pool ('Abzu pond', by analogy with the Mesopotamian underground ocean, or *abzu*).

The largest of the early temples is the 'Kalkstein-tempel' (Limestone temple) (Uruk V-IVb) (76m × 30m). A central oblong space – it is not certain whether it was open to the sky or covered – (*c.* 9m × 58m) was surrounded by four subsidiary rooms on each side, which were all accessible from outside. The walls consisted of limestone blocks and were corrugated with niches more elaborate on the inside than the outside. The classical period of Uruk's architecture was reached in levels IV b-a. There was a rapid succession of strata, and new buildings were continuously erected over and next to existing structures. The considerable variety of ground plans and architectural detail emphasise the creative surge of this period. The various structures cannot be regarded as isolated buildings but as part of an overall design which subtly related the various buildings to a coherent whole. Temple G is similar to the monumental concept of the Kalkstein-tempel and Temple H is another example for the classic Uruk temple. The 'Steinmosaik-gebäude' (IVb), an L-shaped terrace built of large 'Patzen' bricks, consisted of two parts set at right angles to each other. They enclosed a courtyard (*c.* 27m × 19m) decorated with cone mosaics which were laid in courses rather than stuck into the wall. It linked the new main Temple D (see below), erected over the old Limestone temple, with Temple A, a com-

paratively small and plain mudbrick building, with the typical oblong central room flanked by chambers on either side. In front of the NE terrace was a colonnade (*c.* 30m wide). Two rows of massive, pillar-like supports (over 2m in diameter) were engaged to the wall on the N side and also covered with cone-mosaic decoration.

Temple D (IVa) (45m × 80m) had a cruciform central cult room (consisting of a *Rumpfbau* and *Kopfbau*) and its walls were articulated by elaborately stepped niches. On the short walls the niches were three-stepped, and along the long walls they deeply penetrated the body of the temple into funnel-like cruciform openings. The niches surrounding the transverse top part (*Kopfbau*) may have been open to the sky. Temple C also had a cruciform hall with symmetrically arranged chambers along the sides, but no niches.

The religious function of 'Temple E'

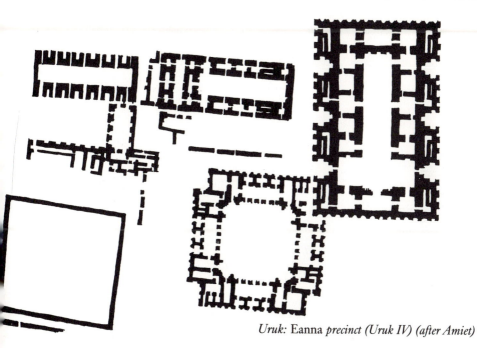

Uruk: Eanna *precinct (Uruk IV) (after Amiet)*

(IVb-a) is still disputed (Lenzen calls it a palace. Schmidt is in favour of the temple). A central square courtyard (20m × 20m) was surrounded on each side by a hall (15m × 5m), with five entrances opening onto the court, separated by four pillars (2m × 2m) which were richly recessed with niches. Each hall was connected to three chambers leading to the outside with diametrically positioned doorways. All facades were rhythmically articulated by stepped recesses.

The dating and purpose of the enigmatic *Riemchengebäude* is equally uncertain. A rectangular enclosure (18m × 20m) was built around an inner room (6.5m × 4m), and the whole interior was filled up with débris including numerous artifacts. At the end of the 4th millennium, all these monuments were systematically destroyed, maybe because of a major religious reorientation, and there is a sharp break in the architectural tradition in the following Jemdet-Nasr period (Uruk III).

The Uruk III *Eanna* precinct was dominated by a raised terrace on which a High Temple is thought to have stood (height and dimensions of this terrace changed through the various building phases of this period). Round the terrace various other buildings, such as houses, administrative quarters etc, were grouped around courtyards. The clarity of design and high quality of execution, which distinguished the structures of the Uruk VI-IV period, were lost. The new buildings have comparatively small interior spaces, enclosed by heavy mudbrick walls built of 'Patzen bricks'. The outstanding monument of this period is the so-called Anu Ziggurat and the 'White Temple'. The 'ziggurat' is an artificial hill (c. 13m high) overlooking the flat plain of Uruk. It had irregular outlines and battered, buttressed walls. A ramp-like stairway against the NE face led to the summit, where the old small sanctuary (17.5m × 22.3m) was preserved under the ruins of much later

235

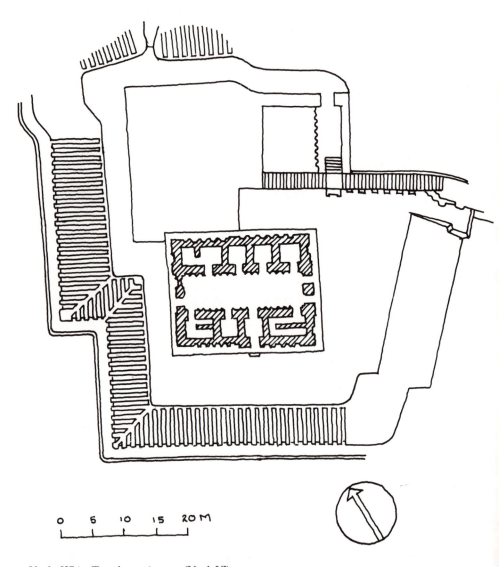

Uruk: White Temple on ziggurat (Uruk VI)

structures. The plan shows an oblong cult room flanked by smaller chambers along the sides. The furnishings of the shrine include a platform or altar with some steps in the NE corner, an offering table and a semi-circular hearth built of brick. The outside as well as the inside walls were plastered and white-washed and structured by stepped niches. This building has marked similarities with the *Eanna* precinct temples of the previous period (temples C, D).

Noteworthy among the buildings of later periods is the Karaindash temple

*Uruk: temple of Inanna, built by Karaindash
(Kassite period)*

(15th C BC), an oblong structure with a long rectangular cella and ante-cella surrounded by corridors and an external wall with bastions at the corners. The walls on the outside were decorated with moulded bricks forming a high relief of male and female figures (water-gods?).

During the Neo-Babylonian and Seleucid periods (1st millennium BC), many temples and palaces were built in and around the *Eanna* precinct. The principal temple, the so-called *Bît Reš*, was a huge complex (213m × 167m) with a double temple dedicated to Anu and Antu that was surrounded by twenty-two chapels.

Detailed excavation reports are published in 'Vorläufige Berichte über die von der Deutschen Orientgesellschaft in Uruk-Warka unternommenen Ausgrabungen'

(UVB), I-XI, *Abhandlungen der Preussischen Akademie der Wissenschaften*, Philosophisch-Historisch Klasse (1929-1940); UVB XII-XXXII (1956-1983)

Heinrich, E., 'Die Stellung der Uruk-tempel in der Baugeschichte', *Zeitschrift für Assyriologie* 49, *Neue Folge* 15 (1949) 21-44

Lenzen, H.J., 'Die Bauwerke von Eanna am Ende der Uruk IV Periode', *Comptes rendus de la XXième rencontre internationale d'Assyriologie* (Leiden 1935) 35-42

Lenzen, H.J., 'Die Tempel der Schicht Archaisch IV in Uruk', *Zeitschrift für Assyriologie* 49, *Neue Folge* 15 (1949) 1-20

Lenzen, H.J., 'Die Architektur in Eanna in der Uruk IV Periode', *Iraq* 36 (1974) 111-128

vault

Primarily found preserved in subterranean structures, mainly tombs. Due to the denuded conditions of Ancient Near Eastern buildings in general, relatively few examples for the use of vaulting as a means of covering spaces above ground are known, though the technical expertise which produced the underground vaults would have been applied more generally. By analogy with contemporary Near Eastern building traditions, and considering certain architectural dispositions, vaulted spaces were probably much more common than it appears from archaeological records alone. Thick walls enclosing relatively narrow transverse spaces were probably roofed by brick vaults rather than the much lighter flat roofs composed of timber and mudplaster. The advantages of vaults are primarily economical: they were cheaper to build and easier to maintain than flat roofs, and they provided higher internal spaces which could be lighted by clerestory windows.

The most widespread techniques of vaulting avoided the use of CENTRING. The high cost of the relatively great quantity of timber required for the temporary structures would have made them too expensive. Most popular for small rooms in private houses throughout the Near East was the corbelled vault. As in the corbelled dome, it distributes the weight gradually over the individual components of the structure, since each brick or stone receives the load of the projecting one above (eg in some of the mid-3rd millen-

nium Royal Tombs of UR, the gatehouse at Tell Taya – see Reade, J., *Iraq* 30, p. 247; the posterns of Alishar, BOGHAZKÖY and RAS SHAMRA (2nd millennium BC); tomb 3 at MEGIDDO).

The earliest surviving examples of barrel vaults or tunnel vaults in brick were found in I Dynasty tombs in Egypt (tomb 3357 in SAQQARA). They were more commonly employed in the New Kingdom and the later periods (especially during the Graeco-Roman). They were used mainly to cover broad halls or corridors and were constructed either with a centring of wood or sand infill (in small structures), or by inclined courses resting against an arch or temporary wall. The voussoirs could be edge-shaped or curved but conventional, rectangular bricks were used more often, with small stones or sherds filling the gaps between them on the outside curve. The bricks usually had a higher proportion of chaff-temper than ordinary bricks to make them lighter. Finger-marks or vertical grooves along the surface allowed them to stick together by suction. The average span of a brick barrel vault was *c.* 3.25m; the largest recorded span, 8.60m, occurred in the royal stables at MEDINET-HABU. The best-preserved Egyptian brick vaults were found in the magazines surrounding the mortuary temple of Ramesses II (Ramesseum) in western Thebes – they were four bricks thick and spanned about 4m.

Ribbed vaults may have originated from curved reed-structures supported by rings of bundled reeds. A series of semi-circular

Corbelled vaults, royal tombs, Ur (Ur III period)

Barrel vault at Deir-el-Medineh, Ptolemaic temple

flat-ribbed arches was filled in with transversely laid bricks and plastered with thick layers of mortar (eg in the mastabas of GIZA). Brick extrados may even have been supported by plastered reed bundles originally (URUK IV engaged columns, see Al-Khalesi, *Mesopotamian monumental architecture*, 107).

A series of arches and short barrel vaults, probably flat domes too, were used to span the rooms of Elamite palaces (up to 5m wide). At SUSA XIV, vaults were sprung from the pilasters at the corners longitudinally to the axis of the room. This in turn supported another vault sprung perpendicularly and resting against the right wall. The long hall (20m × 4.80m) was thus divided into three spaces. The Achaemenians may have used similar devices and perhaps passed on the technique to the Parthians, but there is little archaeological evidence in support of Achaemenian vaults being an important feature.

Pitched vaults were used for corridors and square spaces. Like leaning vaults, they were built against a stable element that propped up the initial courses which were laid at right angles to the wall. The subsequent courses rested against the first ones. Pitched vaults over a square space were begun simultaneously at each of the four corners, and a course was added to each vault until they met, forming a dome and producing a characteristic diamond pattern (eg TELL AL-RIMAH). True vaults or domes, built with radiating voussoirs and centring, were found at an early date in Mesopotamia (royal graves at UR: mid-3rd millennium BC). They were constructed with bricks, like those at TEPE GAWRA VIII or in the palaces at BABYLON.

239

*Mudbrick vault with inclined courses,
Ramesseum, Western Thebes, Egypt
(XIX Dynasty)*

At ASSUR, in the royal tombs, they were made of stone. Also in North Syria: tombs at TELL HALAF, or in the palace at Alalakh (TELL ATCHANA).

Pointed vaults were occasionally used to roof passages; the one in the NE palace at Tell Halaf consisted of three concentric layers with a particularly strong middle section made of specially hard bricks which were composed of clay, gypsum and pebbles. The rock-cut corbelled vaults of the postern mentioned above were also pointed (triangular in section). False vaults could be made by hollowing out the underside of a thick stone roof. This was the common practice in Egyptian stone buildings, especially in rock-cut tombs (eg BENI-HASAN) or certain shrines dedicated to chthonic deities (ABYDOS: temple of Seti-I, Hathor chapels etc).

Besenval, R., *Technologie de la voûte dans l'orient ancien* (Paris 1984)

Fathy, H., *Architecture for the Poor* (Chicago, London 1973) 8-12

Kawami, T.S., 'Parthian Brick Vaults in Mesopotamia', *Journal of Ancient Near Eastern Studies* 14 (1982) 61-67

Spencer, A.J., *Brick Architecture in Ancient Egypt* (Warminster 1979) 123ff

wall

Some form of screen or fence, which surrounds and divides the living space, is one of the most basic elements of human dwellings. These could be made of skins and cloth, reeds or wood. In sedentary communities, where permanent lodgings are the rule, such transient fences are substituted for solidly built walls, meant to last for at least a generation and more. The first solid walls mark the beginnings of architecture, which in the Ancient Near East can be traced to the 9th millennium BC (Palestine). Whether these early walls enclosed the actual living spaces as we would understand today, or whether they were primarily built to preserve and protect goods and agricultural produce, is not certain. The advantages of a permanent shelter must have been obvious, as the steady technological development of building walls over the ensuing millennia clearly shows. Furthermore, the whole settlement could be more effectively protected against the elements (floods, sandstorms, wind); wild animals or hostile human beings, by a strong wall.

Such free-standing perimeter walls had only a few openings which had to be made secure for structural as well as defensive reasons. Sheer vertical walls are not very stable on their own, and various different solutions were found to overcome this statical problem. The most common was the use of battered walls with a triangular section. In Egypt, wavy and undulating brick walls of great thickness surrounded sanctuaries. Buttresses also improve stability. The ultimate development of the original fence around a camp is the huge fortified enclosure wall of the Iron Age, complete with bastions, towers and broad battlements (eg BABYLON, KHORSABAD, BOGHAZKÖY).

Load-bearing walls which supported the flat or vaulted roofs were almost always vertical, though additional strengthening by buttresses or pillars occurred, particularly in monumental structures. Openings were kept to a minimum, with few doorways and small windows.

The choice of material for the building of walls depended on tradition as well as local availability. The brick wall is the typical type of wall in the Ancient Near East, even in areas where stone was readily available, such as Anatolia and Egypt. Brick walls need protection from rain and erosion by the application of plaster on the outside, and some insulation is needed against rising moisture from the ground (sand, layers of reed, a few courses of stone). Massive brick walls have ventilation holes or intermittent layers of reed mats (Egypt, Mesopotamia). Various ways of bonding ensured the internal cohesion of the brickwork. In Anatolia and North Syria, the areas most affected by earthquakes, timber beams were imbedded in the brick walls, either in horizontal layers or in a frame-system, which made the whole structure more elastic (eg Alalakh (TELL ATCHANA), CARCHEMISH, Boghazköy).

Stone walls could be built in different techniques. The simplest and most

Phoenician stone wall, Palestine (after Albright)

ancient type is the dry-stone wall. Blocks and stones in their natural state were fitted together, with the smaller stones filling out any gaps; no mortar was needed. Such walls were common in Palestine during the early Neolithic period before brick-making was discovered, and in Anatolia especially for perimeter walls. During the Bronze Age, dry-stone walls became more regular and the blocks became larger, resulting in cyclopean masonry on the one hand, and the use of orthostats for the outer socle on the other (Anatolia; Boghazköy). Dressed-stone walls were composed of regular, quarried blocks with straight edges (see MASONRY). In Egypt such walls were used exclusively for temples and tombs. The best stone walls of the Ancient Near East were produced by the Phoenician masons in the Levant (eg RAS SHAMRA, MEGIDDO, SAMARIA).

Brick walls with stone foundations or substructures were the most common type of wall, especially for fortifications, with the exception of Southern Mesopotamia and Egypt, where brick prevailed. *Pisé* walls were found mainly in archaic structures in Mesopotamia (URUK) and Iran (Smith, P.E., *Iran* 8 (1970) 179).

window

Archaeological evidence for windows is limited to few actual examples from buildings in stone (Egypt, Anatolia, Persia). Otherwise, the appearance and placement of windows in Ancient Near Eastern buildings can be reconstructed only on the basis of ancient architectural representations, or by parallels with present-day traditional practices. On the

Mudbrick walls, Uruk, Mesopotamia

whole, windows in hot climates do not combine the three functions of providing light, air and ventilation in one architectural element. The primary source of light was the doorway, and additional ventilation could be achieved by vents or MULQAFS in the flat roof.

The simplest type of window was a narrow, slit-like opening (about the width of a brick), directly under the roof-line or high up on the facade, in order to minimise the weakening of the wall and capture the breeze. Sumerian reliefs also show small triangular openings alternating with rectangular ones (an early example in a stone building is the Valley Temple of Chephren at GIZA). Larger windows needed some *brise-soleil*, provided by horizontal or vertical divisions in stone, wood or brick. Egyptian houses and palaces could have more elaborately stylised window-grilles in the shape of hieroglyphic signs or plant motifs.

Large windows as a monumental feature of a facade were found only in Hittite and Achaemenian architecture. The Great Temple at BOGHAZKÖY, for instance, had some forty windows set just above the ground (20cm to 1m). They were probably closed with wooden shutters and may also have had frames covered with transparent hides to keep out the cold of the Anatolian winter. The window frames of stone (curiously carved of a single block or fitted from several corner pieces), set into the brick walls of the palace of Darius at PERSEPOLIS, are the only elements of the facade left standing.

CLERESTORY windows are documented for Egyptian temples and private houses from the New Kingdom onwards (eg

KARNAK: Great Hypostyle Hall). Else-where, the lack of archaeological evidence need not necessarily imply that such facilities were not used. Together with upper storeys protruding above the sur-rounding roof-terraces, they must have constituted a feasible and convenient means of conducting light into otherwise completely secluded interiors, especially in densely built-up agglomerations such as palaces.

wood

Wood probably played a considerably more important part in Ancient Near Eastern architecture than is often assumed. It was used for the beams of the flat roofs, for doors, posts and columns, interior panelling etc. The species of tree used for building varied in the different geographical regions. In Anatolia and Northern Mesopotamia, large forests of deciduous trees (oak, ash etc) existed in antiquity which have long since dis-appeared, not least because of the lavish use of timber in building (see below). Even more famous were the pine and cedar forests of Northern Syria. Southern Mesopotamia and Egypt lie in the date-palm zone, and this tree, which had been cultivated since prehistoric times, supplied most of the timber needed for domestic buildings. Beams of greater length and strength which could span larger spaces were imported in great numbers from the northern Levant. The large palaces throughout the Ancient Near East must have used vast quantities of timber, espec-ially if one assumes that upper storeys were common; the heavy conflagration of

Timber-enforced wall, Ankara

such structures is an indication of the large amount of wood used. In the wooded regions of Anatolia one would expect to find a true wood-based architecture, but there is little archaeological evidence unless the pitched-roofed MEGARON may derive from such a vernacular tradition. The use of wood along with mudbrick, however, was very widespread in Anatolia. It resulted in timber-grid structures on stone foundations, filled in with mudbrick. Interior panelling with wood was also common.

Yazilikaya

Anatolia, see map p. xv. Hittite open-air sanctuary near the capital Hattušaš (= BOGHAZKÖY). The carved reliefs, featuring the assembly of divine beings meeting the king, are preserved on two natural rock galleries. Excavations have revealed that the sanctuary was originally screened by various buildings, including a propylon with a flight of steps, a courtyard and a temple, with the portico leading into the rock galleries.

Bittel, K., *Yazilikaya: Architektur, Fels-bilder, Inschriften und Kleinfunde* (Leipzig 1941)

Hittite rock-relief, Yazilikaya (Anatolia)

Z

ziggurat

Religious structure of considerable height which dominated the skyline of most Mesopotamian cities. They were composed of numerous layers of solid mud-brick, with an outer casing of baked bricks. Most ziggurats (the Akkadian word from which the name is derived means 'to be high') are severely eroded and there are very few original texts which throw any light on their function and appearance.

Only the exterior of these solid monuments could be utilised, and ramps and stairways gave access to the top. One unique sanctuary on the summit of a ziggurat was found (at URUK) and it is not certain whether the later (2nd and 1st millennia BC) structures also had 'High Temples'. Herodotus (*Hist.* I. 185) describes a ritual known as the Sacred Marriage, which culminated in the sexual union of a priestess and the king to symbolise the communion of mankind and the gods; this was supposedly celebrated in a temple on top of the ziggurat. There is, however, no support for this account in Akkadian texts, and the association of the ziggurat with Sacred Marriage rites, which was assumed as factual in most earlier ~~b~~lications discussing ziggurats, needs to ~~be~~ revised. It has been suggested (Lenzen) ~~that~~ the ziggurat developed from the ~~re~~gular socle or platform of early ~~Meso~~tamian temples.

~~O~~f the earliest excavated examples ~~qua~~rter of the 3rd millennium BC) ~~ca~~lled Anu Ziggurat in Uruk ~~h~~ad an irregular outline and a ramp parallel to one of the outer faces, which were inclined and articulated with buttresses. The shrine on top, the so-called White Temple, has the architectural features of the period. The great age of the ziggurat, however, coincides with the great age of Mesopotamian architecture, the Ur III period. The best preserved example is the ziggurat built by Urnammu at UR. It stood within its own enclosure or *temenos*, was oriented to the points of the compass, and access to the first stage was by three ramps, the middle one of which rose from the ground at right angles to the outer face. The mudbrick core was carefully drained with clay pipes and there were internal layers of rush-matting and reeds to even out the pressure. Only the first two stages have survived and nothing is known about the upper parts of the structures.

The northern ziggurats (MARI, TELL AL-RIMAH, ASSUR etc) were not entirely free-standing structures, but were attached to lower temple buildings, the CELLAE of which were hollowed out of the ziggurat's core. If these monuments had any shrines on top, which is not certain, access must have been *via* the roof terraces of these temples. In the 1st-millennium Assyrian temples, such comparatively small ziggurats were annexed to most major temples (in the case of the double sanctuary of Anu and Adad in Assur, one for each).

The Elamite ziggurat at CHOGA ZANBIL was probably inspired by the Meso-potamian prototype, but had many

Ur: **Enunmah** *and ziggurat (Ur III period)*

peculiarities such as numerous chapels on the upper stages and vaulted chambers inside the lower courses.

The 'Tower of Babel' (see BABYLON), called *Etemenanki*, is particularly badly eroded, due to the punitive measures of Xerxes who re-channelled the course of the Euphrates. But it was already in ruins when seen by Herodotus, who relied on hearsay for his description. The measurements and data found on a cuneiform text, known as the Esagila Tablet, seem to tally most closely with archaeological evidence (91.5m at the base; probably 92m high; seven storeys, triple access on the South side).

Amiet, P., *Revue d'Assyriologie* 45 (1951) 80-88; 47 (1953) 23-33

Heinrich, H., 'Von der Entstehung der Zikkurate', in Bittel, K. (ed.), *Vorderasiatische Archäologie: Moortgat Festschrift* (Berlin 1964) 113-125

Lenzen, H., *Die Entwicklung der Zikkurat* (Leipzig 1941)

Panitschek, P., 'Mesopotamische Religion bei Herodot: Die Frau auf dem Turm', *Grazer Morgenländische Studien* 1 (Graz 1986) 43-50

Parrot, A., *Ziggurats et la Tour de Babel* (Paris 1949)

Schmid, H., 'Ergebnisse der Grabung am Kernmassiv der Zikkurat in Babylon', *Baghdader Mitteilungen* 12 (1981) 87–136

Zinjirli (ancient Sam'al)

North Syria, see map p. xix. Excavations have concentrated on the citadel on top of the mound, which was built during the Syro-Hittite period in the 8th C BC. The citadel was surrounded by a strong wall (3.50m thick), roughly circular (720m diameter) in shape, with round towers at regular intervals. The fortified gate had projecting gate-towers decorated with sculpted orthostats. An inner chamber led into a forecourt. From there a second gate, set in a wall articulated with round and rectangular buttresses, gave access to the second courtyard behind which the palace buildings were situated. There were five BÎT-HILANI-type palaces with transverse or oblong main halls, flanked by smaller rooms, bathrooms with drains and impressive porticoes with columns of wood on carved stone bases. The city walls were built of mudbrick, with an interior timber grid on rubble-stone foundations.

Luschan, F. von, *Ausgrabungen von Sendschirli Königliche Museen in Berlin*, Mitteilungen aus den orientalischen Sammlungen, XI-XIV (Berlin 1893-1911)

ALPHABETICAL LIST OF ENTRIES

Index

INDEX

Note: page numbers in **bold** refer to main entries; in *italic*, to illustrations.

Fisher